— Quests: —

The Complete History of the National Football League's Championship Series

by Kelly Bell

iUniverse, Inc.
New York   Bloomington

Quests
The Complete History of the National Football League's Championship Series

Copyright © 2008 by Kelly Denny Bell

All rights reserved. No part of this book may be used or reproduced by any means, graphic, electronic, or mechanical, including photocopying, recording, taping or by any information storage retrieval system without the written permission of the publisher except in the case of brief quotations embodied in critical articles and reviews.

The views expressed in this work are solely those of the author and do not necessarily reflect the views of the publisher, and the publisher hereby disclaims any responsibility for them.
iUniverse books may be ordered through booksellers or by contacting:

iUniverse
1663 Liberty Drive
Bloomington, IN 47403
www.iuniverse.com
1-800-Authors (1-800-288-4677)

Because of the dynamic nature of the Internet, any Web addresses or links contained in this book may have changed since publication and may no longer be valid. The views expressed in this work are solely those of the author and do not necessarily reflect the views of the publisher, and the publisher hereby disclaims any responsibility for them.

ISBN: 978-0-595-52258-3 (pbk)
ISBN: 978-0-595-62314-3 (ebk)

Printed in the United States of America
iUniverse Rev Date 03/20/2009

Contents

Genesis 1
1933 Chicago Bears versus New York Giants

Those Sneaky Giants 4
1934 New York Giants versus Chicago Bears

Renaissance 6
1935 Detroit Lions versus New York Giants

Where in Wisconsin? 8
1936 Green Bay Packers versus Boston Redskins

Sammy Who? 10
1937 Washington Redskins versus Chicago Bears

War of the Walking Wounded 12
1938 New York Giants versus Green Bay Packers

War for an Afternoon 14
1939 Green Bay Packers versus New York Giants

Custer's Revenge 16
1940 Chicago Bears versus Washington Redskins

The Forgotten Championship 19
1941 Chicago Bears versus New York Giants

The Return Engagement 21
1942 Washington Redskins versus Chicago Bears

Farewell to Bronko 23
1943 Chicago Bears versus Washington Redskins

A Reversal of Form 25
1944 Green Bay Packers versus New York Giants

Farewell to Sammy 27
1945 Cleveland Rams versus Washington Redskins

The Scam 29
1946 Chicago Bears versus New York Giants

And the Last Shall Be First 31
1947 Chicago Cardinals versus Philadelphia Eagles

The Snow Show 33
1948 Philadelphia Eagles versus Chicago Cardinals

The Flood of '49 35

1949 Philadelphia Eagles versus Los Angeles Rams

Storybook Beginning 37
1950 Cleveland Browns versus Los Angeles Rams

The Flying Dutchman 41
1951 Los Angeles Rams versus Cleveland Browns

The Texas Connection 44
1952 Detroit Lions versus Cleveland Browns

Strike Three 46
1953 Detroit Lions versus Cleveland Browns

Fourth Time Charm 48
1954 Cleveland Browns versus Detroit Lions

Last Time Around 50
1955 Cleveland Browns versus Los Angeles Rams

Giants Indeed 52
1956 New York Giants versus Chicago Bears

One Last Time 54
1957 Detroit Lions versus Cleveland Browns

The Baltimore Who? 56
1958 Baltimore Colts versus New York Giants

The Best in the West? 59
1959 Baltimore Colts versus New York Giants

Beginning and End 61
1960 Philadelphia Eagles versus Green Bay Packers

Packer Power 64
1961 Green Bay Packers versus New York Giants

Another Day at Work? 66
1962 Green Bay Packers versus New York Giants

The Party's Over 68
1963 Chicago Bears versus New York Giants

The Cleveland Caper 70
1964 Cleveland Browns versus Baltimore Colts

Of Mud and Men 73
1965 Green Bay Packers versus Cleveland Browns

The $15,000 Question 75
1966 Green Bay Packers versus Kansas City Chiefs

Vince's Curtain Call 79
1967 Green Bay Packers versus Oakland Raiders

A Man of His Word. 82
1968 New York Jets versus Baltimore Colts

Anniversary 86
1969 Kansas City Chiefs versus Minnesota Vikings

A Defender's Point of View 89
1970 Baltimore Colts versus Dallas Cowboys

Doomsday 93
1971 Dallas Cowboys versus Miami Dolphins

Nobody's Perfect? 96
1972 Miami Dolphins versus Washington Redskins

Valhalla 99
1973 Miami Dolphins versus Minnesota Vikings

At Long Last 102
1974 Pittsburgh Steelers versus Minnesota Vikings

Worthy of the Name 104
1975 Pittsburgh Steelers versus Dallas Cowboys

Raiders on a Rampage 107
1976 Oakland Raiders versus Minnesota Vikings

Clash of Emotions 109
1977 Dallas Cowboys versus Denver Broncos

The Greatest Show on Earth 113
1978 Pittsburgh Steelers versus Dallas Cowboys

To the Bitter End 117
1979 Pittsburgh Steelers versus Los Angeles Rams

Earning Their Wings 120
1980 Oakland Raiders versus Philadelphia Eagles

Gold Rush 123
1981 San Francisco 49ers versus Cincinnati Bengals

The Capital Connection. 126
1982 Washington Redskins versus Miami Dolphins

Buccaneer's Bonanza 129
1983 Los Angeles Raiders versus Washington Redskins

The Wild West 132

1984 San Francisco 49ers versus Miami Dolphins

Valley Forge Revisited 135
1985 Chicago Bears versus New England Patriots

New York, New York 139
1986 New York Giants versus Denver Broncos

Kings of the East 142
1987 Washington Redskins versus Denver Broncos

What a Way to Go! 145
1988 San Francisco 49ers versus Cincinnati Bengals

San Francisco Quake 148
1989 San Francisco 49ers versus Denver Broncos

Start Spreadin' the Word 151
1990 New York Giants versus Buffalo Bills

Way of the Warrior 155
1991 Washington Redskins versus Buffalo Bills

Shuffle off to…Pasadena 158
1992 Dallas Cowboys versus Buffalo Bills

Play it Again, Emmitt 164
1993 Dallas Cowboys versus Buffalo Bills

An Empire Strikes Back 169
1994 San Francisco 49ers versus San Diego Chargers

Duel in the Desert 172
1995 Dallas Cowboys versus Pittsburgh Steelers

Green and Gold Bowl 178
1996 Green Bay Packers versus New England Patriots

Resurrection 183
1997 Denver Broncos versus Green Bay Packers

King of Hearts 190
1998 Denver Broncos versus Atlanta Falcons

One for the New Age 195
1999 St. Louis Rams versus Tennessee Titans

Nice Guys Finish Second 200
2000 Baltimore Ravens versus New York Giants

Shadows of September 205
2001 New England Patriots versus St. Louis Rams

Clash of Corsairs 213
2002 Tampa Bay Buccaneers versus Oakland Raiders

North and South 218
2003 New England Patriots versus Carolina Panthers

Three by Three. 223
2004 New England Patriots versus Philadelphia Eagles

On the Road...Together. 228
2005 Pittsburgh Steelers versus Seattle Seahawks

Like Father... 234
2006 Indianapolis Colts versus Chicago Bears

A Giant Upset 241
2007 New York Giants versus New England Patriots

Yesterday Once More 249
2008 Pittsburgh Steelers versus Arizona Cardinals

Bibliography 255

Genesis
1933 Chicago Bears versus New York Giants

By 1933 the National Football League was nothing new, but suddenly a few things about it were. Through rule changes and a new way of deciding its champion the league was maturing into an American institution.

The fiery owner of the Boston Redskins, George Preston Marshall, was the catalyst for this reformation. Marshall led the faction demanding the NFL be split into divisions whose leaders would meet at season's end in a concluding, Homeric contest to decide unquestioningly which was the dominant faction.

In the 1930 league meetings Marshall had successfully demanded rule changes he believed would add color to the game and ultimately improve attendance. Prior to that year a passer had to be at least five yards behind the line of scrimmage before he could legally pass the ball. Marshall argued that, as entertainment, football needed to be as exciting as possible, and that this rule handicapped it. The rule was removed. He also was instrumental in having the goal posts moved from the back of the end zone to the goal line in order to increase scoring through more field goals. For placekickers the target was now ten yards closer.

In the irony already becoming characteristic of the game, the owner who led the crusade for these improvements would not see his beloved Redskins in the first-ever interdivisional league championship. George and his men had to stand aside and watch as the Chicago Bears and New York Giants determined who was the toughest kid on the block.

As was already, increasingly the case the Bears were favored to win. With such two-way players as Carl Brumbaugh, Bill Hewitt and Gene Ronzani carrying the load they were a fairly safe bet to prevail, but there was much more. Bronko Nagurski carried the ball for the Bears, who were blessed to have him on their side. At 238 pounds Nagurski did not have to run very far to make it seem like he was, especially for people who got in his way.

Coached by starting right tackle Steve Owen, the Giants were a team without an overpowering superstar, although their quarterback Harry Newman *was* the season's top-ranked passer. They had beaucoups talent spread throughout their roster, especially in the critical area of the backfield. Newman, Ken Strong, Dale Burnett and Bo Molenda did their jobs well, as many rueful opponents had learned.

26,000 hardy souls braved the frigid Illinois elements to view their heroes' expected inaugural triumph. The Bears opened by treating their following to an utterly tedious attack. This was not altogether unexpected since Nagurski's straight-ahead power plunges were not that scintillating. What *was* surprising was Chicago's early inability to get Bronko and his football over the goal line. After New York initially drove deeply into Bear territory only to falter and come up dry at the fifteen-yard line, Chicago pushed right back, but could not cross the enemy sixteen, where Jack Manders kicked a field goal. It happened again early in the second period, only from forty yards as Marshall's portable goal posts made it ten yards easier.

The Giants tired of this monotony and put together a spicy drive combining long runs and passes ending with Newman's thirty-nine-yard touchdown throw to Red Badgro. The first half ended with everyone (the New Yorkers included) rather surprised at the 7-6 NYC edge.

After intermission the Bears resumed their dreary style of play as Manders again split the uprights, from twenty-eight yards. With the score just up to 9-7 Chicago, the fans were becoming impatient for something besides their pocket flasks to warm them. Newman decided he would liven things, and started throwing. Sixty-one yards later, from the Chicago one, Max Krause bucked over for the Giants. 14-9, New York.

The Bears kept being predictable, but finally did it right. After Nagurski's bulldozing took them far into Giant territory they again took advantage of Marshall's rule changes. The big man took another ordinary handoff and pounded for the center as the battered defense braced for impact. The defenders were astonished as Bronko stopped a couple of yards shy of the line, hopped into the air and passed to end Bill Karr for the first Chicago touchdown.

Quests

A 16-14 lead was far from secure as the final quarter began. New York constructed a lovely, balanced drive that carried to the eight-yard-line before things got weird. From here Strong took the snap and faded, but the frantic Bears would not make it easy for him. Flattening blockers they poured in upon Strong who, for want of anything better, turned and lateralled to Newman. Admirably overcoming his astonishment, Newman scrambled for a moment then saw, of all people, Strong alone in the end zone. If Newman was bewildered at having the ball, Strong was equally shocked to be so splendidly wide open as Newman threw it to him. No one was really certain what had happened until the scoreboard flashed—21-16, Giants.

Now Chicago had to contend with the clock, so quarterback Brumbaugh loaded his big gun, repeatedly sending Nagurski into the swarms of defenders. After carrying the ball four times on this drive he had his team on the New York thirty-six. Of course Brumbaugh gave the ball to him again, and naturally the defense again plugged the middle, so when the Bronk jumped high to throw for the second time they were not as surprised, but every bit as horrified.

Bill Hewitt gathered in the toss, and Burnett immediately hit him. Hewitt lateralled to Karr on the twenty-five. The only man with a chance to stop Karr was the indomitable Strong, who instantly drew a bead on the Bear halfback, but as Strong cut down the angle on Karr, he himself was being targeted by Ronzani, who decked Strong to send Karr unimpeded into the end zone. It was the game's sixth lead change, and the clock mercilessly ticked off the final seconds as the Chicago Bears won, 23-21.

The Bruins banked $210.23 apiece for establishing themselves as the league's first interdivisional champs. The sum sounded suspiciously like the score, but that was just a fluke.

Those Sneaky Giants
1934 New York Giants versus Chicago Bears

Every layman knows elements of one sport seldom make themselves felt in a game of a different genre. This makes the 1934 NFL title game all the more in-a-class-of-its-ownish. Basketball came to the rescue of the New York Giants.

It had been a painful season for those opposing the Chicago Bears as they bludgeoned their way undefeated to the championship match with these very Giants they had tossed aside twice during the regular season. Everyone knew the New Yorkers would crumble beneath the Chicago onslaught, and everyone was almost right.

The first half was all according to script as Bronko Nagurski's rushing took him into the end zone once, and close enough for a Jack Manders field goal after Ken Strong placed the Giants on the score board first with a conversion of his own. The game would have been far easier for the Bears had their star rookie halfback Beattie Feathers been active, but Feathers' career had recently been interrupted by a severe shoulder injury just after he became the league's first-ever 1000-yard season rusher via his unbelievable 9.1-yard average per carry that year.

By halftime New York, though battered, trailed by only 10-3, yet the margin felt much wider. At this point Giant head coach Steve Owen recalled a suggestion his friend Ray Flaherty had made before the game. Ray said basketball sneakers were known to give traction on surfaces that were impervious to cleats. The problem was in how the December weather had transformed the game site, the New York polo grounds, into a fair imitation of an ice skating rink. The Giants could not keep their feet under them long enough to get the ball past the skilled Bears.

At intermission Owen sent clubhouse attendant Abe Cohen off to Manhattan College on a quest for the precious footwear. New York trainer Gus Mauch got in touch with an official at the school who let

Cohen into the gymnasium to grab every sneaker upon which he could lay his frozen fingers.

The round-trip subway ride was time-consuming, and there were just ten minutes remaining in the game when Cohen slid into the Giants' bench with nine pairs of sneakers of about as many different sizes. Calling timeout the harried New Yorkers rushed to the sideline to try on their sudden salvation. By this time the score is 13-3, but abruptly the Giants were very much in business.

The rout started with quarterback Ed Danowski fading to pass in front of the stumbling Bears. Ed fires toward Ike Frankian twenty-eight yards downfield. After snatching the almost-interception from Chicago's Carl Brumbaugh, Frankian falls into the end zone and the Giants trail by three.

After the kickoff the Bears go nowhere and have to punt. Ken Strong grabs the ball and scampers forty-two sure-footed yards to take the never-expected lead.

Again New York kicks off to the Chicagoans, who use the next three downs to gain eight yards. The worried Bears have no thought of punting, but see Nagurski hurled backward for no gain on fourth down at midfield. Starting from here the running of Strong and Danowski carried the Giants to the eight-yard-line from where Strong scored easily.

One last, futile time Chicago takes possession only to have Brumbaugh intercepted, setting up the final score. New York 30, Chicago 13.

For the first time a title contest spawns mass pandemonium as shivering Giants fans swarm onto the field to embrace their heroes. In the final ten minutes the New York Giants scored twenty-seven points to claim the crown few expected. They deserved every hug.

— Renaissance —
1935 Detroit Lions versus New York Giants

Few teams in any sport have ever overcome more that 1935's Detroit Lions did in reaching a goal. At the three-quarters point in the season they possessed a drab 3-3-2 record and faint hopes of overtaking the Green Bay Packers in the National Football League's Western Division. Detroit decided to sneak up on the Packers, and took the last four games, nosed out the Pack and earned its first championship appearance in the young interdivisional playoff format.

The defending champion New York Giants were prohibitive favorites after waltzing to dominance in the Eastern Division. However, during its infancy, the championship game would see its first great victory of speed and finesse over bare-knuckled brute force.

Detroit head coach Potsy Clark was aware of his weapon of surprise, and made full use of it. He pounded the message into his charges during daily scrimmages, with emphasis on stifling the marvelous passing tandem of Ed Danowski to rookie sensation Tod Goodwin. The fates had already blessed the Lions via the severely infected hand of key Giant receiver Dale Burnett, which banished him to the sideline.

The night before the game fortune pulled its final switchblade on the hapless New Yorkers as torrents of freezing rain deluged the game site, the University of Detroit Stadium. After a mid-morning respite the elements again cut loose, this time as a blizzard. The Giant passing game was under wraps before the contest commenced.

The fired-up Lions assailed New York early with a long pass from Ed Presnell to Ed Klewicki who caught the ball after it bounced off Danowski and set Detroit up on the two-yard line. Former Giant Ace Gutowski scored the touchdown for a 7-0 Lion lead with the game six plays old.

Minutes later the Motor City watched or listened gleefully as its beloved runner Dutch Clark charged through the secondary forty-two yards for his side's second score. With the count now 13-0 for the Lions the Giants mustered for an impressive march downfield to the ten-yard line. Detroit's defense stiffened here, though, and the downs slipped away as New York was held on four straight and left the field at the half still trailing by thirteen.

Still, a certain degree of momentum had been established, and five minutes into the third period Danowski managed a forty-two-yard end zone shot to Ken Strong. With the difference shaved to six the Lions were warned to stay on their toes, so at the start of the fourth quarter they worked their way toward the distant goal line as their scared opponents tried vainly to regain possession. At the tail-end of this drive Detroit was on the four when Presnell took the snap and handed off to Gutowski sweeping right. Seemingly. To their horror the pursuing defenders realized Gutowski's hands were empty and that Eddie Caddel was behind them, curling left and untouched into the end zone.

After a final score from nine yards out by future Lion coach Buddy Parker the only league championship game that would ever be played between these teams ground to a chilly close with Detroit on top 26-7. Bad breaks and the unanticipated ability and resolution of their adversaries had been too much for the incumbents, but their days were coming.

— Where in Wisconsin? —
1936 Green Bay Packers versus Boston Redskins

There was something very novel about the Green Bay Packers, besides the odd name. This had been a promotional gesture to honor their original sponsor, the Indian Packing Company of Green Bay, Wisconsin—wherever that was. Still, the impact of this small town team would be overpowering.

The Boston Redskins had finally made it to the championship game their owner George Preston Marshall had been instrumental in creating—not that their city much cared. Bostonians were devoted to college teams from Boston College, Holy Cross and Harvard, and ignored the successes of their hometown professionals. The talented Redskins could vanquish other football teams, but could never hope to prevail against a stadium full of empty seats. In desperation, Marshall moved the site of 1936's title game to a neutral location—New York's Polo Grounds. Perhaps George also hoped the small town Packers would be overawed by the vastness of New York City. The Green Bays never gave much thought to the Big Apple's immensity, however, they only had eyes for the Redskins.

What Marshall had in mind was to take the league championship then move his franchise to Washington, D.C., thumbing his nose at apathetic Boston while also finding greener pastures. Sure he would.

Green Bay had its heart set on the title, and had the talent to realize the dream. Especially in the passing department. For the third time Packer quarterback Arnie Herber had led the league in passing, but there was quite a bit more. One of Herber's receivers held football's coming, aerial era in his soft hands.

Since joining the club a year earlier, Don Hutson had been overhauling the sport via his pass-catching ability. Herber repeatedly laid the ball into Hutson's huge mitts, and then crowds would look on as the Alabama Antelope lived up to his hard-to-live-up-to moniker.

The game began in standard Green Bay fashion as the Packers marched methodically to the Boston forty-three-yard line, and then got spectacular. Dropping back among typically splendid protection Herber spied Hutson running free and whipped the ball to him. The absurdly simple play gave Green Bay a 7-0 lead three minutes into the first quarter.

The 'Skins quickly clamped Hutson with multiple coverage, and the rest of the quarter was scoreless. It was time for the Pack to look for alternatives, but first their opponents had a drive.

Early in the second period Boston started from its twenty-two and marched to six points. Everyone wondered if the missed extra point would matter. It would not. Early in the second half the Hutson-conscious Redskins kept the lethal wideout encircled by defenders, and the first alternative Herber found was end Milt Gantenbein, who caught an eight-yard scoring pass in the third period.

Not a great deal happened the rest of the game as the Packers used as much time as possible when they had the ball, and stymied their opponents with resolute defense the rest of the time. One last touchdown completed the test as Green Bay won 21-6, and finally Packer head coach Curly Lambeau was content. After sixteen years on the job he could tell people he coached in Green Bay, Wisconsin and have them know where he meant. Coming seasons would insure they would never forget.

Sammy Who?
1937 Washington Redskins versus Chicago Bears

By 1937 the now-Washington Redskins were a better team than the one that had quailed under the passing blitz of the Green Bay Packers in the previous year's league championship, and it was more than the motivation of playing in the nation's capital. The lesson had been painfully administered, and the Redskins made the most of their experience. Possessing the second overall choice in the '37 college draft owner George Preston Marshall knew exactly whom he wanted—Sammy Baugh of Texas Christian University. On draft day Marshall was a nervous wreck, he just knew he would lose his man, but did not and gleefully made his selection.

In college Sammy had starred in baseball as well as on the gridiron, and the Redskins had to shell out a hefty sum to entice him away from the baseball St. Louis Cardinals. It was the best investment an NFL team had ever made.

At first, many in the league were dubious of Baugh's potential. He was so lean he hardly cast a shadow, and at first glance he looked like he would never be able to rise after being laid horizontal by a hard-charging defensive lineman, who averaged bigger, stronger and faster than collegians.

The knowledgeable ones were not giving much thought to the possibility that Sammy might be much tougher than he looked, or that he was as great a passer as his new owner kept claiming. Not only had Washington just signed one of the greatest passers the game would ever spawn, but in Cliff Battles it had the season's top rusher.

The Redskins' opponents for the title game were the Chicago Bears, and as kickoff neared yet another factor arose that would supposedly affect Baugh's effectiveness. It began to snow. Sammy had never played football in snow before, especially this kind. The blanket was so thickly crusted on top that a man could break his fingers on it.

Quests

The Redskins and their young leader would not be dismayed by the elements, and started the game in spectacular fashion. Stuck at his own nine on his first possession Baugh dropped into his own end zone in punt formation, but instead of kicking the ball he heaved it forty-three yards to Battles. The Bears had never heard of anyone passing from behind his own goal line, and before they could recover from the shock they trailed 7-0 after Battles finished the drive with a seven-yard charge.

Stung, Chicago soon tied the game on Jack Manders' ten-yard run. Manders not only scored the touchdown, but kicked the extra point. The Redskins saw more of the troublesome Manders as he caught quarterback Bernie Masterson's thirty-seven-yard scoring pass that sent his side into intermission with a 14-7 lead.

In the second half Sam Adrian Baugh grimly set himself to his task, and passed Chicago dizzy. He wound up with 335 yards through the air and three touchdowns. Early in the third quarter Baugh found end Wayne Milner clear for a fifty-five-yard throw that tied the game at fourteen. The Chicagoans pulled away one last time by bulling their way straight downfield with Manders, Ray Nolting and Bronko Nagurski carrying the load. At the Washington three, with the defensive line expecting another straight-ahead power plunge, Masterson tossed the ball to end Ed Manski for a 21-14 Bear lead.

From this point Sammy forever silenced his critics. From his own twenty-three Baugh hit Milner on the Chicago forty-eight. Manders and Nagurski gave futile pursuit as the tying score covered seventy-seven yards.

Several minutes later, with the Bears having been stopped on offense, Sammy was among the first to use a killer tactic that would spell defeat for many future teams. He looked at end Charles Malone and pumped his arm, then reversed himself and threw to halfback Ed Justice as the anguished secondary tried to cut back. It was to late, and the thirty-five-yard completion won the contest 28-21 to the despair of the Wrigley Field crowd.

Sammy Baugh had proven himself and dawned a new, aerial era. He also did it in the backyard of the team that would be his worst enemy for many, many more years.

—War of the Walking Wounded—

1938 New York Giants versus Green Bay Packers

Few teams have ever paid more pain for a goal than the 1938 New York Giants. They shelled out the price willingly, for none could have wanted the title more. It had been a long journey back from their trouncing in Detroit three years earlier, and they had no intention of repeating that demoralizing script. Still, the many breaks and bruises of this regular season were a big factor in the Giants' championship test with the powerful and hale Green Bay Packers.

Granted, the Packers were handicapped in one vital respect in that their legendary receiver Don Hutson was hobbled by a bad knee that kept him on the sideline for most of the contest. It was just enough.

The Giants put on an inspiring display of unflinching courage and resolution in the first half despite the Packers' relentless attack, and, aided by a blocked kick, managed to leave the chilled Polo Grounds at intermission leading 16-14. This was particularly praiseworthy since New York's pivotal, league MVP center Mel Hein had been knocked senseless early in the game and did not return until much later.

The Giants also surprised their opponents and fans when, due to the many injuries, they inserted seldom-used Hap Barnard into the lineup. Barnard raised eyebrows and hopes throughout the arena when he caught quarterback Ed Danowski's pass for the touchdown that gave New York the halftime advantage.

Early in the third quarter Green Bay kicker Tiny Engebretsen salvaged a drive that had stalled on the Giant fifteen when he pierced the uprights to give his team a tenuous 17-16 edge. At this point New York head coach Steve Owen realized his men who played primarily offense were nearing the end of their endurance, and called together the eleven of them with the fewest hurts to tell them that if they did not score on the next drive chances were they would not score at all until the next season. Infused with the hard desperation of necessity they limped determinedly onto the field.

In later years Giant fullback Hank Soar would umpire baseball in the major leagues, but right now all he had on his mind was football and the Packer line. Owen instructed Danowski to employ a rudimentary form of misdirection, so Danowski repeatedly faked handoffs in one direction before turning and giving the ball to Soar heading the other way. The Green Bays were unaccustomed to this sort of attack, and had much difficulty trying to contain it. Soar twice picked up precious first downs on third-and-long when the defense was expecting a pass.

Then the Giants found themselves stymied with a fourth-and-one on the Packer forty-four. After a brief consultation with Owen, Danowski returned to the huddle with the only possible instructions. Both men sensed the battered New Yorkers would not likely be able to recover should they give up the ball now even though a considerable portion of the game remained to be played. Owen told his players to go for it.

The Packers knew there was no one the Giants could give the ball to except Soar, yet when Hank took the handoff and pounded into the swarm of defenders he bulled just far enough to keep his outfit's hopes breathing. This gritty, gutsy style of play carried New York to Green Bay's twenty-five where Danowski shocked the stadium by *throwing* the pigskin to Soar for the winning touchdown.

For the Giants the final quarter was the most nerve-wracking ever played. The Packers repeatedly lunged for the goal line, only to be turned back each time by the desperate home team. Concussion notwithstanding, Hein had to return to battle the relentless Pack who, despite Hutson's absence, took to the air in their attempts to score one last touchdown. The Giants knocked down passes in bunches, and were saved when an official ruled end Milt Gantenbein was an ineligible receiver on what could have been a crucial completion to the New York forty.

The quarter would be scoreless, and the bandaged New York Giants won their title 23-17. The bruises, they decided, were worth it.

A year later the Pack would take its vengeance.

War for an Afternoon

1939 Green Bay Packers versus New York Giants

The New York Giants had very little going for them the afternoon they played the Green Bay Packers for the 1939 National Football League championship. Not only was the game in frigid Green Bay, but their rivals were thirsting to retaliate for the title victory New York had eked out over them the year before.

Midway through the first period the Giants punted and saw the ball go a very short distance. Taking over on the New York forty-six, the Packers drove to the seven. Quarterback Arnie Herber sent his magnificent wide receiver Don Hutson to the left, and as the Giant secondary scampered after him Herber fired the ball to end Milt Gantenbein for the game's first points.

The remainder of the first half was scoreless as a swirling, thirty-five-mile-per-hour wind pinned down both offenses. The breeze did not hinder the Packers from administering a brutal physical pounding to their opponents, who came into the game much healthier than when they left.

New York's defensive line had rolled many offenses into their own backfields during the regular season, but it never had a chance against the vengeful Pack. At the start of the third quarter Tiny Engebretsen drilled a field goal from the Giant twenty-nine for a 10-0 Green Bay lead as the Packers were finally getting started on the scoreboard.

After accepting the kickoff the New York offense quickly stalls when Gantenbein intercepts an Ed Danowski pass and returns it to the Giant thirty-three. Green Bay wastes little time as Cecil Isbell takes the snap and takes off, seemingly trying to sweep outside on a keeper play. As the secondary rushes to meet him he suddenly halts and throws to wide-open halfback Joe Laws for a 17-0 advantage as the period, much to the Giants' relief, ends.

Quests

The fourth quarter is no gentler on the visitors as the Packers continued to hammer them. On fourth down at the New York thirty-seven, Green Bay surprisingly sends in substitute Ernie Smith for the field goal attempt instead of the expected Engebretsen. Replacement or not, Smith splits the uprights to run the score to 20-0.

When the Giants got the ball again Bud Svendsen immediately picked off a pass and ran it back to their fifteen. This leads to Eddie Jankowski's one-yard dive to arrive at the final bulge of 27-0, Green Bay.

After the final gun Packer fans showered the Giants with bottles and other debris as the losers painfully climb aboard their buses. No one listens when end Jim Lee Howell exhorts them to smile. "After all," he says, "We got out alive." Some of his teammates did not feel safe yet.

Yet, the next title game would make this one seem like cricket.

Custer's Revenge
1940 Chicago Bears versus Washington Redskins

Everyone knew the Chicago Bears of 1940 were a great team. Even their mortal rivals from Washington, D.C. acknowledged it to a certain point, despite having beaten the Bears 7-3 during the regular season. Something monumental happened after this game.

Redskin owner George Preston Marshall told reporters that Chicago was strictly a first half club that would eventually give way to any team that refused to be intimidated. "The Bears," said George, "fold up when the going gets rough." The Windy City flattened its ears at the insult. When the Bears earned the right to play for the league title their joyous anticipation was spawned less by the shot at the championship than by the fact that the Redskins had also qualified, and the Chicagoans had their chance at lusted-after vengeance.

The Bears were obsessed with Washington. They viewed Redskins as more malevolent than any witch dragged from the depths of Grimm's Fairy Tales, and Chicago readied to slay its dragon. Bear eyes swelled and ached from long hours in the projection room studying every move made by every Redskin on every play of the earlier game. By game time it had only been a week since Chicago owner/head coach George Halas had installed the T formation, in which for the first time the quarterback became the central figure on offense. This revolutionary, still-unfamiliar alignment took the 'Skins totally by surprise this sun-drenched afternoon in Washington's Griffith Stadium, rendering the old single wing and double wing formations eternally obsolete as this one game forever changed American football.

Besides the drastic, unexpected tactical lesson he was about to spring on the Redskins, Halas never lost sight of how vital it was to keep his men seething. As game time approached he kept reminding them of what Marshall had said. As far as the weather and the Bears were concerned, the nation's capital was ideal for football that monumental Sabbath, and the teams quickly got serious.

After his side took the opening kickoff, Chicago quarterback Sid Luckman tested the Redskin secondary on whether it would react as it had in the regular season game. Indeed it did. On the first play Luckman handed off to his runner over tackle for an eight-yard gain while Sid watched the defensive backs. He had sent rookie end Ken Cavenaugh wide left, and halfback Ray Nolting to the right. Both men were covered by defensive backs whose absence from the ball carrier's vicinity enabled him to pick up his yardage. Luckman reasoned that if he could earn eight yards this way he should be able to stretch the distance yet more.

On the next down Cavenaugh again headed right, and this time George McAfee went left. Luckman took the snap and turned toward Nolting, approaching from the right, as if to hand off to him. Luckman suddenly spun and thrust the ball into the midsection of Bill Osmanski coming hard from the opposite direction. Osmanski was supposed to cut inside the defensive left end, but the defensive tackle plugged the hole. Bill slashed back outside, rounded the end and pelted down the sideline. Ed Justice and Jimmy Johnston moved to cut off Osmanski and force him out of bounds, but they had eyes only for the runner. Bear end George Wilson threw his history-making block at this point as he crashed into Justice so violently that Ed slammed sideways into Johnston. Neither Redskin had seen Wilson coming, and as they gazed stunned into the clear blue sky while flat on their backs they wondered who had thrown the lightning bolt. More were coming.

Although nobody even touched Osmanski on his sixty-eight-yard scoring run, Washington was still convinced of the truth of Marshall's words—all they had to do was refused to be cowed and the visitors would crumble. For a moment it seemed to be happening as Redskin passer Sammy Baugh steadily marched his squad downfield. It was not a long drive because Max Krause had returned the kickoff sixty-two yards.

Baugh aimed to get the equalizer immediately and turn the contest's momentum his way, so he sent right end Charlie Malone on a post pattern. Malone ran a perfect route, and Baugh spun the ball straight into his chest, but made one mortal mistake. His shadow was in front of him. When Malone looked back all he could see were the blinding rays of the December sun, and not the ball, which he dropped.

The defense stiffened at this point. The Redskins could not pick up a first down, and missed a field goal attempt. Hereafter the saga becomes solely that of Luckman & Co. Taking over on his own twenty he drove his offense to its second touchdown as the massacre commenced. Considering the final score the 28-0 halftime difference was surprisingly close.

At intermission Marshall repeated to his men his prediction of a third quarter Bear collapse, but the faint hope these words brought was fleeting. In the third period Chicago scored four more touchdowns, and another three in the fourth. After the ninth score the supply of balls was nearly depleted. In those days there were no nets behind the goal posts, and footballs kicked through the uprights for field goals and extra points became fan souvenirs. With just one ball left the Bears ran on the PAT attempts after the final pair of TDs. It was the only drama remaining. Chicago won 73-0. The T formation gave its creators and users a career's worth of retribution in one day.

During jubilant postgame interviews Halas was careful to not berate *his* (very) defeated rivals, and told the mob of newsmen merely, "We deserved to win." One of them referred to this championship posse as the "Monsters of the Midway" for the first time.

Not for the last.

—The Forgotten Championship—

1941 Chicago Bears versus New York Giants

So many things were happening that December. The National Football League championship was played on the twenty-first—two weeks after the Japanese had made their ill-advised trip to Pearl Harbor. Now the New York Giants made an equally unwise journey to Chicago.

The most unexpected thing about this contest was the very presence of the Giants at Wrigley Field. For a year everybody had assumed the title game would be a rematch between the Bears and Washington Redskins, who were dying to atone for the 73-0 crucifixion of 1940. The wily New Yorkers added fleet George Franck to their backfield, and after coaxing passer Ed Danowski out of retirement made their unheralded way to the lakeshore, hoping to play David to the Chicago Goliath.

The Bears had added massive fullback Norm Standlee to their already punishing ground attack, but the Giants, with an unexpectedly tenacious defense, were able to deny their foes the end zone throughout the first half. In the first and second quarters New York used a five-man defensive front bolstered by three linebackers. This alignment effectively neutralized the inside rushing of Standlee and George McAfee.

The Giants surprised the assembly by scoring the sole touchdown of the half on a pass from fullback Tuffy Leemans to Franck. It was not enough for a lead as Chicago led at intermission 9-6 on three Bob Snyder field goals. Early in the third quarter kicker Ward Cuff drew New York even 9-9 with his thirty-nine-yard placement. From this point the Bears ruled.

Deciding he was going to have to get really serious in this game after all, Chicago head coach George Halas ordered quarterback Sid Luckman to send Standlee and McAfee around the ends. The weary Giants could not stop them. Luckman threw the ball enough to keep the defense off-balance, but this was not often now that he had established his running game.

In the third period Standlee had three- and seven-yard scoring runs, and at the beginning of the last quarter Chicago center Bulldog Turner intercepted a pass to start the next touchdown drive. A pass interference call against New York's Chet Gladchuck put the ball on the Giants' five, from where McAfee scored easily.

The scoring ended with Ken Cavenaugh grabbing a New York fumble and returning it forty-two yards for the final bulge of 37-9, Chicago. The outright victory had been taken for granted, and this was the biggest problem for the home team. Only 13,341 fans showed up to witness the inevitable, and each Bear received just $430.34 as their winner's share of the gate receipts. One of the greatest teams in history won barely enough for Christmas shopping.

Much worse was coming. World War II would soon decimate the champions.

The Return Engagement
1942 Washington Redskins versus Chicago Bears

Maybe they were not the team they had been. The Second World War was thinning the ranks of more than military units—it had seriously drained the roster of the defending NFL champion Chicago Bears. Ball-carrying marvels George McAfee, Norm Standlee and Ken Cavenaugh were serving overseas, much to the advantage of the Washington Redskins, who were to play the Bears in the 1942 league championship. During the regular season Chicago had also lost starters Bill Osmanski and Joe Stydahar to the military, but this crucial duo were granted special leaves to play in the title game.

Despite the absence of so many key players the Bears did not lose a game in the regular season. In fact, going back more than a year, they had won twenty-four in a row.

Not many Washingtonians dared raise their hopes as kickoff drew nigh. The 73-0 shellacking of two years earlier was an aching, still-fresh memory. Yet 36,000 showed up for the rematch. It commenced in sluggish fashion with the first quarter melting away scorelessly. Then, midway through the second, the action started.

At midfield Redskin quarterback Sammy Baugh took the snap and turned to hand off to fullback Andy Farkas. The connection went awry and the ball bounced loose. Bear tackle/placekicker Lee Artoe scooped up the fumble and dashed fifty yards to realize every lineman's dream of scoring a touchdown in a championship game. The ideal would have been perfect had Artoe not missed the extra point. 6-0, Chicago.

Memory of past disaster spurred Washington to desperate efforts. Farkas was especially eager to atone for his miscue as the Redskins pushed to the Bear twenty-five, where Baugh found Wilbur Moore with a scoring pass that gave their side a 7-6 halftime edge.

In the second half Chicago's defense concentrated on pass rushing, so Baugh repeatedly handed off to Farkas during the drive for the clinching touchdown. During this possession Andy gained eighty yards through the snarling Bears. He finally powered across the goal line from a yard out to produce the final margin of 14-6.

For the Redskins (especially their unspeakably relieved fullback) revenge was sweet. Yet their future with the Chicago Bears would be bitter.

Farewell to Bronko
1943 Chicago Bears versus Washington Redskins

The monotony was building. Could no one besides the Chicago Bears and Washington Redskins make it to the finale? Not lately, but even if it did have the same old contestants the game could not help being interesting. Chicago's Sid Luckman and Washington's Sammy Baugh had a way with footballs.

Both teams (especially the Bears) did have problems with player attrition due to military service, and this made the 1943 title game all the more remarkable. Bronko Nagurski made a final appearance.

Bronko had hung up his leather helmet after the 1938 season, feeling, at age thirty, too venerable for this most violent of professions. He stayed retired five years until a desperate Chicago Bear owner/head coach George Halas convinced him to make a comeback.

The game itself gave early indication of the bloody clash it would be when Baugh was so severely pounded in the first quarter by the marauding Bears that he had to be led to the locker room for examination by the team doctor. He had been the season's leading passer, but during his absence Luckman began to steal the show. Washington tried hard, and even scored first, but there was little question of who would win after Luckman started throwing and Nagurski started running.

Back on November 14 Luckman had heaved seven touchdown passes during one incredible afternoon at New York. In this more-important matchup he would connect with the end zone five times, setting an enduring postseason record in his last game before reporting for service in the merchant marines. Still, everyone's heart belonged to Bronko.

The first period provided lots of hard hits, but no points. On the first play of the second quarter Andy Farkas rammed over from the three to give the Redskins a fleeting 7-0 lead. Three minutes later Luckman passed thirty-one yards to Harry Clark for the equalizer, and the Bears never looked back.

Washington had sheathed its offensive sword for the rest of the half, but Chicago was out for more. Starting on their own thirty-one the Bears marched on Bronko's legs. The drive reached the Redskin three-yard line. Sid gave the ball to Nag, who plunged into the right side and disappeared into a swarm of defenders. Just as everybody decided it would take another down or two the Bronk tore free from the mass of men and tumbled into the end zone.

34,320 fans sprang to their feet and hollered in delighted unison. To be able to say they watched Bronko Nagurski score his last touchdown was why they would remember this game. They knew he would not likely be back, so they took this last-ever chance to let him know how much he was loved.

Chicago widened the difference in the second half as Luckman threw the rest of his home run shots. Ringing ears or no, Baugh had to return in the forlorn hope of salvaging some sort of miracle. He managed a couple of TD tosses, but the last Redskin hope died in the fourth quarter when Baugh was knocked senseless in a violent collision with Luckman, who was returning one of Baugh's own punts.

Washington would lose 41-21. In this, the last title game that would ever be played between these teams, the Bears had the last laugh on their bitter foes from Capital City.

A Reversal of Form

1944 Green Bay Packers versus New York Giants

The Green Bay Packers had atonement on their minds when they came to New York to play the Giants for the 1944 NFL Championship. A month earlier they had been whitewashed 24-0 by the New Yorkers at these same Polo Grounds. Because of the war both sides had a fair share of overaged players on their skimpy rosters, but these somewhat senior citizens fought each other with truly youthful abandon.

The first quarter was scoreless as the contestants tested each other for weaknesses. Early in the second period the Packers found one. Starting on the New York forty-eight Green Bay re-introduced fundamentals. Surprising their foes with unexpected simplicity they bulled for the game's first touchdown—almost running out of downs at the end, but Ted Fritsch managed to power his way into the end zone on fourth-and-goal from the two.

The Giants were keeping a fearful eye on the Pack's brilliant receiver Don Hutson, who had led the league in scoring five straight seasons. He was cloaked with multiple coverage throughout the afternoon, but as the final seconds of the second quarter ticked down the wily flanker got loose for the only time all day.

Green Bay quarterback Irv Comp took the snap at midfield and faded. Spying a tiny seam he threaded the ball to Hutson. The reception put the Pack on the New York twenty-six, and there was time for one more play.

Comp sent his star pass-catcher to the right, and looked at him all the way. As Irv had expected, the entire Giant secondary chased Hutson, and there was no one near Fritsch when he caught the pass on the left sideline. Ted scored easily, giving the Packers a 14-0 halftime lead.

In the third quarter New York found its offensive legs largely through quarterback Arnie Herber's right arm, and worked its way to the Green Bay one as time expired. On the first play of the final quarter Ward Cuff scored the touchdown, cutting the difference to seven after forty-year-old Ken Strong kicked the extra point.

After their score the Giants had trouble converting third downs as Green Bay's defense dug in and its offense took no chances, staying on the ground and using booming punts to lock the home team in its own territory. It was the clock, though, that was the best defender. With time almost gone, New York kicked up a final flurry that ended when Paul Duhart intercepted a Herber pass deep in Packer territory as the 14-7 lead became the final score.

Don Hutson caught just one ball, but his presence on the playing field worried the Giants into losing. It was the last championship game for one of the greatest receivers in the history of football, and he had been typically pivotal. It would be many, many seasons before his team returned to the summit.

Farewell to Sammy
1945 Cleveland Rams versus Washington Redskins

1945 was a good year for the people of Cleveland, Ohio. Apart from the blessed conclusion of the war, it marked the first title appearance for their Cleveland Rams. The Rams had always tried hard in the past, but never got above .500 in the win-loss column. Yet this was the year a golden rookie named Bob Waterfield joined the club.

Waterfield had more than his bountiful athletic prowess going for him. Fresh from the UCLA campus he radiated charm and confidence, and was the husband of movie starlet Jane Russell. He would soon be back in California as the Rams were preparing to move their franchise to Los Angeles.

There was something else of note about this contest—it was the final championship appearance for Sammy Baugh. The Slinger had passed his Washington Redskins into the title test yet again, and his throwing would determine the winner in a way none could have anticipated.

At the kickoff the temperature in Cleveland stood at six degrees above zero, but the players were affected surprisingly little by the cold. The bizarre, game-deciding play came early.

The initial scoring threat came from the Rams as they drove to the Washington five-yard line and tried to score a touchdown on fourth down rather than kick an easy field goal. The Redskin defense smothered the play, and Baugh lined up his offense backed against his own goal line.

First down accomplished little, so on the next play Baugh dropped into his own end zone in punt formation. It was nothing new—Sammy was known to punt before fourth down when his team was in a deep hole. With his leg even stronger than his storied passing arm he would generally boot the ball deep into opposition territory, setting up his defense to its advantage. The Rams knew all this and prepared to field a kick, so when Baugh took the snap and cocked his arm to throw they were Pearl Harbor-surprised. End Wayne Milner was wide open, but the pass never reached him.

Fifteen years earlier Redskin owner George Preston Marshall had convinced the league to move the goal posts from the back of the end zone up to the goal line in order to increase scoring by making it easier to kick field goals. On this frostbitten Sabbath Marshall's portable posts made a difference he had never anticipated.

Baugh fired a pass toward Milner, but the ball struck the upright and ricocheted into the Washington end zone, where Sammy alertly fell on it before the Rams could recover it for a touchdown. It went for a safety and 2-0 Cleveland lead. Shortly afterward Baugh was hit hard and limped from the field, not to return until much later.

Frankie Filchok took over at quarterback for the Redskins, and promptly gave his side the lead when he found receiver Steve Bagarus in the clear. The pass was high, but Bagarus pulled it down and ran the rest of the way on the sixty-two-yard scoring play.

Shortly before intermission Waterfield drilled a thirty-seven-yard touchdown to Jim Benton, and it was time for the goal posts again. Waterfield doubled as placekicker, but his extra point attempt was deflected and hit the cross bar. The Municipal Stadium assembly gasped as the ball perched momentarily, then tumbled over for a 9-7 Ram lead at the half.

At the start of the third quarter the home team only ran the ball out to the nineteen-yard line, but they did not stay there. They drove to their opponents' forty-four and Waterfield hit Jim Gillette for a 15-7 score that stayed that way as this extra point attempt sailed wide.

The last score of the day came when Filchok found Bob Seymore in the end zone to narrow the difference to 15-14. It became the final as the Redskins missed two field goal attempts in the scoreless fourth quarter.

Despite the eyelash-thin result the Washingtons posted some dismal statistics. As a team they rushed for only thirty-two yards, while Gillette led all rushers with 101 steps. The immortal Sammy Baugh's last championship match-up saw him complete one pass for one yard. The Rams, meanwhile, left frozen Ohio in a blaze of glory.

A year later the league made it clear that crime does not pay.

The Scam

1946 Chicago Bears versus New York Giants

Few would have ever heard of one Alvin Paris if not for one thing—he tried to fix the outcome of the 1946 NFL Championship. Two New York Giants were implicated in the football version of the Black Sox scandal. They were running back Merle Hapes and recently acquired quarterback Frankie Filchok.

Paris offered the men $2500.00 apiece to sabotage the upcoming title game with the Chicago Bears. Although both players turned down the bribes, they failed to report Paris. This alone was a serious breach of league policy.

Whereas Hapes admitted being approached by Paris, Filchok denied it. After years of playing second-fiddle to Sammy Baugh in Washington he could not bear to not be permitted his first shot at championship glory, so he lied about being offered the bribe. With insufficient time to adequately investigate the affair, Commissioner Bert Bell took Filchok's word and considered him innocent until proven guilty. He ruled that Hapes would not be allowed to play in the title game, but Filchok would.

It was a memorable matchup for more than the aura of subterfuge. A record attendance of 58,346 paid $282,955.25 to view the contest, and Filchok may have sensed it was his last chance to prove himself. He put more effort into this cold afternoon's work than many had thought possible against Chicago's ravenous Bears. Soon after entering the game he suffered a broken nose that made just focusing his bleary eyes a painful endeavor. He kept them open, though, and fought the favored Bruins with desperate abandon.

Several notable records fell. Bear quarterback Sid Luckman broke Baugh's marks for postseason passing yardage and aerial touchdowns. Additionally, the winners received $1975.82 apiece as their shares of the gate receipts, and the losers each got $1295.57. More all-time highs.

The press caught wind early of the Paris situation, so no one thought about much else, except for the players. The visitors opened the scoring with Luckman's twenty-one-yard TD toss to Ken Cavenaugh. Soon afterward Dante Magnani picked off a Filchok pass and returned it thirty-nine yards for a 14-0 edge.

Just before the half, Filchok, despite the awful throbbing in the middle of his face, managed a thirty-eight-yard touchdown throw to Hank Liebel. The bedeviled Giant signal caller made it clear he was not trying to throw the game when he found Steve Filipowicz open for the score that evened the game at fourteen in the third quarter.

Had the New Yorkers been able to upset the Monsters of the Midway, Frankie Filchok might have been forgiven for not reporting the bribe he had been offered, or maybe not. It would be a moot point since Chicago cracked down on its recalcitrant foe in the final period when Luckman scored on a surprise nineteen-yard keeper play. Frank Maznicki sealed the victory with a twenty-six-yard field goal. The Bears won 24-14.

Filchok's efforts had been Herculean. He passed for two touchdowns through a team that was easily the class of the decade. New York head coach Steve Owen later told newsmen, "It choked you up knowing how hard that boy was trying," but Filchok and Hapes were permanently suspended from the league after the former confessed his scant but definite intercourse with Paris. There was no other way. The National Football League had to keep its integrity unconditional.

— And the Last Shall Be First —
1947 Chicago Cardinals versus Philadelphia Eagles

Until the late 1940s most teams looked forward to playing the Philadelphia Eagles and Chicago's stepchild, the Cardinals. As all knew, the Bears owned the Windy City. In the distant past the Cardinals had had a respectable enough record, but their more recent tally was dismal. The Eagles had an even less-distinguished chronicle.

By 1947 the Cards had developed a powerful, backfield-centered offense headed by rifle-armed quarterback Paul Christman and the ball-carrying tandem of Pat Harder and Marshall Goldberg. Runner Charley Trippi rounded out what owner Charles Bidwell called his "Dream Backfield."

Philadelphia had its own offensive powerhouse in tailback Steve van Buren who, despite a crippled arm, ran into the Hall of Fame. Fullback Joe Muha made it risky for defenses to key on van Buren, and quarterback Tommy Thompson ignored near-blindness in his left eye as he habitually set up behind his weighty offensive line and drilled sniper-accurate passes to his flock of gracile receivers.

The game was played in Chicago's Cominsky Park, and the Eagles quickly found themselves at odds with the officials. The December cold had hardened the field until it felt like the floor of a garage. The Cardinals came out wearing basketball sneakers, but the Philadelphia players trotted out wearing standard shoes whose cleats were sharpened to points. Five minutes after the kickoff the officials spotted these needle cleats, ruled them "illegal equipment," and forced the Eagles to don sneakers.

The game opened up midway through the first period when Trippi took a handoff and turned on his afterburner. Fifty-four yards the speedy, bruising ball carrier galloped for the game's first score just minutes before Elmer Angsman did the same thing, only from seventy yards.

Trailing 14-0, Philly got untracked when Thompson hit Pat McHugh with a fifty-three-yard touchdown pass in the second quarter. At the half the visitors trailed 14-7.

Late in the third period Chicago resumed its spectacular style of play as Trippi fielded a punt on his own twenty-five. It seemed every Eagle on the field had at least two shots at Charley as he churned downfield. None got a solid grip and the Card lead again swelled to fourteen.

Philadelphia started its next drive on its own seventeen and eventually scored on van Buren's one-yard plunge, but if the Eagles felt they had seen enough of Angsman for one afternoon they were mistaken. Moments later he tore off another seventy-yarder for a 28-14 lead as the stumbling, cursing Philadelphians reeled in futile pursuit.

The time-bereft Eagles scored a last time on Thompson's second touchdown pass as the Chicago Cardinals won their only title, 28-21. These teams would again clash the following year in a snowy sequel that would further distance them from their old domain of doormats.

The Snow Show
1948 Philadelphia Eagles versus Chicago Cardinals

Outside Philadelphia's Shibe Park shivering scalpers peddled their tickets with little success. Few could be convinced to pay money to sit through a blizzard even if the football game they would be watching was the 1948 NFL championship between the Philadelphia Eagles and Chicago Cardinals.

The scene was ripe for this rematch, and the Eagles wanted the Cardinals badly. The scintillating long runs of Elmer Angsman and Charley Trippi in the previous title test were still fresh, painful recollections. There was also triple-threat Card Pat Harder, who for the second straight season had topped the league in personal point production.

Philly was obviously eager to erase the hurt of the last year's finale, but at the moment the elements seemed bent on erasing the yardage markers. In some spots on the field the snow was almost a foot deep. Surprisingly, the game started only half an hour late.

Eagle quarterback Tommy Thompson was one of the most accurate passers the game has ever spawned, and had led the league in throwing that season. He wanted to give his adversaries a shot of their own, spectacular style early, so from his thirty-five he went deep. The intended receiver was end Jack Ferrante, who, despite his huge size, was pronghorn-swift. Jack flew through the secondary, gathered in his pass and never looked back the whole sixty-five yards. It was indeed too good to be true. One reason Ferrante so totally outdistanced his coverage was that he broke from the line a count early. Instead of a promising early lead Philadelphia was penalized five yards for offsides. It was the game's most exciting episode.

The Eagles repeatedly had breaks come their way as they recovered fumbles and intercepted passes, only to consistently fail to capitalize. Trippi and Angsman were stymied, but so was Philly's great Steve van

Buren. Yet the snowstorm and the Cardinals would not stop van Buren and his mates on this frozen day of great possibilities as one last chance presented itself.

Philadelphia placekicker Jim Patton had missed three field goal attempts, one of just twelve yards. Then the home team got another shot as time dwindled in the third quarter. Eagle punter Joe Muha had pushed Chicago back to its own nineteen with a towering kick. On the next play the Cards made their last mistake.

Quarterback Ray Mallouf took the snap and turned to hand off, but nobody was there. A lineman slammed into Mallouf and the ball popped loose. Philadelphia's Bucko Kilroy recovered at the seventeen. As time expired in the period the Eagles' Bosh Pritchard made it to the eleven. Muha carried the ball three more yards, and then Thompson bootlegged to a first-and-goal on the five.

It was time to ignore the numbing cold, to toss aside finesse and the blizzard-neutralized passing game. It would be impossible to surprise the defenders—as if they did not already know, the fans were telling them. "GIVE THE BALL TO STEVE!," screamed thousands of ice-crusted throats. It was not only the popular course, but also the only one.

Van Buren snatched the pigskin, slashed into a snowy sliver of daylight opened by his splendid offensive line, and Philadelphia had its first NFL title.

Patton kicked the extra point to close out the scoring—the least ever in a championship game. Philadelphia 7, Chicago 0. In the City of Brotherly Love this ice age ended on a warm note, but weather was not finished participating in title games.

The Flood of '49
1949 Philadelphia Eagles versus Los Angeles Rams

The cavernous Los Angeles Memorial Coliseum seats over 70,000 people, but not on December 18, 1949. Despite tons of sunny promises to the contrary in sundry travel brochures, southern California was on the brink of washing away on this day of the seventeenth NFL Championship game.

The storm did not worry the visiting Philadelphia Eagles. For them this weather was an improvement over the previous title game's blizzard. Besides, every casual fan knows that rain affects passing far more than it does running, and the Eagles were the best running team in the league. For the third straight season their Steve van Buren had topped the pros in rushing, and was as unstoppable as ever. The hometown Rams, meanwhile, were dangerously dependent on the passing of quarterbacks Bob Waterfield and Norm Van Brocklin.

There were other worrisome implications to the meteorological situation. Neither team stood to profit much by performing on a field surrounded by empty seats, which was certain to happen in this deluge. Despite the clear advantage the weather afforded them the Philadelphians did not object when Rams owner Dan Reeves proposed telephoning Commissioner Bert Bell to request permission to postpone the game a week, playing it on Christmas Day. The Birds took for granted they could beat L.A. *under* water, should that be where they played them. Yet their magnanimity would not matter. Bell, mindful of radio commitments to broadcast the game nationwide, denied Reeves' request.

The visitors' overconfidence was squelched the night before the game by a terse pep talk from tackle Al Wistert. By game time the Eagles were primed. Sure enough, just 22,245 fans glowered from the waterlogged bleachers at the kickoff, but despite the low final score they would not be bored.

The alternating passing tandem of Waterfield and van Brocklin would complete only ten of twenty-seven attempts for ninety-eight yards, while the other Dutchman, van Buren, splashed for a record 196 yards. Ironically, Steve would score no touchdowns.

Van Buren once got loose on a forty-nine-yard run to set up a seemingly certain touchdown, but Pat Parmer fumbled the possession away on the seven-yard line. Steve later rattled off a twenty-three-yarder that came to naught when quarterback Tommy Thompson threw an interception. Yet the scoring was there as Thompson took advantage of the absence of injured defensive back Gabby Sims to drill Pete Pihos with a thirty-one-yard paydirt pass to give Philadelphia a 7-0 halftime lead.

If Waterfield's passing was rained out, he almost made up for it with his punting. Bob repeatedly shoved the Eagles deep into their own territory via towering kicks that scraped the low-hanging clouds before descending, but it did not last.

Standing on his own five-yard line in the third period Waterfield readied to uncork another of his altitudinous punts. But when center Don Paul snapped the ball he gave it too much arm, forcing the Rams' multitalented passer/kicker to leap to snare it. By the time he landed and regained his balance the Eagles' Ed Skladany was upon him and blocked the kick. Skladany then seized the ball and charged across the goal line for a 14-0 score.

Any chance for scoring in the final quarter was washed away as Philadelphia sponged off its second straight title. It would be one to savor and remember.

During the following pre-season injuries to key personnel rendered the Eagles' magnificent offense impotent, and eleven years would pass before Philly saw another championship. Meanwhile, an incredible chapter was to be written in Cleveland.

Storybook Beginning
1950 Cleveland Browns versus Los Angeles Rams

Like everything else, football teams have beginnings. When the Cleveland Browns played their first season in the NFL one might have thought they were in their infancy. Not so—the Browns had opened for business four years earlier as part of a rebel league called the All-America Conference (AAC.)

The rival club had come about because of the old guard's strong anti-expansion faction. When the National Football League refused to grant new franchises, those who had sought admission set up their own shop.

From the outset the Browns were the AAC's dominant team, winning every one of its championships and fifty-one of the fifty-eight games they played while the league lasted. When it folded after the 1949 season the NFL grudgingly admitted four of its teams, the Browns, Baltimore Colts, San Francisco 49ers and New York Yankees.

Paul Brown was Cleveland's brilliant head coach, and destined to make an immense splash in the big times. He had painstakingly handpicked and taught a roster that was not only superior to those in the AAC, but to any in the established league even if the NFL did not yet realize it. To further strengthen his squad Brown scanned the ranks of players cast adrift when the All-America Conference collapsed. He signed the most talented of these free agents for his already irresistibly skilled team. This influx of new players also made it difficult for upcoming NFL opponents since the newcomers would not be in evidence when opposing coaches and players viewed game films made before the free agents arrived.

The boys in the established camp can be forgiven for looking with sneering overconfidence upon the new Cleveland team. After all, the lineups it had manhandled in the defunct league were not considered world-beaters—especially by NFL standards. Paul Brown did not mind his outfit's being underestimated. He knew it was a great advantage.

As if to put the Brownies in their place right away the schedule makers slated them to meet the defending champion Philadelphia Eagles in the first game of the 1950 season. Philly's marvelous offense had been ravaged by injuries during the pre-season, but most figured it would not matter. It did. Cleveland 35, Philadelphia 10. This game showed that the new kids were for real. The rest of the regular season went to proving they were title contenders.

When December rolled around, Cleveland was indeed in the finale, and the irony was rich at whom they would play. The Los Angeles Rams were paying a visit to their old stadium five years after ducking out to the West Coast. Now that a new team had filled the void in embarrassingly spectacular fashion, a soap opera confrontation was inevitable. During the twelve-game regular season the Browns gave up just 154 points, but had not played the Rams, who scored 466. In a game with Green Bay, Los Angeles had scored forty-one points in the third quarter alone.

The Rams went against what was considered the norm. Other teams established a running game first, and then threw. L.A. was wont to take to the air from the beginning and keep throwing throughout the contest. While their opponents lusted after optimum field position, the Rams concentrated on touchdowns. It seemed head coach Joe Stydahar knew what he was doing. He was in the title game, and his team had averaged over 300 passing yards per game that year.

With quarterbacks Norm van Brocklin and Bob Waterfield, the California marvels were justified in their style of offense. Receivers Tom Fears and Elroy Hirsch caught 126 balls between them in the '50 season. The Rams even had a powerful *running* game in their "Bull Elephant" backfield of Paul "Tank" Younger, Dan Towler and Ralph Pasquariello. Both teams felt at home in Cleveland's Municipal Stadium for the Christmas Eve game, and most of the fans had cheered lustily for the *Rams* in the past. It was just five years since the Bighorns had brought Cleveland its first pro football championship. Yet this wide-open game would put history to shame.

Broken ribs had sidelined van Brocklin in the previous week's playoff game with Chicago, but Waterfield was hale and eager. When his side returned the opening kickoff only to the eighteen-yard line he more than made up for the short runback on the first play from scrimmage.

Bob knew the Browns would go to extreme efforts to shut down his deep threats Hirsch and Fears, so he and Stydahar devised a stratagem specifically for this afternoon. On first down Fears, Hirsch and Verda "Vitamin T" Smith ran pass routes to the right while halfback Glen Davis hesitated in the backfield as if to block. While the secondary frantically chased the apparent three-pronged receiving pattern Davis, unnoticed, suddenly took off down the left sideline. Waterfield's pass caught up with him at midfield and the All-American from Army outran late-arriving defenders Ken Gorgal and Tommy James for an eighty-two-yard scoring play that gave L.A. a 7-0 lead with twenty-seven seconds elapsed.

The home team swiftly retaliated as they huffed to the Rams' thirty-one where quarterback Otto Graham hit flanker Dub Jones for the TD that tied for Cleveland. The visitors came back with a lovely drive ending with Dick Hoerner's three-yard smash on the game's fifteenth play. 14-7, Rams. Four minutes into the second period Graham found end Dante Lavelli on a twenty-six-yard toss to finish what would have been a playbook-perfect drive had not Lou Groza missed the extra point.

After so many early fireworks the defenses suddenly began to assert themselves, and the score remained 14-13 until halftime. At one point the West Coast offense lost thirty-eight yards during one series of downs.

In the third quarter the excitement returned as the Browns marched seventy-seven yards for a 20-14 lead on Graham's second touchdown pass to Lavelli—this one from thirty-nine yards. Minutes later the Rams stormed back as Waterfield passed his team to the Browns' seventeen, then astonished onlookers by handing off to Hoerner seven straight times into the pass-conscious defense. The last was from the one-yard line on fourth down to give Los Angeles a 21-20 edge.

On the first play after the kickoff the Browns' huge fullback Marion Motley fumbled. Defensive end Larry Brink grabbed the loose ball and lumbered into the end zone for his side's second TD within twenty-five seconds. 28-20, Rams.

Paul Brown and his men refused to be dismayed by the unfortunate turn the game had abruptly taken for them. A whole quarter remained to be played. Cleveland began the final touchdown drive of the day after Warren Lahr picked off a Waterfield pass early in the final period.

The Browns displayed extreme resolution (and more than a hint of desperation) on this march as they twice refused to punt on fourth downs, and both times achieved the priceless conversions. Finally, end Rex Bumgardner made a spectacular nineteen-yard catch of a Graham pass in the end zone to pull Cleveland to within a point.

After the kickoff Los Angeles was quickly forced to punt when Waterfield was sacked by defensive end Len Ford. Ford had missed most of the regular season with a broken jaw, and was another grim surprise for the visitors.

With three minutes to play, Graham had his offense on the Ram twenty-four. A field goal at this point would have been easy enough for Groza (who was eager to atone for his earlier missed PAT,) but Otto wanted to get closer still and eat up as much clock as possible. He tried to run for extra yardage, but linebacker Mike Lazetich crunched him from the blind side. Graham fumbled and Lazetich recovered.

Stydahar instructed Waterfield to take no chances, and keep the ball on the ground. The three running plays Bob called gained just six yards, but used up more time. Out of field goal range, Waterfield popped a fifty-one-yard punt that many thought would be the game-winning play.

Cliff Lewis managed to return the kick to his own thirty-two, and with one minute and fifty seconds left, the Browns were not the fans' choice to pull off the scoring drive through the determined Los Angeles defense. Spectators were streaming toward the exits.

Graham had no time to worry about this lack of faith as he ran, passed and cajoled his squad down the field. He drove them to the Ram sixteen where he risked a quarterback sneak to give Groza a better kicking angle in the tricky crosswind. This time Otto did not fumble as he gave Groza optimum position in the middle of the field, and called timeout.

Big Lou jogged in for the biggest kick of his life. He tried to forget how momentous it was. "I didn't hear the crowd. I blotted out the distance, the time left, even the score. All I had to do was kick the ball."

Groza did kick the ball, and could not have kicked it better. The chip shot gave Cleveland the lead, game and title, 30-28. It was a season-long feat not likely to ever be repeated as the Cleveland Browns won the NFL championship their first year in the league. They were just getting started.

— The Flying Dutchman —
1951 Los Angeles Rams versus Cleveland Browns

Very swiftly the Cleveland Browns had earned more than respect and a title. The NFL was frankly terrified of these splendid newcomers who had squeezed into the club, then promptly and against its will forced their way into its throne room. Still, not everyone was intimidated. Their championship victims of the previous post-season were thirsting for vengeance, and had done plenty to assure they would be quenched.

1951 was just the second year in the league for the Browns, and they had torn through their opposition as easily without the element of surprise that had so aided them the previous season. There were many who had suspected that the no-longer-overconfident big league franchises would firmly put the gatecrashers back in their place, but the only game Cleveland lost all year was its season opener to San Francisco—another All-America Conference refugee. It was true that the Brownies did not need to sneak up on their foes to defeat them, but these were not quite the same teams that had met in the last title confrontation. The Los Angeles Rams had a new look

The veteran core was still the mainstay, yet the class of '51 included thirteen fresh-faced rookies whose contributions to the team's quest for a rematch were inestimable. With 5506 the bomb-tossing Rams had rolled up more yards than any team in history, and despite their aerial predilection they had amassed 366 *rushing* yards in a regular season game with the New York Yankees. A record 59,475 fans were accordingly excited as they filed into the Los Angeles Memorial Coliseum.

Like the year before it was the Rams who scored first. Dick Hoerner punched across from one yard out after a pass interference penalty set the home team up with optimum field position. This touchdown may be regarded as strictly a bonus since Cleveland was not playing the type of defense Los Angeles had expected. Ram head coach Joe Stydahar had stationed a "spy" in the Browns' hometown to observe their practice sessions. The man supposedly told Stydahar they were planning to use a six-man defensive line, so the Bighorns were taken aback when Cleveland came at them from their standard, four-man alignment.

The visitors got on the board with Lou Groza's fifty-two-yard field goal and quarterback Otto Graham's seventeen-yard touchdown pass to Dub Jones for a 10-7 halftime lead, but in the second half the action strayed from the script. In a regular season meeting Graham and his Browns had raked these youngsters 38-23. The Los Angeles defense may have suffered from a slight case of diaper rash, but had grown up some since that last encounter and was determined to not be humiliated again.

Midway through the third quarter defenders Larry Brink and rookie Andy Robustelli knocked the ball loose from Graham on the Cleveland forty-one. Robustelli snatched the fumble and rumbled to the two-yard line before being caught by fullback Marion Motley. Dan Towler scored the touchdown for a 14-10 lead.

As soon as his defense regained the ball Stydahar replaced uncharacteristically ineffectual quarterback Bob Waterfield with Norm van Brocklin. Back in September the Dutchman had presented a passing clinic the like of which has been seen just that once in football. He shredded the New York Giant secondary for 554 yards in a 54-14 rout. Having stood on the sideline for most of the afternoon he had had plenty of time to observe and digest what was and was not working for Waterfield. Nevertheless, the first series of downs with van Brocklin at the helm was spectacularly unsuccessful. L.A. drove effortlessly to the one-yard line, where everything fell to pieces.

On the next three plays the defense shoved the Rams from the one back to the eighteen, then snowed under Glen Davis on an attempted reverse out of a fake field goal attempt. After regaining possession they had it happen again, only this time they stopped themselves as two penalties pushed them from the one out to the eleven. Los Angeles did not come up totally dry this time as Waterfield converted a field goal for a 17-10 advantage.

With time dwindling, the Rams figured Graham would try to pass his way to a tie, so they lined up with seven defensive backs. Otto was too wily a field general to do what his opposition expected, so he moved on the ground toward the score. The TD drive covered seventy yards (with Graham picking up thirty-four on one scramble,) and ended with Ken Carpenter's five-yard rush to even the game at seventeen.The Browns had assigned a flock of defensive backs to wide receiver Elroy Hirsch, who had topped the season with sixty-six receptions for 1495 yards and seventeen touchdowns while his fellow wideout Tom Fears was hobbled by a sore knee. Fears' legs would prove as sound as van Brocklin's mighty right arm midway through the final period as, while the defense worriedly surrounded Hirsch, they would nail down the game.

The Rams had a third-and-three on their own twenty-seven. With the defense expecting a run van Brocklin sent Fears wide left, and at the snap Tom sprinted down the sideline then cut to the right at midfield. At this point the Dutchman unloaded what Fears later called, "The best-thrown pass I ever caught in my life." He was in full stride and pulling away from hopelessly beaten defenders Cliff Lewis and Tommy James when the ball reached him. The play covered seventy-three yards, giving Los Angeles a 24-17 lead. The Browns had one more chance.

Cleveland threatened one more time, but running back Dub Jones was dropped for a two-yard loss on fourth-and-two from the L.A. forty-two, and the acne-faced Ram defenders did not let the Eastern Division champs out of their own territory for what was left of the contest. With a 24-17 victory the West Coast got its first taste of pro football championship glory, and showed the rest of the league Paul Brown and his pack were only human. It would not be the last time.

After the win the youngsters tried to carry their beaming, huge Coach Stydahar off the field on their shoulders. It was the hardest job they faced all afternoon. They dropped him.

The Texas Connection
1952 Detroit Lions versus Cleveland Browns

It had been a long wait for the sports-minded folks of Detroit. Seventeen years is quite awhile for loyal fans to bide their time while their team works its way back to the rainbow's end.

That long-ago title squad had featured an outstanding ball carrier named Buddy Parker, who was back with the team as head coach. Buddy achieved sterling success by dredging up talent where no one else bothered looking. Parker adopted players who were disillusioned, disgruntled or simply could not fit into their former teams' systems onto the team he was now springing upon the NFL. Foremost among this group of former castoffs were a couple of Texans who had been with the Lions since before Buddy took charge—quarterback Bobby Layne and halfback Doak Walker.

The Lions' opponents for the 1952 title game were the Cleveland Browns, who were anxious to atone for the previous year's (to them) inexplicable championship loss to the L.A. Rams. The game was played in Cleveland, and the first quarter ended scorelessly, but late in the period the league's leading punter, Cleveland's Horace Gillom, got off a dismal kick that fluttered just twenty-two yards before bouncing out of bounds at midfield. Layne positioned the touchdown with a couple of key passes to ends Bill Swiacki and another Texan, Cloyce Box. Layne ran for the TD from one yard out for a 7-0 halftime edge.

Walker had spent most of the season sidelined by a severe muscle pull. Today the injury came in handy since it meant the Browns did not expect much trouble from the ball-toting marvel from Southern Methodist who had scored seventeen touchdowns his first two years in the pros, but none in this, his third.

On his own thirty-three Layne sent Box deep to the left, took the snap, furtively handed off to Walker, and then faded as if to pass. Walker shot through the left side of the line, cut to his right and pounded sixty-seven yards to a 14-0 lead.

Four minutes later Cleveland achieved its only score on a seven-yard run by Harry Jagade. Browns quarterback Otto Graham tried mightily, but did well to throw for a modest 157 yards. Pivotal receivers Mac Speedie and Dub Jones both missed the game due to injuries, and Otto's shrunken catching corps was unable to shake off the sticky Detroit secondary.

The Browns' running game seemed hearty enough when thirty-two-year-old fullback Marion Motley ripped off a forty-two-yard fourth quarter sprint that placed the ball on the five. The boisterous Municipal Stadium crowd loudly awaited the tying score, but grew silent watching its team being shoved back to the twenty-two by the resolute Lion defense, and coming up empty-handed.

After Detroit running back/place-kicker Pat Harder drilled a three-pointer the Clevelanders came close once more, but a fourth down pass from Graham to Pete Brewster for an apparent touchdown was nullified when the officials noticed end Ray Renfro, who in this play's alignment was an ineligible receiver, tip the ball before it reached Brewster.

Statistically, the home team dominated, but the final score favored the Lions, 17-7. Buddy Parker and his posse of refugees had the last laugh on more teams than just the Browns, but in the future they would keep laughing at the Browns.

Strike Three

1953 Detroit Lions versus Cleveland Browns

The Cleveland Browns had been impatient for the 1953 season to begin, and especially for it to end. Two straight NFL championship game losses made them forget the regular season victories they had accumulated in bunches. To win that last game was all that mattered. Again their opponents were the Detroit Lions, and Motor City's Briggs Stadium was typically jammed.

The Lions had a rookie middle linebacker named Joe Schmidt who gave warning of his coming greatness on the second play of the game when he blitzed the ball loose from Cleveland quarterback Otto Graham. Detroit's Les Bingaman recovered the fumble on the Browns' thirteen-yard line. Doak Walker finished the short drive by scoring the only touchdown of the first half, which, after he and Browns kicker Lou Groza swapped field goals in the second quarter, ended with the Lions ahead 10-3.

Detroit's defense stifled Graham's passing attack all afternoon, but the Clevelanders were just too good to be denied the end zone. Harry Jagade's scoring run in the third period, and two more Groza field goals gave the Browns a 16-10 fourth quarter edge and a relentless determination to protect their precarious lead.

Jim Doran and Leon Hart had come to the Lions as wonderfully gifted receivers, but their team's defensive secondary was critically deficient, and opposing passers threw with ease through the porous coverage. Then the coaches discovered Doran could defend passes as well as catch them. Indeed, it often seemed his job had changed little as he latched onto almost as many balls as a defender as he had from the offensive side. Hart's emergence as a top flanker made the shift an unconditional success.

Late in this championship game a knee injury felled Hart, leaving head coach Buddy Parker no choice but to send Doran back to the offense. Defensive back Warren Lahr found himself one-on-one with the swift Doran, whom Cleveland had not expected to be used as a receiver. Doran made two crucial receptions on Lahr which, between them, sewed up the game.

The first catch was an eighteen-yard gain to the Browns' forty-five on a key third-and-ten with just under three minutes remaining. Detroit quarterback Bobby Layne next picked up another fresh set of downs via a surprise, third down running play to the thirty-three, then called time out to discuss strategy.

Doran realized he could beat Lahr deep, and kept urging Layne to throw long. On the Cleveland thirty-three, Bobby reasoned that if he pushed much deeper he would not have room for a bomb, and Doran's advantage of speed would be negated.

At the snap, Doran shot straight ahead then cut to the inside. He left Lahr far behind and took Layne's heave in for the winning touchdown in a 17-16 decision.

Moments later a desperation Graham pass was intercepted to nail down Detroit's latest title. Coach Paul Brown and his athletes had fallen short for the third straight year, and left a trail of tears all the way back to Ohio. Yet this latest loss birthed a determination that would steamroller all opponents the following year.

Fourth Time Charm
1954 Cleveland Browns versus Detroit Lions

In the misty days of yore the Detroit Tigers had a pitcher named Frank Lary who held an unending victory streak over the New York Yankees. Lary consistently pitched his team past the otherwise indomitable Yanks, who kept vowing a vengeance that never came.

Motor City had the upper hand in another running feud, this one in football. The Detroit Lions alone held championship sway over the Cleveland Browns. Counting exhibition games the Lions had bested the Browns seven out of the last eight times they had met—the lone exception being a pre-season tie. Most painful for the Brownies were the back-to-back league title games they had dropped to Detroit.

Maybe it was something psychological. Cleveland had too talented a team simply to be outclassed repeatedly. The law of averages decreed Detroit's hold over the Browns had to end. In this Year of Our Lord 1954 the Clevelanders were in their fifth straight National Football League championship game, but had lost the last three in a row.

Another factor stated something had to give. The Browns' quarterback incomparable Otto Graham had announced the game would be his swan song after nine years as signal caller. Otto's teammates could not abide the thought of him going out a loser. Game day saw Cleveland's Municipal Stadium holding 43,827 hopeful partisans come to witness the great Graham take on the bane squad that had frustrated him so long.

At first the script appeared distressingly familiar when Detroit fullback Bill Bowman crashed through the center of the line and into the clear on what would have been a touchdown had it not been for an early season leg injury that still slowed him enough that the Browns were able to catch him from behind. The visitors got no points off that play, but an intercepted Graham pass later set up the game's first score—a thirty-six-yard field goal by the Lions' Doak Walker. A combination of panic and grim resolve settled on the home team, and despite being the year's highest-scoring franchise, Detroit was no longer a match for these angry, vengeful Eastern Division champs.

Graham completed scoring shots to Pete Brewster and Ray Renfro for the first touchdowns of the game. Late in the first period Cleveland's Billy Reynolds returned a punt to the one-yard line, and on the first play of the second quarter Otto called his own number and sneaked the ball across for a 21-3 advantage.

An eleven-yard TD toss by Detroit quarterback Bobby Layne cut the lead to 21-10, but Graham was just getting started. He scored on a five-yard run, and seconds before intermission he speared Renfro with a thirty-one-yard throw for a 35-10 halftime bulge. The second half was no more merciful to the Lions as their opponents rang up three more touchdowns to amass a final margin of 56-10.

The crowd gave Graham a standing ovation every time he stepped on the field. A solid wall of joyful noise celebrated his passing for three scores and running for three more against the most appropriate team possible. The taste of victory was too sweet to walk away from just yet, and Otto Graham would change his mind and return to lead his beloved Browns on another quest for championship glory.

Last Time Around

1955 Cleveland Browns versus Los Angeles Rams

It was a short retirement for Otto Graham, but for the Cleveland Browns it seemed eternal. Without him their offense fumbled impotently through the 1955 exhibition schedule. Before long head coach Paul Brown called, and Graham agreed to don his pads for one more season. Responding beautifully to his skilled leadership and play, Cleveland cruised to the top of the Eastern Division. This cast of grizzled, fire-tested veterans earned the right to travel to Los Angeles to contest for the league title with the bomb-tossing Rams.

Through sheer, gutsy determination the Rams had managed to win the Western Division despite what should have been a fatal number of injuries. Billy Wade and Norm Van Brocklin shared quarterbacking duties, much to the displeasure of van Brocklin, who could not gracefully accept playing second-fiddle to anyone. Likely for this reason the Dutchman (who was slated to start) was determined to put more effort into this game than any other. Perhaps he tried too hard, but he would not be lonely as a record 85,693 fans squeezed into the Los Angeles Coliseum to witness their heroes' struggle with the heavily favored Browns.

Van Brocklin's long day started early when Don Paul intercepted a first period pass intended for Skeet Quinlan and returned it sixty-five yards for the first score. The

crowd's hopes were already starting to fade.

Trailing 10-0 shortly before halftime Dutch again called on Quinlan, hitting him with a sixty-seven-yard touchdown pass to cut the Cleveland lead to three and momentarily shift momentum to the Rams. Had they been able to break for intermission right then the Bighorns might have made a game of it in the second half, but in the few seconds remaining in the second quarter Graham ran the home team's impetus (and hopes) into the Coliseum turf.

The cagey passer sent two receivers down the right sideline as decoys while end Dante Lavelli slipped off to the left. As the defense concentrated on the twin receiving threat to the right, Lavelli threw off his coverage by cutting diagonally across the field and catching Graham's throw in front of the surprised deep defenders, who were then blocked out by the receivers they had been covering. The play went fifty yards for the back-breaker, robbing Los Angeles of hope, and leaving it demoralized and baffled.

The Browns could do no wrong in the second half, rolling up and down the field, devouring the clock and scoring three more touchdowns while van Brocklin continued to force the ball into the secondary. He wound up with six interceptions.

Cleveland won 38-14 behind the typically expert quarterbacking of Graham, who ended the day and his career with 202 yards on fourteen completions off twenty-five attempts for two touchdowns. He ran for two more.

The great grid general went out with a fittingly superb performance the like of which he made commonplace during his tenure as the only starting quarterback in the team's history. With him over center the club's NFL record was 58-13-1, and his absence in coming seasons would emphasize his true value. It was nine years before the Cleveland Browns won another league title.

Giants Indeed

1956 New York Giants versus Chicago Bears

It was ten years since the league's foremost rivalry had met in a confrontation of championship proportions. The dimensions of this game would be grand, but it was not a contest.

Right up until the end 1956 was very good to the Chicago Bears. Their quarterback Ed Brown led the league in passing, and the 363 points they amassed were far more than the season total of the New York Giants, whom they would face in this title game. The Giants were hungry. It had been eighteen years since they had taken home the shiny trophy reserved for those at the top, and this drought was ending with a flood. Jim Lee Howell had played on that long-ago championship team. Now he was head coach, leading another squad to this last game of the quest for the tardy title.

To no one's surprise, New York was cold on game day, although nobody much noticed except for the Bears. For them the afternoon lasted all winter. The Giants received the opening kickoff, which went to a fumble-prone return man named Gene Filipski. Gene did not fumble this time as it took the visitors fifty-three yards to catch him. The long return set up fullback Mel Triplett's seventeen-yard touchdown run to give New York a permanent lead. At the end of the first quarter the Giants led 10-0, and by halftime the difference had swollen to 34-7 as the underdog home team ruthlessly
pressed its advantage.

The Bears' league-leading rusher Rick Casares was the center of his team's fondest hopes, but other than a nine-yard scoring run just before halftime, Casares was well neutralized. Despite intense preparations the Chicago offensive line was unable to stop future Hall of Fame middle linebacker Sam Huff. Huff let his fellow defenders worry about the other Bears while he concentrated solely on Casares. Devised by New York defensive coordinator Tom Landry, this strategy was unbeatable.

Six Giants scored touchdowns as the splendid backfield trio of Triplett, league Most Valuable Player Frank Gifford, and Alex Webster galloped with killing impunity through the demoralized Bears. On defense other men besides Huff laced into the Bruins.

End Andy Robustelli had played for the L.A. Rams' 1951 championship team. Now he brought his talent and ability to bear on the previously free-scoring Chicagoans. Former Steeler Ed Modzelewski got his first-ever taste of title glory as he helped shut down the lethal Bear attack.

Back in October the Yankees had breezed to victory in the World Series. Now, as the Giants polished off Chicago 47-7, and 50,000-plus delirious fans pulled down the goal posts, for the rest of the sports world the New York holocaust was complete.

One Last Time

1957 Detroit Lions versus Cleveland Browns

Just when it finally appeared someone besides the Detroit Lions and Cleveland Browns would fight it out for the NFL throne each year, these same teams squared off for the fourth time in six years. For more reason than one, it would be a season to recall and savor.

1957 was a strange year for the Lions, starting back in August. At a pre-season banquet for players, coaches and club officials head coach Buddy Parker rocked the assembly by abruptly announcing his resignation. The next day assistant coach George Wilson took over for Parker, who stated in his farewell message, "When you get to a situation where you can't handle football players, it's time to get out!"

Late in the season, against these same Browns, ace quarterback Bobby Layne suffered a broken leg. Tobin Rote, who had just come to the club from Green Bay, took over as starter.

December 29 was sunny and cold in Detroit as the finalists lined up in Briggs Stadium, and things started off to the crowd's delight as the Lions piled up a 17-0 first quarter lead. Still, the game was not yet secure. It the rookie year of up-and-coming running back Jimmy Brown. Early in the second period Brown took a handoff twenty-nine yards around right end for the score that gave the Brownies a fighting chance.

Rote realized the game's momentum could easily swing to Cleveland. The tough campaigner decided to spring a surprise that had just occurred to him.

On fourth down at the Browns' twenty-six Coach Wilson sent in his field goal unit, fully expecting it to go for the three-pointer, but in the huddle Rote changed the play. Rather than hold for kicker Jim Martin he grabbed the snap and rolled out to his right. Wide-open receiver Steve Junker caught the pass at the five and strolled untouched into the end zone. The visitors were devastated by this unexpected ploy, and folded completely.

The Detroiters well recall the post-season shellacking they had taken from this same outfit three years earlier, and never ease their assault today. Surrogate quarterback Rote finished with 296 yards passing and four touchdowns as the Big Cats pulverized their foes 59-14.

The shell-shocked Browns would never be the same after this pounding, taking seven years to make it back to the title game. The arch-rivalry of the decade was over. In coming years players and fans would wait vainly for the customary annual Cleveland-Detroit shootout, but as seasons and post-seasons dragged past and other teams and dynasties stepped forward, the old passions faded. Yet for some sports fans who watched and listened as the Cleveland Browns and Detroit Lions took six titles in eight seasons the Eisenhower years will always have a rich flavor.

The Baltimore Who?
1958 Baltimore Colts versus New York Giants

The Baltimore Colts had quite a bit of history for team that had only been in the league seven years. As part of the late All-America Conference the club was absorbed by the National Football League upon the AAC's collapse, but one year later the Colts sank into bankruptcy and disbanded. In 1953 an energetic young businessman named Carroll Rosenbloom purchased the financially ailing Dallas Texans and moved them to Baltimore, giving them the old name.

With the city having no major college or university the Colts stepped into a ripe football vacuum where throngs of previously teamless fans adopted their newly arrived professionals lovingly. For some time opponents looked forward to playing the Ponies, who were looked upon as the league's pushovers. Then in 1956 Baltimore picked up a twenty-three-year-old quarterback named Johnny Unitas whose name was on an old waiver list. A year earlier Johnny had been a low draft pick of his hometown Pittsburgh Steelers, who released him without giving him any playing time. After being waived, Unitas took a job as a construction worker and spent his spare time quarterbacking a local semi-pro team called the Bloomfield Rams. A Ram fan wrote an enthusiastic letter about him to Colt head coach Weeb Ewbank, who passed the tip to general manager Don Kellett. Kellett made the best sports deal in history by investing eighty cents in a long-distance phone call to ask Unitas if he was still looking for a team.

Shortly after Johnny's arrival an injury sidelined the Colts' starting quarterback George Shaw, who never regained his job. By 1958 Johnny U was making Baltimore look like his last stop en route to Canton, Ohio and the Hall of Fame. In that season, despite suffering broken ribs and a punctured lung in a 56-0 midseason rout of the Green Bay Packers, he threw nineteen touchdown passes against just seven interceptions in the twelve-game schedule. It was a sweet schedule, too. On November 30

Johnny's old team, the lowly Steelers, upset Chicago to give the Colts a shot at the Western Division title. Baltimore snatched the opportunity, stampeding back from a 27-7 halftime deficit to drop the San Francisco 49ers 35-27 and secure its first-ever post-season appearance.

The plot was different in New York. The Giants were unable to repeat their sparkling 1956 showing, ending a distant second to Cleveland in the Eastern Division in '57. They clawed their way back to the divisional crown this following year. With middle linebacker Sam Huff and his tigerlike defense carrying the load, quarterback Charlie Conerly and his careful offense squeezed out enough points to land them in the big game versus up-and-coming Baltimore. Under the brilliant direction of offensive coordinator Vince Lombardi and defensive coordinator Tom Landry an early-season contest between these teams had ended with a dramatic 24-21 New York victory that provided it with the momentum needed for the run to this sequel.

The game would feature everything necessary for it to become known as the "greatest game ever played." The visiting Colts had things pretty much their own way in the first half, going into the locker room at the half leading 14-3. Yet the Giants had too much class, pride and determination for the matchup to become a blowout. In the third period the momentum abruptly, drastically shifted on the home team's one-yard line. It was first-and-goal for Baltimore, and another touchdown would have probably slammed the door on valiant but slightly overmatched New York. Even Colt fans were not too eager for a crushing defeat. The closest margin of victory in the last four championship games had been twenty-four points, and viewers and listeners across the country were ready for some hair-pulling suspense. They got it from the Giant defense as it fashioned a goal line stand such as could be recalled by very few, holding Baltimore on four straight and taking away the ball when Huff dropped fullback Alan Ameche for a four-yard loss on fourth down. Four years earlier Ameche had won the Heisman Trophy his senior year at Wisconsin. He would make certain this setback was only for the moment.

Inspired by its defense's heroics, the New York offense generated two long drives to take a 17-14 lead late in the fourth quarter. Hoping to pick up a first down and run out the clock, Conerly handed off to halfback Frank Gifford on third-and-four. Baltimore tackle Gino Marchetti flew into this pivotal play with such abandon that he broke his own ankle while stopping Gifford barely shy of the first down marker.

Colt chances did not look rosy after an altitudinous punt set them back to their own fourteen with slightly under two minutes to play. Unitas came out pitching, though, and ate up the yardage with precise passes to his ends Lenny Moore and Raymond Berry, the year's leading receiver.

There were seven seconds left in regulation time when Ewbank sent kicker Steve Myra after the field goal to tie the score at seventeen. Myra came through and the NFL title game would require an unprecedented overtime. The Giants received the fifth period kickoff, but Baltimore's defense forced a punt. The home team would not see the ball on offense again.

The Colts took over on their own twenty, and with the clock no longer an enemy their incomparable quarterback drove them home. Berry was again central as he took all but one pass on the winning drive.

Once, when Unitas had called a pass in the huddle, he bent over center and noticed Huff was lined up deeper than usual in anticipation of the throw. Johnny audibled to a different play and sent Ameche up the middle on a lovely trap for twenty-three crucial yards.

The weary New York defense could no longer stop the brilliant signal-caller and his hungry teammates as they bulled to a first-and-goal at the eight-yard line. Most looked for Ewbank to send in the reliable Myra to close the deal, but Steve stayed on the sideline as Unitas shocked the assembly (his coach in particular) by *passing* to Jim Mutscheller, who twisted to the one.

After the game Ewbank revealed how his quarterback's choice of plays had floored him. Of *course* a pass was too risky for that situation, and it took the Giants by surprise. None could argue with the result after the next play as Ameche drove through a ragged wound in the line for the winning touchdown.

No longer would a football-bereft Maryland have to look on unrepresented as other locales savored all the gridiron glory. The 23-17 final score sent the state into delighted delirium and was close enough to satisfy a drama-starved sports world.

For Unitas such heroism would always be typical.

The Best in the West?
1959 Baltimore Colts versus New York Giants

In a curious act of divisional positioning the NFL placed the Baltimore Colts in its Western Division despite their proximity to the eastern seaboard, while the nearby New York Giants were in the Eastern Division. The alignment was painful to other western teams as the Colts lived up to their newly earned reputation following their arresting overtime win over the New Yorkers in the '58 title test.

Long-maligned Giant quarterback Charlie Conerly was showing what he could do when finally surrounded by a quality cast, statistically outstripping even the Colts' new superstar Johnny Unitas, and leading the league in passing. Determined to achieve a rematch with its new archrivals, New York dominated the east in 1959.

57,000-plus fans jammed Baltimore's Municipal Stadium for the confrontation, and quickly had cause to cheer. In the first quarter Unitas fired a fifty-nine-yard touchdown heave to Lenny Moore.

The play scared but did not rattle the visitors as they immediately drove toward the tying score, but the Baltimore defense stiffened deep in its own territory and forced the Giants to settle for a Pat Summerall field goal. In the second quarter Summerall drilled a thirty-seven-yarder, and his defensive mates rose to their pugnacious reputation by shutting out the Colts the rest of the first half, which ended with them clinging to an eyelash-thin 7-6 advantage.

Summerall added another three-pointer for the only scoring in the third period and gave his team a 9-7 lead. Late in the quarter, though, New York found itself stymied with a fourth-and-one on the Baltimore twenty-nine. Giant head coach Jim Lee Howell recalled the previous year when he punted rather than go for the first down, and lost the title. This time he told Conerly to go for it, but when Charlie handed off to power runner Alex Webster the defenders sprang off the snap so fast the offensive linemen did not have time to brace themselves. Webster did not get his yard.

Early in the fourth quarter Unitas scored on a four-yard run, and the Ponies were off to the races. Defensive back Johnny Sample became very offensive-minded in the final period, stealing two Conerly passes and returning one forty-two yards for a score. Andy Nelson intercepted another to set up a twelve-yard TD pass from Unitas to Willie Richardson.

For most of the game the Giants had stifled Unitas' deep passing attack by double-covering his favorite receivers, Raymond Berry and Jim Mutscheller. With twelve minutes remaining he began sending his running backs on deep pass routes. This left him unprotected in case of blitzes, but forced single coverage on his receivers. Besides, with so many pass catchers to guard no defensive backs were free to blitz. Also, early in the quarter, New York's best pass defenders, Jim Patton and Linden Crow, left the game with injuries.

The game became a rout in those final twelve minutes as Baltimore scored twenty-four points to win 31-16. It was a day for non-Packer fans to relish. A new dynasty was emerging in the far north.

Beginning and End
1960 Philadelphia Eagles versus Green Bay Packers

The teams that met in Philadelphia's old Franklin Field to contest for 1960's NFL crown were amazingly dissimilar. The Green Bay Packers were young, hopeful and terribly talented in every area. Their head coach Vince Lombardi had been offensive coordinator for the great New York Giant teams of the late 1950s, and he now brought his philosophy of adherence to fundamentals to a team that had been a laughingstock. Lombardi believed there to be no defense for a properly executed play, and seemed to have a point since his squad had earned the right to play for the title. His quarterback Bart Starr would rarely set the league aflame in this running-centered attack, but he had a knack for doing whatever it took to win. Running backs Paul Hornug and Jimmy Taylor would come to be considered the greatest backfield combo in league history. Hornug scored a record 176 points that season while running with, catching and placekicking footballs. Middle linebacker Ray Nitchke led a bulletproof defense that, with the rest of the team, would one day crowd into the Hall of Fame.

The Eagles were a tattered collection of aging warriors who had played their hearts out all year in hopes of a final (in many cases an *only*) championship before the final gun. Head coach Buck Shaw had acquired the fabled Dutchman, quarterback Norm Van Brocklin, from the Rams before the season. Shaw planned on this game being the swan song of his coaching career.

A pulverizing hitter named Chuck Bednarik played center for Philly, and owing to a late-season injury to left linebacker Bob Pellegrini, he would also play linebacker. In fact, Chuck played fifty-eight of the game's sixty minutes. Bednarik was one of a handful of Eagles left over from the franchise's last championship cast eleven years earlier. Born into a blue-collar immigrant family eking out an existence in Pittsburgh steel mills he had worked himself through the University of Pennsylvania, twice winning the Maxwell Trophy as college football's top player. When Philadelphia won its second straight league title his rookie season prospects looked rosy for his sparkling NCAA career to slide smoothly into a professional dynasty. High hopes crumbled quickly as injuries decimated the powerhouse around him while moving into a decade dominated by teams from Cleveland, Detroit and Baltimore.

When Shaw arrived and commenced reconstructing the downtrodden assembly he found in Bednarik an invaluable example of hardworking, talented determination whose splendid attitude spread easily to the growing pool of Eagle recruits, new and used, who would briefly return the team to its long-vacated nest at the summit. The resurrection would not likely have happened without the constant contributions, physical and emotional, of this gritty athlete.

Despite their grim resolution the Eagles got off to a dismal start in the title game, with their first two possessions ending in turnovers. The first time they got a reprieve when their defense held the Packers on four straight plays, taking the ball back on downs on their own five-yard line. After the offense moved to its twenty-two it fumbled, but again the defense held. Lombardi did not disdain the three points this time and Hornug's placement gave Green Bay the first lead, 3-0.

After another Packer field goal, van Brocklin spotted a weakness in the Green Bay secondary. Speedy flanker Tommy McDonald could get loose outside when his standard, inside route lulled the defense into assuming he would go that way on every down. Dutch called McDonald's number from the Packers' thirty-five and the surprise outside post play worked for a 7-6 Philadelphia lead. A fifteen-yard Bobby Walton field goal minutes later gave the Birds a 10-6 halftime edge.

Defensive heroics kept the third quarter entertaining but scoreless, but on the last play of the period something very interesting occurred. It was fourth-and-eleven when Green Bay wide receiver Max McGee dropped back in punt formation deep in his own territory. Max never laid his foot into the ball—instead he tucked it into his arm and sprinted all the way to the Eagle forty-six. Earlier, a violent tackle by Bednarik had sent a dazed Hornug to the bench for the rest of the afternoon, but his replacement Tom Moore now alternated with Taylor in hammering at the Philadelphia line, which was still in shock from McGee's run. Max fittingly finished the drive he had saved. After pushing to the seven-yard line Starr tossed the ball to McGee in the end zone for a 13-10 lead.

It would take more than one big play to beat these powerful young visitors, so Ted Dean returned the kickoff clear to the Packer thirty-nine before getting shoved out of bounds. Next came the final drive of van Brocklin's career, and the Green Bays have never forgotten it. Using his runners and receivers expertly he drove his offense to the five-yard line. Dean took van's handoff and followed guard Gerry Huth around left end for the winning score.

Starr & Co. conceded nothing to the valiant vets from the City of Brotherly Love as they embarked on an inspiring but eventually fruitless trip down Franklin Field. They used all their times out on this drive, and on the game's final play Starr could find no one open but Taylor, who was far short of the goal line. Big Jim gathered in the throw and shook off every tackler until he reached the nine-yard line, where Bednarik waited. Chuck met him head-on and clung tight until 270-pound tackle Jess Richardson arrived to sew up the kill. Lombardi's dream of his first championship fell nine soupy yards short.

Shaw and van Brocklin retired while on top, and without them the Philadelphia Eagles slid back into obscurity. The Packers, meanwhile, had quite a bit of future coming.

Packer Power
1961 Green Bay Packers versus New York Giants

It had been a close call back in the 50s. Green Bay, Wisconsin almost lost its NFL franchise through financial woes. When the danger of bankruptcy passed, everyone decided to get optimistic. Things could only improve, right? Sort of. The ledgers looked better, but on the field few teams performed as dismally as the Pack. Seventeen seasons had passed since Green Bay last won it all. Coming close the year before was nowhere near good enough, especially for miracle working head coach Vince Lombardi.

Lombardi bullied his players into a state of near-perfect physical condition and infused an absurdly simple, effective philosophy. He hammered into his men the message that if each of them did his job properly on each play then each play could not help being successful. Proper *execution* was the key. He told them this repeatedly and loudly.

From a personality standpoint Bart Starr, Paul Hornug, Jimmy Taylor, Max McGee, Ray Nitchke and their teammates represented a sprawling spectrum, but on the field they were no longer an assortment of immensely talented individuals. They were an irresistible, single force performing with flawless precision. They were the penultimate *team*.

1961 had a new look for another franchise with which the Packers were well-familiar. The New York Giants had showed considerable class and ability by beating out defending champion Philadelphia by a half game mainly by following their example of trading for a veteran quarterback who both knew how to win and who had more football left in him than his former team had realized. Hopes in the Big Apple were pinned on a balding Texan named Yelberton Abraham Tittle. He found a chance for a championship in New York after many seasons of frustration in San Francisco, and soon learned his new team wanted the crown as badly as he did. By dropping deep passes to receivers

Frank Gifford and Del Shofner, Y.A. guided his outfit to his first title confrontation. New head coach Allie Sherman figured a few of Tittle's home run heaves and a virtuoso showing by his powerful defense might be just enough to undo the Packers.

The game was played on a glacial New Year's Eve in Green Bay, and the Giants' strategy came unglued early. It was the third straight year Packer halfback Paul Hornug had led the league in scoring, and this afternoon he set a one-game record for post-season points.

The visitors' defensive plan was to stop the inside power rushing fullback Taylor, but they never had the chance. Taylor was nursing a sore back and used mostly as a decoy while Hornug swept outside. Earlier there had been some question as to whether Green Bay's star runner would play at all. He had been summoned to Ft. Riley, Kansas for service in his Army Reserve unit. A special leave was granted for Private Hornug, and New York has never forgiven the military. Nitchke had also been called for reserve duty because of the Berlin Crisis, but he too got a hard-case pass.

While Hornug was running and place-kicking his way to a record nineteen points, his defensive teammates never gave Tittle and his offense a moment's respite. When Y.A. was not being sacked by swift defensive end Willie Davis or by blitzing linebackers, he was watching an aroused, alert secondary intercept four of his passes. His counterpart Starr lived up to his name by throwing for three touchdowns. He had time to do it because guard Fuzzy Thurston and center Jim Ringo kept pushing feared middle linebacker Sam Huff out of the way with relentless double-teaming. The home team won 37-0.

It was a New Year (and era) to celebrate in Green Bay. The Packers and their fans no longer needed to look hopefully to a distant future, for that tomorrow had finally arrived...with a dynasty.

— Another Day at Work? —
1962 Green Bay Packers versus New York Giants

There being no such thing as a routine title contest the Yankee Stadium crowd was typically huge and enthusiastic the wintry afternoon the New York Giants and Green Bay Packers met to play for 1962's bragging rights. The rematch alone stirred enough notice, but there were other points of interest. The Giants were smarting from the savage loss inflicted on them by the Pack in the previous championship. The New York offensive line was infused with a burning determination to protect recently injured quarterback Y.A. Tittle, who was finishing his fifteenth season.

Back on October 28 in this same arena Tittle had completed twenty-seven of thirty-nine throws for 505 yards and seven touchdowns in a 49-34 slugfest versus the Washington Redskins. The last TD had come with a full eight minutes remaining in the game, but Y.A. was too classy to run up the score just to achieve an NFL-record eighth touchdown pass. He kept the ball on the ground and ran out the clock rather than garner yet more of the spotlight. "It wouldn't have been in good taste," he explained afterward. "It would have looked like too much individualism." Such unselfishness and high regard for his teammates despite his own phenomenal ability made Tittle perhaps the league's toughest act to follow. His defense would try, though.

A year earlier the Giant defenders had been burned by swift Packer tailback Paul Hornug after they had carefully prepared for fullback Jimmy Taylor. Since he was healthy this time there was little doubt Big Jim would tote the biggest burden, but the aged New Yorkers would nevertheless keep a wary eye on the golden-haired Hornug. It made sense. With their simple, grind-it-out-in-the-mud running style the Green Bays had led the league in scoring with their 415 points.

The main difference for Hornug this season was his being relieved of placekicking duties by guard Jerry Kramer. Jerry had a gruesome medical history far from confined to hurts suffered on gridirons. A car crash, hunting accident and a mishap involving him backing into a table saw in a high school shop class all left scars, but the most significant of his boyhood misadventures occurred on his family's Idaho farm in 1946. Kramer was chasing a calf when the animal stepped on the end of a plank that had been broken off at the opposite end. The broken, jagged end tilted upward and young Jerry, running along behind, was impaled. The wound in his groin was improperly treated, with three sharp, fountain pen-sized slivers of wood inadvertently left inside. By 1962 they were giving the excellent pulling guard a great deal of pain which he ignored as he gave an All-Pro account of himself that year.

Green Bay had rebounded admirably from a thorough defeat and physical pounding suffered at Detroit on Thanksgiving Day that saw quarterback Bart Starr thrown for 110 yards in losses. They would not again take anyone lightly.

As the title game got going, it soon became apparent neither side planned to surprise the other. Taylor was the visitors' bread and butter with eighty-five yards through the fired-up Giants. Hornug was held to thirty-five steps.

As always Tittle's passing was the center of his team's fondest hopes, but the elements helped the Packers cancel this strategy. Gusts of freezing wind corkscrewed through the stadium all during the game, and Tittle's passes described curious, boomerang-like loops when caught in this low-altitude Gulf Stream.

A field goal by Kramer and a seven-yard scoring run by Taylor gave the Packers a 10-0 halftime lead that looked secure considering how the weather and Green Bay defense were stifling the New York attack, but home hopes briefly glimmered in the third quarter as the Giants' Erich Barnes blocked a Max McGee punt and Jim Collier fell on it in the end zone for a touchdown to cut the difference to 10-7. Even this big play could not shake off the stranglehold head coach Vince Lombardi's defense held on the New York offense.

By the fourth period the temperature had dropped to five degrees above zero. Starr was little more effective than Tittle, completing just nine of twenty-one passes into his receivers' numbed mitts. He was able to avoid being intercepted, and eased his offense close enough for Kramer, ignoring the awful pain in his guts, to add two more short field goals for a final score of 16-7 and title #2 of the Great Packer Empire.

For Tittle, one more heartbreak was coming.

The Party's Over

1963 Chicago Bears versus New York Giants

Y.A. Tittle had started chasing his dream of a championship many seasons earlier in the long-dead All-America Conference, but rarely came close during his years in Baltimore and San Francisco. At age thirty-four he became a New York Giant, and three years and two lost title games later opportunity for the Grail knocked for the last time.

New York's passing game was as lethal as ever, with split end Del Shofner having caught 185 passes for 3439 yards and thirty-two touchdowns over the last three regular seasons. In 1963, thirty-seven-year-old Tittle's thirty-six touchdown passes pointed his team to Chicago to contest with its oldest adversary for the league crown, and his teammates had to have him. In an early season game with Baltimore, Tittle was scissored on a rare bootleg, suffering a cracked breastbone and partially collapsed lung. With him on the sideline the following week, and with a running game defused by age and injuries the Giants were crushed by the lowly Pittsburgh Steelers 31-0.

Other than winning, the Bears had little in common with their opponents. Owner/head coach George Halas directed a team built around a pulverizing defense. Larry Morris, Fred Williams, Joe Fortunato, Ed O'Bradovich and their unit were known to stymie even offenses of New York's standing.

The game was played in Chicago's Wrigley Field, and Tittle realized he needed to stand fast and establish momentum. Surprising the Bruins by staying on the ground with draw plays to runners Phil King and Joe Morrison, Tittle ended the opening, fifty-nine-yard drive with a sudden fourteen-yard scoring pass to Frank Gifford for a 7-0 first quarter lead. The home team would not be tricked again, so on the next Giant possession linebacker Morris picked off a pass and returned it sixty-one yards to the New York five-yard line. Quarterback Billy Wade sneaked across the equalizing score two plays later.

A close game was expected to favor the visitors since their kicker Don Chandler had topped the league in scoring that year. A second period Giant drive carried to the thirteen where a third down pass was dropped in the end zone, and Chandler converted for the last lead his side would see.

The 10-7 advantage was as fragile as Tittle's legs, and when pass rushers decked him just before intermission he had to be carried from the field, wincing at the pain in his left knee. Although he returned, the Bald Eagle was ineffectual from then, and the Giants were scoreless in the second half.

Tittle knew he had no choice but to keep throwing against that defense despite being repeatedly intercepted. Later his team doctor found he had played the whole second half on torn knee ligaments. Unable to set up properly it is little wonder he kept spinning the ball to the wrong people. At least Chicago was not getting any points out of it. Yet.

Deep in his own territory Y.A. aimed a screen pass at Morrison. He was under the usual heavy pressure from another linebacker blitz, and his throw was deflected into the hands of O'Bradovich, who stumbled to the New York fourteen. Wade passed to tight end Mike Ditka, who twisted to the one, and then Wade dove for his second scoring sneak and a 14-10 lead that was enough to win.

It was a game to be remembered for more than the Chicago Bears defeating the New York Giants for 1963's NFL Championship. It should be recalled as the final title contest that would ever be played between these ancestral rivals, but most of all it lives on for those who venerate the memory of Y.A. Tittle the player. It was the marvelous old pro's last big game.

Meanwhile, the next championship contest would be a big surprise.

The Cleveland Caper
1964 Cleveland Browns versus Baltimore Colts

Most agreed that the game itself was a formality. In a few hours the Baltimore Colts would be the 1964 National Football League champions. Quarterback Johnny Unitas and his supercharged offense had only to manhandle the Cleveland Browns' allegedly wispy defense while the feared Colt defenders would presumably find an antidote to the yardage-gobbling triumvirate of quarterback Frank Ryan, running back Jimmy Brown and rookie receiving sensation Paul Warfield. Baltimore head coach Don Shula had watched his defense bottle up capable offenses all season, and it seemed likely little would change this blustery afternoon in Cleveland's Municipal Stadium.

Two years earlier a player revolt had brought on the firing of Browns head coach Paul Brown, whose technical brilliance had not been sufficient to prevent an undercurrent of resentment and disaffection from surfacing and growing. His players accused him of being too set in his ways. They said his resistance to change and development stifled athletes by not giving them the chance to show what they could do in a more diversified, accommodating game plan. A new management fired Brown and replaced him with a diplomatic assistant named Blanton Collier who soothed the hurt feelings, gave the men the opportunities they desired and got their minds back on football.

In his second season at the helm, Collier coached the team to the top of the Eastern Division and earned it the right to contest for the title against the resurging Colts, who had finally made it past Green Bay. The Ponies may have figured that taking the division away from the Packers was the tough part. The Browns spent *their* time getting very ready for the game.

The Cleveland coaches knew Baltimore was the year's top-scoring team, that the main reason was Unitas' right arm, and that they would have to devise something novel to shoot down this flying circus. There was also the matter of Colt running back Lenny Moore, who had scored twenty touchdowns in fourteen regular season games.

Among all the talk about the balanced Baltimore attack and the Browns' offense everyone seemed to overlook the Cleveland defense. The home team owned a fine line anchored by Bill Glass, Dick Modzelewski and Jim Kanicki. If these behemoths could be given time to reach Unitas the Colts would be in unexpected offensive trouble.

Said Collier, "With Baltimore we felt the only chance we had to stop Unitas was to shut off his first or primary receiver. That was the only chance we had for our pass rush to get to him because in looking for the second receiver he'd use up the valuable half-second more our pass rush needed to penetrate."

Defensive back Walter Beach would cover feared Colt tight end Raymond Berry one-on-one. Beach would stick closely to his man while always staying between him and Unitas. This single coverage was a gamble, but held a bonus if successful—Cleveland's linebackers would be freed to blitz. During the season the Browns had rarely blitzed, but played back and waited for the opposing passer to make a mistake. It worked well enough with other teams, but Collier knew Unitas seldom made mistakes. Johnny U had thrown nineteen touchdown passes against just six interceptions that year, so the

defensive game plan would have to be adjusted. Baltimore knew nothing of this.

On offense it was also a story of change through necessity as Collier concocted another crafty stratagem. It was certain the Colts would keep their eyes on Brown and Warfield, so he would use them primarily as decoys. Gary Collins played across from Warfield, and Collier would make unheralded Collins his hot receiver.

At kickoff a twenty-mile-per-hour wind was blowing into the stadium through its open end, and the Browns exploited this, too. When Baltimore's offense had the wind at its back the Cleveland secondary played deep. When the Colts tried to advance into the gale the deep defenders used it as an extra defensive back, blowing Unitas' passes back in his teeth as they crept closer to the line of scrimmage to help with the run defense.

The first half was scoreless as the Cleveland defensive strategy took hold and the offense took no chances. In the first pair of quarters the home team defensive linemen concentrated on stopping Moore while blitzing linebackers harried Unitas. Baltimore did manage to reach the opposing twelve-yard line in the first quarter, but the drive came to naught when the holder fumbled the snap for a field goal attempt. The visitors never again threatened.

Early in the third period forty-year-old Lou Groza stood with that wind at his back and booted a forty-three-yard placement. The quietly confident Clevelanders were off and running.

The Colts were getting impatient on both sides of the line, and tired of watching a Jimmy Brown who was not carrying the ball, so they were shocked when he ripped off a forty-six-yard gainer to their eighteen. They went back to guarding Brown, but on the next play Ryan threaded the first of his three touchdown passes to Collins.

With the Baltimores now playing catch-up and having to throw on nearly every down the defensive line was able to take its eyes off Moore and start rushing Unitas. The linebackers eased off their blitzing and dropped back to bolster the already-sticky pass coverage.

After watching his defense bury another Colt possession Ryan zipped a forty-two-yard scoring shot to Collins. He next worked his squad close enough for another Groza field goal, and hit Collins for a third touchdown in the fourth quarter as the seven-point underdogs slapped a 27-0 whitewashing on the Western Division's embarrassed champs. After the final gun a bloody Unitas offered no excuses—just congratulations.

Cleveland's tradition of brilliant coaching gleamed as brightly as ever. It would take a dynasty to stop it.

Of Mud and Men
1965 Green Bay Packers versus Cleveland Browns

The ground crew tried hard all morning, but it was the weather rather than the field that needed improving. The snow came down in fat, wet globs that melted upon landing—especially when trampled by assorted Packers and Browns. The irascible climate of Green Bay, Wisconsin is renowned for being almost as troublesome for Packer opponents as are the Packers themselves. On this gray, winter Sabbath nobody was surprised.

The defending National Football League champion Cleveland Browns had visions of winning this 1965 title and resurrect their franchise's dynasty of the 1950s. The fabulous offense was still there, but an empire was difficult to imagine for this team without its immortal runner Jimmy Brown, and he would be retiring after this game. He and the other big guns of the Cleveland turbocharge were impatient to repeat the previous year's stunning title triumph, in which they had been far greater underdogs than they were today.

The Pack was back in the money after a two-year layoff caused mainly by an epidemic of injuries that affected them still. Few Green Bay starters were not bothered by some nagging hurt, and this made most prognosticators feel the game was a tossup despite the Packers' home field advantage and the weather, which favored their head coach Vince Lombardi's straight-ahead running game.

The contest's early minutes brought surprise when Packer quarterback Bart Starr uncorked a forty-seven-yard touchdown pass to end Carroll Dale. This was startling not only because the elements did not favor passing, but also since Starr was one of Green Bay's walking wounded. His badly bruised ribs had led most to assume he would not be able to throw a deep pass.

The Browns took the ensuing kickoff and moved with ease to the home team's fourteen, where last year's hero, wide receiver Gary

Collins, grabbed quarterback Frank Ryan's toss to move them to within one point of a tie. Forty-one-year-old Lou Groza had converted ninety-six consecutive extra points when he lined up to even the score, but his holder fumbled the wet football and the tally stayed 7-6. Groza did manage two short field goals before halftime, but so did Packer kicker Don Chandler to give his team a dainty 13-12 lead at intermission.

Lombardi's strategy was slow in taking hold, but began to make a difference in the second half. The Green Bay secondary, aided by the weather, choked off Ryan's feared aerial attack to his marvelous receiving combo of Collins and Paul Warfield, and Brown's renowned end sweeps were also neutralized.

Again the wet playing surface aided the Packers by making it virtually impossible for Brown to turn either corner without losing his footing. When he tried the center he kept colliding with middle linebacker Ray Nitchke, who took his cue from Brown's every move. Nitchke's strength and quickness shut down Brown's inside rushing to take away Cleveland's last weapon.

Green Bay's rushing tandem of Jimmy Taylor and Paul Hornug was not so hampered by the soupy field. Their offensive line gouged gaping avenues in the Brown's defense as Taylor carried for ninety-six yards, and Hornug wound up with 105. A thirteen-yard scoring run by Hornug in the third period and a twenty-nine-yard fourth quarter field goal produced a final of 23-12 as the Green Bays nailed down their third title in five years.

Earlier in the day the governor of Wisconsin had tried to fly in for the game, but his plane was grounded by the snowstorm. Apart from the Cleveland Browns he was the only disappointed person in this deliriously delighted state.

It was the end of an era. This was the last game played under the old championship format. The following season two leagues would come together in a way never before seen in professional football, but this would not slow down the Packers.

The $15,000 Question
1966 Green Bay Packers versus Kansas City Chiefs

Ending a war by playing a football game may seem bizarre, but this war between football leagues was not really ending. It was simply taking on a different tone. Back in 1960, scions of Texas oil millionaire families, Lamar Hunt and Bud Adams, got ambitious and organized the nucleus of a rebel league to challenge the established National Football League. They called their outfit the American Football League, and its eight teams had more desire than talent, but had no intention of staying that way or of doing the NFL any favors.

The Nationals refused to acknowledge the existence of or make any kind of treaty with the insurgents, and a blistering financial war commenced over the services of talented college players. It was a good time to be entering the pro ranks. When the AFL's New York Jets shelled out a signing bonus in the neighborhood of $400,000.00 to entice University of Alabama quarterback Joe Namath away from the NFL's St. Louis Cardinals the exasperated old guard sued for peace. With the leagues bidding themselves into bankruptcy, a merger was the obvious solution. They reached an agreement in which the larger National League would absorb the newcomers, a mutual draft would be conducted instead of separate ones with ensuing bidding contests, and most importantly the top two teams from each league would meet at each season's end in a game of unprecedented proportions. This contest would later be called the Super Bowl, but the first one, to determine the professional football champs of 1966, was given the nondescript title of NFL-AFL World Championship.

Each league's top echelons decided to award the players of the winning team $15,000 apiece. It was a spirited regular season as this purse gave players more motivation than they had ever had.

Head coach Vince Lombardi and his Green Bay Packers earned the right to represent the NFL by winning a free-scoring playoff game in

Texas, where they nosed out the Dallas Cowboys 34-27, holding off a furious Dallas rally in the closing moments. This experience in post-season pressure was something their AFL opponents lacked.

The Kansas City Chiefs were a fitting team to be facing the Pack in this game. Their owner Lamar Hunt was a catalyst in the league's formation, and both he and his team wanted to show the world they were for real. The previous year a huge factor was created in K.C.'s rise to championship caliber when its marvelous, quiet young running back Mack Lee Hill died during knee surgery. Dedicating the '66 campaign to their late brother infused the Chiefs with a determination no AFL opponent could withstand.

Other than a smattering of standouts the defense was nothing to write home about, but head coach Hank Stram's jet-propelled offense scored enough points to offset this weakness during the regular season. In the league title game with defending champion Buffalo, Kansas City never knew an uneasy moment as it cruised to a 31-7 triumph. This type of easy victory was commonplace for the Chiefs and left them unprepared for the pressure and distractions surrounding the first Super Bowl.

The Packer lineup was the same one fans had come to recognize—for the most part. Golden runner Paul Hornug was suiting up to spend this last game of his career as a spectator because of a pinched nerve that shot spears of pain through him every time he tried to run. Elijah Pitts started in his place.

Another hero of yore, Max McGee, was not slated to start. His thirty-four-yearold legs had seemingly carried him through more pass routes than they could recover from now, but there was a possibility. Starter Boyd Dowler was the unhappy possessor of two damaged shoulders that might banish him to the sideline at any moment, in which case the fun-loving McGee would get another shot.

The game was played in the Los Angeles Memorial Coliseum, and when Kansas City's Mike Mercer kicked off to Green Bay the pro football leagues became blood brothers. On the second play from scrimmage Dowler threw a block on Chief linebacker Fred Williamson, aggravated a tender shoulder, and McGee jogged into the sunshine.

To get things started, the teams traded punts, and then the Packers got serious. It cannot be said the Kansas City defenders underestimated McGee. They knew far too little about their adversaries to take anything for granted. Nevertheless, old Max had his day of glory. Green Bay quarterback Bart Starr had just completed his best-ever regular season, leading his league in passing. Taking the snap on the Chief thirty-seven-yard line Starr drilled the ball to McGee, who outran much younger cornerback Willie Mitchell to the end zone.

In 1962, 1964 and 1966, the same years Starr had led the NFL in passing, Kansas City quarterback Lenny Dawson topped the American League in aerial stats. Dawson had thrown 132 touchdown passes during his five years with the Chiefs, all of them after five unhappy seasons spent sitting on the benches of the Cleveland Browns and Pittsburgh Steelers. Despite his impressive credentials Dawson was allotted little hope against the Green Bay colossus, but Lenny directed an impressive drive to the Packer seven, from where he tossed a touchdown to running back Curtis McClinton. In fact, K.C. outgained Green Bay in total yardage 181 to 164 in the first half while outscoring it 10-7 in the second period to hold the Nationals to an unexpectedly slender 14-10 edge at halftime.

Lombardi was terrified by the prospect of humiliating the established league by losing to these upstarts. During intermission he administered one of his storied locker room tongue-lashings to his men, reminding them they represented the NFL, and would be letting down the whole league if they lost.

Dawson's stabbing, play-action throws had given the Packers fits in the first half, so Lombardi and defensive coordinator Phil Bengston devised a cure. Early in the third quarter the Chiefs had a third down at midfield. Hoping to fool the linebackers into thinking another play-action was coming, then throw deep, Dawson sent both running backs on pass routes to the weakside. Rather than cover the backs the linebackers uncharacteristically blitzed, and without his runners a shocked Dawson had nobody to block the blitzers and no time to wait for his receivers to break into the clear. Forced to throw before he was ready he got off a pass that linebacker Dave Robinson deflected into the hands of safety Willie Wood, who returned the interception to the Kansas City five-yard line. Pitts scored on the next play and Green Bay never looked back.

McGee and Pitts each scored again for a final of 35-10. Lombardi's legions not only defeated the rebels, but they did so decisively.

Despite the outcome the Chiefs had come too far to feel ashamed, and the $7500.00 they each received as losers' share was more than any previous AFL *winner* had pocketed. It candy-coated a bitter pill and left them very hungry. Their day was already looming.

Vince's Curtain Call
1967 Green Bay Packers versus Oakland Raiders

More than one kind of speculation was running wild prior to the second NFL-AFL championship game, and thousands of typewriters chattered the intricacies of each. Green Bay's Packers were again stepping forward to defend the National Football League's claim to superiority, but another story held a major share of avid interest.

Over a rather short stretch Green Bay head coach Vince Lombardi had earned respect and adulation of proportions transcending awe. He was now a legendary institution within football. In 1967 he steered, prodded and led his roster of aging, aching vets to the threshold of their fifth pro title in just seven years. If this towering opportunity were not enough motivation for his team on the eve of the second Super Bowl, it was rumored Lombardi would be retiring after this game. The specter of him going out a loser was not one his players could abide.

The Oakland Raiders were the opponents for Vince's warriors in the coming collision, and despite their physical prowess and brash confidence they were not counted worthy adversaries for the dynasty. For the second straight year the Packers would face a team unaccustomed to the incredible pressure that is part of this game. The Raiders had lost just once in the regular season, and then thrashed Houston 40-7 for the American Football League championship. It was all so easy.

Although most refused to believe it, Green Bay was fading rapidly, and had to struggle mightily for every win while staggering to the top of the NFL's Western Division with a 9-4-1 record and losing their last two regular season games. Ailing quarterback Bart Starr threw nine interceptions in the first two games of the year, then sat out three weeks to recuperate. He came back in time to get his team into the playoffs, where for the second straight year it nosed out the Dallas Cowboys in a hair-tearing thriller. The Pack won on Starr's one-yard sneak with sixteen seconds to play, no times out and the temperature fifteen degrees below zero. This familiarity with tension coupled with grim resolution to win a beloved coach's last game would be too much for the hopeful young Raiders, who would also do themselves no favors with their execution.

Oakland quarterback Daryle Lamonica had spent five years fretting on the Buffalo Bills' bench before being traded west. In his first season there he gained the starting job by dropping long scoring passes to his splendid wide receivers Fred Biletnikoff and Warren Wells. His backup, George Blanda, was discarded a year earlier by Houston as too old to contribute as a passer or place-kicker. Blanda's right foot was something his head coach John Rauch had high hopes for in the coming match in Miami's Orange Bowl.

With the biggest man in post-season history, seven-foot Richard Sligh, only a second-stringer the Raider defense was clearly constructed with an emphasis on power. If the muscular defenders could give their offensive mates the ball enough times Rauch hoped to push close enough for a handful of old George's three-pointers and win a close decision. This plan unraveled early.

It was *Packer* kicker Don Chandler who led in scoring that warm Florida afternoon. After his first two field goals gave Green Bay a 6-0 lead, Starr sent wide receiver Boyd Dowler on a down-the-middle post pattern so simple it caught the Oakland secondary by surprise. Dowler flew past startled linebackers Dan Conners and Kent McClouglan, grabbed Starr's pass in full stride and pelted the rest of the way for a sixty-two-yard touchdown play and 13-0 lead.

Although the Raiders refused to be intimidated by this gracile bit of bloodletting, scoring a TD of their own via Lamonica's twenty-three-yard throw to tight end Bill Miller, they were devastated by what happened on a Green Bay punt late in the second quarter. Running back Donny Anderson doubled as punter, and with the Pack facing fourth-and-long deep in its own territory he dropped back in kick formation to his own sixteen. Reserve tight end Dave Kocourek almost blocked the punt, but just missed. Oakland's Rodger Bird waited for the ball on his own forty-five, but dropped it. Second-string Packer linebacker Dick Capp pounced on the fumble. Had Kocourek managed to block the kick so deep in Green Bay territory the game's momentum might have swung drastically toward the Raiders. Although the turnover resulted in only another Chandler field goal, the West Coast team was devastated by this turn of events, and the Packers dominated from this point as for the second straight year the AFL representative collapsed in the second half.

Rauch's strategy for Blanda's kicking was not practical for catch-up football, and any chances for an Oakland comeback were fumbled away, killed by dropped third-down passes, interceptions and time-consuming Green Bay drives that brought still more points as the Packers won this last game of the Lombardi era 33-14.

Not everyone noticed, but this match was different from the massacre of the previous year. It was a hard-fought contest that the Pack's advanced years could only partly explain. The champs had *needed* Chandler's accurate toe and the many Raider mistakes to make the score lop-sided, but it would take another season for the old guard to realize the teams of the American Football League were no longer pushovers.

A Man of His Word
1968 New York Jets versus Baltimore Colts

A forgettable pair of years had just passed for the American Football League as its representatives in the first two Super Bowls were sent reeling by a dynastic Green Bay Packer franchise determined to preserve the superior image of the imperial National Football League. After the second Bowl legendary head coach Vince Lombardi resigned, the aging Packers declined, and a team they had long barred from the throneroom, the Baltimore Colts, bludgeoned its way to the top of the NFL.

A damaged elbow sidelined the Colts' great quarterback Johnny Unitas for the bulk of the 1968 season, but head coach Don Shula found a surprisingly able substitute in journeyman Earl Morral. Baltimore was the fifth city for which Morral had played, and he set it alight with his fiery performance. He earned the season's Most Valuable Player award after a fitting finale in Ohio when he directed a 34-0 league title game wipeout of a Cleveland Browns team that had handed the Colts their only regular season loss.

A hefty portion of Baltimore's success came from the defensive front four of Ordelle Braase, Fred Miller, Bubba Smith and Billy Ray Smith, which mashed every offense they faced that year, shutting out four. Of course they would do the same to that of their opponents in the approaching interleague confrontation—the New York Jets.

The Super Bowl might have died out from lack of interest had it not been for the charismatic young quarterback of the third team in three years the AFL would send against the old guard. The man's name was Joe Willie Namath, and he was not about to let his team or league be taken lightly.

Although Namath's knees had pained him since he had wrecked them in a college game against North Carolina State, he was otherwise hale and possessed a great deal of confidence in himself and his teammates. He felt insulted by the reverence shown the Colts and their more established league. The eighteen points by which Baltimore was favored irked and amazed Joe most of all.

The point spread was partly the result of how the Jets had barely survived their league championship game when defending champion Oakland fumbled away a potentially game-winning drive in the final quarter to preserve a 27-23 New York victory. Still, Namath made it clear to all (especially reporters) that the Colts certainly did not intimidate him. In part because he felt Earl Morral, despite his laudable regular season performance, was not only less skilled than himself, but also to several AFL quarterbacks whose teams the Jets had defeated. Taking umbrage to this evaluation, Shula meticulously outlined to the press the differences between Morral's and Namath's styles and in the types of defenses they had faced, but, perhaps unintentionally, he did not compare them head-to-head. By praising Morral without *comparing* him to Namath, Shula sounded defensive and led many to suspect even he considered Joe Willie the better of the two.

Namath also pointed out how he did not feel Cleveland had played well in the semi-final with Baltimore, but these statements were mere preliminaries. Three days before Super Bowl III, Namath told an audience at a private club called Miami Springs Villa that the game's outcome was indeed a foregone conclusion, but not how they expected. "We are going to win," said Joe to the astounded audience. "I guarantee it!"

One might have expected such remarks to motivate the Colts to blow the insolent New Yorkers so far out of the Orange Bowl it would take the U.S. Navy to find them, but as the crafty Namath had foreseen the exact opposite came true. The Baltimores sat back and laughed at how easy it was going to be to crush this band of upstarts who had to talk to work up the nerve to show up Super Sunday. They were already considering how they would spend the $15,000.00 each of them would bank as winners of the formality they were about to play. Forgetting about how they had been upset in drastic fashion four years earlier, by game time the overconfident Ponies were ready to be broken.

"I'm shocked. It all happened so suddenly I haven't thought where I go from here. I'm waiting." These were the thoughts of Weeb Ewbank after being abruptly fired as Baltimore head coach after the 1962 season. He waited until he was hired by the Jets to build their infant squad into a contender, for no new nationwide sports league can hope for true success without a powerful franchise in the media capital of New York City. Weeb did just that, and was now preparing to trim a team he had guided to two NFL championships, for which he had signed Johnny Unitas, and that had repaid him with walking papers. Management replaced him with Shula, who had been a defensive back on the Ewbank-led Baltimore club. Now they were coming together for the greatest reunion professional sports are likely ever to see.

With both of New York's starting running backs, Emerson Boozer and Matt Snell, having undergone knee surgery the previous season the Colts may be forgiven for assuming that Namath was the sole offensive threat facing them. Three gimpy-legged starters in the Jet backfield made the Baltimore defense's optimism understandable, and even if Namath *was* a major danger they did not bother to realize it. Furthermore, Snell was utterly reclusive the days leading up to the kickoff, not even showing up for the team photo session. His visibility was as low as Namath's was high. Between his surgery and virtual invisibility, Baltimore forgot all about him. The operation was a success, and so was Snell.

Early in the game Namath spotted a weakness in the right side of the Colt defensive line where thirty-six-year-old end Braase tried futilely to hide a painful back injury. Joe repeatedly sent Snell into the spongy right side, and by game's end the hard-charging, overlooked runner had amassed 121 yards and a four-yard touchdown run in the second period to give New York a 7-0 halftime lead. By this point the Orange Bowl crowd was deafeningly aware that it was watching history in the making.

After the TD, assistant coach Walt Michaels up in the press box informed Namath of a weakness in Baltimore's zone defense in which split end George Saur could beat eleven-year veteran cornerback Lenny Lyles. This tip-off further enhanced Namath's already-brilliant play-calling as he consistently executed patterns that sent receivers Saur, Pete Lammons and Don Maynard into wide-open spaces created when increasingly frustrated Colt defensive backs resorted to blitzing in the second half.

The Baltimore secondary had not expected to have to defend many passes since it assumed its linemen would flatten Namath every time he tried to throw, but Joe's lightning-quick release and habit of fading back very deeply before throwing thwarted this dread pass rush. Also, the aroused Jet offensive line was moving these feared defensive linemen like they were empty coffee cans.

Everyone pulling for New York gasped in the third quarter when Namath injured his right thumb and temporarily had to leave the game. He worked the soreness from his priceless digit by firing practice strikes to sports writer Lou Sahadi behind the Jet bench.

Meanwhile, the feats of the rebel defense were matching those of its offense as it fought the Colts with a tenacity seemingly saved specifically for this game. It was a unit that had allowed fewer rushing yards than any in the AFL that year, and given up just 178 first downs. Morral threw three interceptions, and the ground game was equally neutralized. Although fullback Tom Matte gained 116 yards, half of this was on one carry. Besides, running is not the best strategy for a team playing come-from-behind football—the unexpected situation in which Baltimore found itself.

Jet strong safety Jim Hudson did a ding-dong job covering Colt Hall of Fame-bound tight end John Mackey. Hudson would pick up Mackey as soon as he crossed the line of scrimmage, and stick closely to him throughout his patterns. What passes Mackey managed to grab he did not carry far with Hudson in his way before and after his catches. Big John took just three receptions for thirty-five yards.

New York kicker Jim Turner had converted a lovely total of thirty-four of his placement attempts that season. Versus Baltimore he drilled field goals to end three second half drives that also ate up generous chunks of time as the Jets moved to a 16-0 fourth quarter lead with the crowd emitting a volcanic crescendo. A desperate Shula finally sent in rusty Unitas, but the living legend had time only to fashion one late score to cut the gap to 16-7 before the clock ran dry and the humiliation of the NFL was complete.

The New York Jets' revolutionary upset of the mighty Colts exposed a previously unnoticed fact—the two leagues had been relatively equal in talent for some time. The only reason for the National League's apparent dominance until now was that one team, the Green Bay Packers, had been dominating *both* leagues, and just happened to be part of the older circuit. Now, with the decline of the Pack, the newcomers were stepping forward for their share of the glory.

Maybe it should not have been so surprising to so many. Namath had said he would win, and he was an honest man.

— Anniversary —
1969 Kansas City Chiefs versus Minnesota Vikings

1969 was a special year for both of America's major professional football organizations. The National Football League celebrated its fiftieth birthday, and the American Football League its tenth. In the fourth Super Bowl the NFL's Minnesota Vikings and the AFL's Kansas City Chiefs wore patches to commemorate these anniversaries. They had little else in common.

Ironically, the Chiefs were the older franchise, having started out as a charter member of the AFL in 1960. The Vikings opened for business in the NFL as an expansion team in 1961. Head coach Bud Grant's Norsemen were a rustic, fundamentalist group much in the mold of Lombardi's Packers, but on offense they had a tendency to spontaneously improvise that was alien to anything Lombardo preached. Minnesota had dropped its season opener to the New York Giants, and the regular season finale to the Atlanta Falcons. In between these interruptions there were twelve straight victories as the Vikes ran away with the last of the old NFL's championships.

This unpredictable offense was the year's highest-scoring unit, and it was built around quarterback Joe Kapp. This hulking transplant from the Canadian Football League took readily to the frigid climate of Minneapolis-St. Paul, and his style of play was reminiscent of Paul Bunyan. In a September 28 game with defending league champion Baltimore, Kapp was superhuman, firing seven touchdown passes to six separate receivers in a 52-14 rout. Should his targets be covered he would often tuck the ball in and run with favorable results. In the NFL title game with Cleveland, Kapp, on a rollout, drove unhesitatingly into Browns linebacker Jim Houston. Kapp knocked the 240-pound Houston unconscious and the Vikings breezed to a 27-7 triumph.

More than anything, though, Minnesota lived off its ravenous defensive line of Carl Eller, Gary Larson, Alan Page and Jim Marshall.

These "Purple People Eaters" had few peers, and throughout the schedule hammered hapless quarterbacks and runners mercilessly.

The Super Bowl's other defense was pretty much the same story, just not as well publicized. The Chiefs had allowed an AFL-low 177 points to close out the decade of the sixties. The defensive squad manhandled by the Packers three years before had little resemblance to the one fielded on this dreary afternoon in New Orleans' Tulane Stadium. Just four starters remained from that earlier bunch, and this meticulously revamped defense was not only superbly talented, but lucky. Blessed with a virtually injury-free season the eleven starters were able-bodied for all seventeen regular season and playoff games, leading their league in seventeen of twenty-four defensive categories.

Pro football was entering a period of innovation, especially on offense. K.C. head coach Hank Stram was leading the way with his mobile, "floating" pass pocket and intricate formations. Quarterback Lenny Dawson had led his team fearlessly through a personally difficult '69 campaign. Against the Boston Patriots in the season's second game he already had two damaged hands when he tore a knee ligament. Fearful of missing the rest of the year while recuperating from the surgery team doctors recommended he "...kept looking until I found a doctor in St. Louis who felt rest might heal the knee." It did, and after sitting out five weeks thirty-four-year-old Dawson was eager as a rookie despite personal pain, guiding Kansas City to a crucial victory in New York immediately after learning of his father's death. Then, a few days before the Super Bowl, his name was mentioned in connection with an underworld gambling figure whose name happened to be Dawson. The link turned to be non-existent. Lenny came to New Orleans to erase a painful, three-year-old memory, and could do so only by sinking a longboat full of supremely confident berserkers.

Many considered the previous Super Bowl's stunning AFL upset a fluke, so Las Vegas installed the Vikings as thirteen-point favorites. They would need more than thirteen.

Soon after the game commenced it became apparent something was wrong. Kapp was not dissecting the K.C. secondary with those wobbly passes of his that so often hit their marks. His runners were not grinding out steady yardage in lengthy, time-consuming drives that ended with touchdowns. Joe was running not because he wanted to, but for his life as his offensive line could not protect him from the brutal charges of Chief linemen Buck Buchanan, Jerry Mays and Curly Culp.

Another newcomer was kicker Jan Stenerud, who had missed just eight out of thirty-five attempts in '69. Today he drilled three quick field goals over the heads of the increasingly frustrated Vikings. Then, late in the second quarter came a crushing blow.

Throughout the game Dawson's offensive line protected him marvelously from Minnesota's amazed front four, but at the end of the game's first touchdown drive they did more than pass block. After a fumbled punt set the Chiefs up with a first-and-goal on the Viking five-yard line Lenny executed "65 toss power trap." He faked a toss to fullback Robert Holmes as tackle Jim Tyrer pulled out to simulate a sweep and lure Marshall to the outside. Page came through Tyrer's vacated spot untouched, but guard Mo Moorman peeled back from the right side and disposed of Page with a pulverizing trap block. Dawson turned and handed off to tailback Mike Garrett, who darted through the gaping hole produced by Moorman's block. Garrett scored easily to give the Chiefs a cozy 16-0 halftime advantage.

Kapp managed to supervise a lovely third period drive Dave Osborn ended with a four-yard run to return the gap to nine points, but a forty-six-yard touchdown pass Dawson threw to wide receiver Otis Taylor gave Stram's red-shirted braves all they needed to wrap up the game and title 23-7 in the last game played by an AFL team.

The terms of the merger were complete and implemented the next season as the old league absorbed the new. Yet none could deny that the American Football League had been a winner.

The coming seasons would be just as dramatic.

— A Defender's Point of View —
1970 Baltimore Colts versus Dallas Cowboys

Going into Super Bowl V the Baltimore Colts were in a position to acquire an amazingly dubious place in sports history. The merger between the American Football League and National Football League was complete, and 1970 saw them compete as one. The Colts, Pittsburgh Steelers and Cleveland Browns were transplanted from the older National League into the ranks of former AFL teams to comprise the American Football Conference. Considering Baltimore's loss to the New York Jets two years earlier while still part of the old NFL the Colts, now about to go against the National Football Conference champion Dallas Cowboys, were in a position to become the only team to ever lose Super Bowls in both conferences.

Under new head coach Don McCafferty, Baltimore had been pre-season pick to win the AFC's Eastern Division in its first year of existence. It had taken awhile to recover from the shock of totally unexpected Super Bowl defeat two years earlier. The season after that game the Colts staggered to a demoralized, injury-plagued 8-5-1 record. Now their bodies and spirits were somewhat mended (and older,) and they were raring to make up for two years' worth of more than one kind of pain. The Cowboys bore a similar cross.

Over the last pair of seasons Dallas quarterback Craig Morton's chronic arm and shoulder problems had short-circuited his team's passing game, but powerful running and impregnable defense carried it to a two-year regular season record of 21-6-1. 1969's number one draft pick, running back Calvin Hill out of Yale, won Rookie of the Year honors by gaining 942 yards despite missing three games with a foot injury. However *this* year's top choice, West Texas State's Duane Thomas, proved such a ravenous ground gainer that even Hill wound up on the bench.

Four straight postseasons had seen the Cowboys' championship dreams go down the tubes with agonizing playoff losses to Green Bay and Cleveland. For a time it looked like they would not even reach the 1970 playoffs because of an unhopeful late-season record of 5-4 that included defeats by such scores as 54-13 and 38-0. All gave up on the lackluster Dallasites, doing them a great favor. Head coach Tom Landry realized the pressure was now off, and told his men they may as well ease up and enjoy themselves, and the best way to do this was to win their remaining games. Dallas not only won its last five, but just the right combination of other teams lost to fan the faint spark of playoff hope into a roaring conflagration as the running game and defense bulled through the playoffs to Miami's Orange Bowl, where Baltimore waited.

The Colts had a mighty defense of their own despite its creaky old age. The game would be a defensive clinic as both offenses were pushed all over the field by the rampaging defenses, which jarred loose and recovered five fumbles, snatched off six interceptions and compelled thirteen punts.

Morton came *into* the game with more accumulated hurts than the Light Brigade. His throwing arm ached with a post-operative shoulder, sore elbow and a deep gash on his hand. He was also coming off a severe case of flu and laryngitis that almost cancelled his appearance. A couple of days before the game he had lost his voice, and it was questionable whether he would be able to call signals on Super Sunday. His vocal chords came through just in time.

The contest started with a pair of Baltimore turnovers setting up Mike Clark field goals for a 6-0 Cowboy lead, but in the second quarter one of the game's controversies occurred. Venerable Colt quarterback great Johnny Unitas aimed a medium-range pass at wide receiver Eddie Hinton. Forced to throw over the towering Dallas rush line, Unitas threw the ball too high. When Hinton stretched for the pigskin he deflected it toward cornerback Mel Renfro, who tipped it into the hands of tight end John Mackey, who galloped into the end zone to complete a seventy-five-yard scoring play. The rules stated that it was illegal for two eligible receivers to touch the ball in succession, and this was very crucial since Renfro vociferously denied touching the football. The officials allowed the touchdown, however, and film replays seemed to indicate that Renfro had indeed gotten a fingernail or two on the ball.

It was only the second TD the Dallas defense had allowed in the last twenty-seven quarters, and even now they blocked the extra point to keep the score tied at six.

Later in the period Morton found Thomas open on a short scoring throw to retake the lead, 13-6. To compound the Baltimore woes, on the first series after the Cowboy touchdown mountainous defensive end George Andrie smashed Unitas and cracked his ribs, sidelining him for the rest of the afternoon.

On the second half kickoff Dallas had its greatest opportunity to put the game away when the Colt's Jim Duncan fumbled and safety Richmond Flowers recovered to give the Cowboys a first down at the Baltimore thirty-one. Moving to a first-and-goal at the two, Morton handed off to Thomas who cracked into the line and fumbled. During the scramble for the ball, defensive tackle Billy Ray Smith jumped up and frantically signaled that his side had recovered. The officials took Smith's word for it and presented possession to the Colts. This touched off a violent argument between the officials and Dallas center Dave Manders, which was understandable since it was Manders who got up holding the ball. However questionable the call may have been, Dallas had lost a Christmas chance for a 20-6 lead that, considering how its defense was playing, would almost certainly have been insurmountable.

The third quarter was scoreless as turnovers and penalties stymied both offenses, but midway through the fourth period Baltimore safety Rick Volk returned an interception to the Cowboy three-yard line. Two years earlier Earl Morral had committed just about every mistake a quarterback can en route to a staggering defeat. Today, again subbing for an injured Unitas, he took no chances as he handed off to power runner Tom Nowatzke for the tying touchdown. 13-13.

Finally, only 1:09 remained, and Dallas had the ball on its own twenty-seven. Morton would surely hand off to his outstanding runners, make prudent use of times out and try to work his way into field goal range, but throbbing arm and all, Craig put the ball in the air in an attempt to connect with running back Danny Reeves. Under a hard blitz by linebacker Ted Hendricks, Morton threw slightly behind Reeves, who had the pass for an instant before he was hit and lost his grip. The ball tumbled into the arms of delighted linebacker Mike Curtis, who returned it to the Cowboy twenty-eight. Two plays later it was on the twenty-five, and there were five seconds left. Enter kicker Jim O'Brien.

O'Brien had missed an earlier attempt plus the extra point, so it cannot be said the twenty-two-year-old rookie was confident as he jogged onto the field. Dallas called a time out to give the youngster some agonizing extra moments to think about how many things could go wrong on the next play. McCafferty looked at his trembling kicker and told Morral, "For heaven's sakes, go talk to the kid, Earl." The grizzled vet spoke a few soothing syllables to the nerve-wracked novice before kneeling to hold for the kick. O'Brien booted a perfect, thirty-two-yard placement that gave the Colts a 16-13 win and a measure of redemption from the galling, two-year-old memory of humiliation in this same stadium.

The Cowboys stamped their cleats and hurled their helmets. It hurt worse every year. Another season as coming, though, and the Dallas Cowboys reached for it hungrily.

Doomsday

1971 Dallas Cowboys versus Miami Dolphins

The Dallas Cowboys had lost this thing before, and the thought of losing it again was so horrid that they refused to let it occur to them. They pushed the possibility out of mind. There had been too much heartbreak during five years of post-season pain. The obsession welled in every one of them as they arrived, silent and angry, in New Orleans.

After beating the San Francisco 49ers in the National Football Conference title game the Cowboys were strangely quiet in their locker room. Safety Cornell Green later wondered, "How could we get excited about going to the Super Bowl? We had already been there and lost. Man, we had been everywhere and lost. Only one thing mattered— *winning* the Super Bowl." It was an attitude his teammates shared. To a man.

The Pokes had surged into the 1971 season seething with determination to capture the long, long-awaited Grail, and corralled one team after another en route. Head coach Tom Landry installed former Naval cadet Roger Staubach as quarterback at mid-season, and the team responded with nine straight victories to surge into old Tulane Stadium as a heavy favorite over the Miami Dolphins.

The Miami who? It was a common question that year. Like Dallas, the Dolphins were an expansion team, and Super Bowl VI was the first one to feature two such outfits. The Dolphins had surprised both their fans and themselves with their glittering '71 performance. The major factor behind Miami's emergence as a top contender was new head coach Don Shula's burning desire to win all the marbles to atone for the galling upset he had suffered in the third Super Bowl, when he was still coaching Baltimore. Shula was fortunate to have taken over a team with so much young talent. He awakened and honed his mens' skills through sweat-soaked workouts that often numbered four per day.

Offensively, Miami was downright dangerous with power runners Larry Csonka and Jim Kiick hammering holes in every defense they had so far faced. Bob Griese was a quarterback who seldom needed to risk making mistakes as he handed off to Csonka and Kiick, and kept defenses honest with occasional, sniper-accurate throws to wide receivers Howard Twilly and recently acquired marvel Paul Warfield. The defense was another script.

This squad had little in common with the so-seasoned vets who plugged holes for Dallas. The Dolphin defense was so young that Landry admitted he could not think of their names—they had not been around long enough to become known. The crucial exception in this post-graduate array was middle linebacker Nick Buoniconti. Nick was a ten-year man who provided a vital dash of skilled stability and leadership to the inexperienced unit around him.

Landry and his assistants figured the best solution for Miami's menacing offense was to keep it on the bench. Long, slow drives that eventually brought points would limit Griese's and his mates' opportunities to score and would force them to play catch-up, but in order to retain possession for long stretches Dallas would have to neutralize Buoniconti. His speed and savvy had carried him and his students through the season because enemy offenses had not been able to elude his quick pursuit and that of his teammates, who followed his every lead. The Cowboys would negate this strategy by running straight at Buoniconti. Repeatedly, runners Duane Thomas, Walt Garrison and Calvin Hill followed at least one hulking interior lineman on plays directly over the increasingly less-sprightly Buoniconti who, along with the whole Dolphin defense, wore out under this crushing assault from a team usually noted for finesse rather than power.

Miami received the opening kickoff and did dandy for one down as Csonka plowed for twelve yards. On the next play he fumbled for the first time that year. Dallas linebacker Chuck Howley recovered.

The young Dolphin defenders had allowed on average less than thirteen points per game during the regular season, but Landry's play-calling was psychic as he seemed to know their plans for every down. Csonka's fumble only brought the Cowboys a field goal, but seemed to rattle the underdogs. What happened minutes later finished them.

On the last play of the first quarter Griese faded to pass, but right tackle Bob Lilly and left end Larry Cole eluded their blockers and stormed in on the unfortunate quarterback. Griese was known as a fair scrambler, but every time he danced away from Lilly, Cole reached for him, and vice-versa. The bedeviled Dolphin kept hoping to escape, but after he had retreated twenty-nine yards Lilly buried him for the deepest sack anybody had ever seen. Whatever composure Miami still had withered away at this point. Considering the degree of Dallas domination, the halftime count was seemingly tight at 10-3. No scoreboard was ever more misleading.

Early in the third period Buoniconti was knocked unconscious. The Cowboy runners, freed from his pursuit, swept outside on a drive that Thomas ended with a three-yard jaunt for a 17-3 lead. Landry's strategy remained flawless as his offense ran off sixty-nine plays to Miami's forty-five, and held possession forty minutes and fifty-nine seconds.

Staubach had drilled a touchdown pass to wide receiver Lance Alworth in the second quarter, and closed out the point gathering with a fourth period shot to tight end Mike Ditka for a final of 24-3, Dallas. Only a late fumble on the Dolphin one-yard line stopped the bulge from swelling further as the Cowboys cruised on a sweet breeze to bring Texas its long, long-awaited first NFL championship. The future, however, was Miami's.

Nobody's Perfect?
1972 Miami Dolphins versus Washington Redskins

Miami Dolphin head coach Don Shula had lost in the very end twice before. Super Bowls III and VI were his nightmares. He was a terrible loser. None worse. Almost.

There *was* his upcoming counterpart in Super Bowl VII—Washington Redskin head coach George Allen. This religious dedication to winning was one of the few features they shared.

Allen told his players how great they were, that he believed in them, gave them chances nobody else would, and rewarded them with splendid contracts. When they did well on the field he leaped and cheered wildly. They could not bear the thought of letting him down.

Shula's men did not *dare* fail him. He worked them relentlessly, releasing those who did not measure up or whose dedication was marginal. When his players did well on the field he grumbled, "It's about time." There was no way he would let his earlier Super Bowl losses be repeated. He had indeed wrought marvels, and neither Washington's "Over the Hill Gang" or all the demons in a dozen hells would come between him and those sparkling champion's rings.

It was only three years since he had taken over the ragged Dolphins and whipped them into contenders, and the mauling they had absorbed in the previous Super Bowl provided all the maturity and motivation they needed for this second run for glory—especially now that Shula's heavy guidance had forced them to realize how great they were.

So irresistible was their determination, leadership and motivation that they tore through the 1972 regular season undefeated and kept their record unblemished through the playoffs. In 1934 and again in 1942 the Chicago Bears had been the only franchise to go through regular seasons undefeated, but both years they lost the title game. If the Dolphins could whip Washington in this confrontation the mythical perfect year would no longer be unknown.

The Redskins' warmest hopes were pinned on the legs of All-Pro tailback Larry Brown. Because he was almost totally deaf in his right ear, Brown had always been forced to line up on the right side of the backfield so that he could hear the snap count. It was not his natural position, and he was not as effective here as he might have been on the other side. Lately he had been wearing a radio-controlled hearing aid in his helmet, enabling him to switch to his called deployment. His powerful running style was fueled by a grim determination that made him seem much bigger than his actual dimensions of 5-11 and 195 pounds. Often this scrappy runner gained extra yardage by simply refusing to be taken down by fewer than three or four defenders. His example was such that prideful men could not abide doing less than their absolute best on the same field with a teammate so willing to spill his guts on the turf in order to earn victory. This team-pervading attitude paced the 'Skins past all NFC opponents.

Today, however, there was a Miami defender whose resolution matched even Brown's. The Dolphins originally signed defensive tackle Manny Fernandez because they hoped to sell a few extra tickets among Miami's sizable Hispanic population, and figured his name in pre-game programs might help. The coaches had not expected much from Manny apart from ticket sales. Besides being almost legally blind, he had not even started at U. of Utah, which was one of the worst teams in the country during his time there. Yet when given a shot at the big leagues he blossomed into stardom. It was primarily Fernandez who shut down the feared Washington running game, which gained just 141 yards.

There was nothing spectacular about this Super Bowl played in the Los Angeles Memorial Coliseum. The Miami secondary limited Redskin quarterback Billy Kilmer to just 104 yards while intercepting him three times.

Dolphin signal-caller Bob Griese faithfully stuck to his coach's dependable, unspectacular philosophy, handing off to his untouched running tandem of fullback Larry Csonka and tailback Mercury Morris. Csonka was especially troublesome to the Washingtons as he pounded out 112 yards.

In the first period Miami opened the scoring with a surprise twenty-eight-yard touchdown pass to unheralded wide receiver Howard Twilley while defenders kept a worried eye on the other wideout, All-Pro Paul

Warfield. A short scoring run by goal line specialist Jim Kiick gave Miami a 14-0 halftime lead and packed its offensive bags

for the afternoon, but this boring game was headed for a bizarre finale.

There were 2:07 remaining in the contest when Shula sent his field goal unit after the placement to clinch the contest. What happened next was the strangest play in Super Bowl history.

The attempt started out ordinarily enough, but kicker Garo Yepremian's attempt was blocked and the ball bounced back to him. The plucky native of Cypress tried to pass to someone whose identity was never established, but the ball slipped from his grasp and fell into the eager arms of Redskin cornerback Mike Bass who hurried forty-nine yards to the Dolphin end zone to avert the shame of being shut out.

Miami defensive back Jake Scott, a former seventh round draft pick, earned Most Valuable Player honors by picking off two Kilmer passes that hazy afternoon as his team won 14-7. The Dolphins had not lost a game since the *previous* Super Bowl, and their perfect 17-0 season is a pro football icon that will likely stand eternally. Even so, this team still had a lot of games to win.

Valhalla
1973 Miami Dolphins versus Minnesota Vikings

Game day for Super Bowl VIII was January 13, 1974, and the teams were the Minnesota Vikings and Miami Dolphins. In Minneapolis the Minnesota Symphony Orchestra's performance for that day had to be postponed from 3:00 p.m. until 7:45 because the musicians took time off to watch the game. They need not have bothered. Their performance was a better show.

1973 was the year head coach Don Shula's Dolphins legitimized their claim as a dynasty, becoming the most prolific winners the league had ever produced over a pair of seasons. Miami's regular season record the last two years stood at 26-2 as they arrived at Houston's Rice Stadium for their record-breaking third straight Super Bowl.

It had taken the Vikings awhile to recover from the shock of thorough, unanticipated defeat. It was four years since their long afternoon in New Orleans, but this one would be no shorter.

Apart from his small stature Minnesota quarterback Fran Tarkenton was the prototype of the modern man under center. He would finish his career with the highest passing yardage total in NFL history to that date, and the only player with 500 or more carries to average over six yards per rushing attempt. His nimble feet, accurate arm and crafty football mind were a winning combo when added to dazzling rookie running back Chuck Foreman and deep threat John Gilliam. The long ball was the Vikings' most effective weapon, but the Dolphin secondary had allowed just five touchdown passes all season. Safeties Dick Anderson and Jake Scott made virtually any post pattern impassable.

Miami's double-barrelled running tandem of Larry Csonka and Mercury Morris was the best the league possessed, and among the very best it had *ever* produced. On this Super Sunday they faced a defense ranked twenty-third out of twenty-six at stopping the run. The Norsemen never had a prayer.

Dolphin quarterback Bob Griese worked his misdirection-style offense splendidly all season. When he was not handing off to the juggernaut Csonka up the middle, he would fake a give to Big Larry, and as the defensive line massed to meet him, spin and toss the ball to Morris sprinting to the outside. Occasionally the process worked in reverse, with the defense chasing the fleet, empty-handed tailback around end only to have Csonka hurtle through the middle after taking a furtive handoff. When the secondary worriedly inched closer to the line of scrimmage, Griese was wont to unload a bomb or two to wideouts Howard Twilley and Paul Warfield. It was all centered around the monotonously effective ball-control running game.

Miami's style of offense won games in bunches, but was boring to watch. As more coaches patterned their attacks after Shula's, most games became low-scoring field goal exchanges. The following year would bring rule changes intended to increase scoring and improve league-wide stadium attendance and television ratings. It was all because of this superteam from Florida. Meanwhile there was a title test to play.

Minnesota won the toss, but went three-and-out. Ten plays later the heralded misdirection broke the ice as the Viking defense fell through it by chasing Morris outside while Csonka churned five yards up the middle for the game's first score.

Tarkenton's offensive line consistently gave him what ordinarily would have been ample time to throw, but he could only wait and wait and wait while Gilliam could not shake off the sticky coverage that would limit him to just forty-four yards.

A short run by Dolphin goal line specializing runner Jim Kiick and a twenty-eight-yard Garo Yepremian field goal gave Miami a 17-0 halftime lead, and only a late fourth quarter run by Tarkenton averted a shutout as the Dolphins rolled tediously to a 24-7 victory. Csonka's 145 yards and two touchdowns broke the Super Bowl rushing record and made him Most Valuable Player.

It seemed the Miami Dolphins were destined to rule the NFL for some time. It was openly stated by many that the '73 edition of this fabulous franchise was the greatest team in history. In its present, intact state it would never know defeat, but the current cast would not be around much longer. The following year more than rules would change. A rival league was forming, and its wealthy owners would use glittering, many-zeroed contracts lure away Csonka, Kiick and Warfield. The retirement of pivotal middle linebacker Nick Buoniconti weakened the defense, and the Dolphins sank into a decade-long sabbatical before their next championship appearance.

It was time for a new empire.

At Long Last
1974 Pittsburgh Steelers versus Minnesota Vikings

Everyone who ever knew Arthur Rooney, Sr. had at least one friend for life. Him. Mr. Rooney's kindness, compassion and generosity made Santa Clause a miser by comparison. This was a problem for him in one respect—he owned the Pittsburgh Steelers. NFL owners with big hearts often have losing teams. Firing losing coaches is something they may be slow to do, and from the time affable Arthur purchased the team for $2500.00 in 1933 until when it won him a divisional title, forty seasons passed.

The turning point came when he hired Chuck Noll as head coach, and like so many former offensive linemen Noll made a wonderful mentor. He did not inherit much. In his first year the team went 1-13, but as he and his staff drafted and coached expertly the team's rise was meteoric.

In Penn State's Franco Harris they found a panther-powerful and cat-quick ball carrier who could squeeze through the slenderest seam in spite of his huge size. Quarterback Terry Bradshaw was the first player taken in the 1970 draft. He had bushels of talent and promise, but started slowly. In earlier years the Steelers had discarded quarterbacks Johnny Unitas, Lenny Dawson and Earl Morral without giving them time to develop. Bradshaw was nurtured along patiently as he passed from pitiful to mediocre to erratic. Late in the 1974 season he nailed down the starting job via a performance worthy of the greatest.

Potent offense notwithstanding, Pittsburgh was carried by a defense known around the league (and beyond) as the Steel Curtain. This bunch had no weak spot. Despite the linebackers and secondary being the best in the business it was the rapacious linemen that earned the formidable alias. L.C. Greenwood, Joe Greene, Ernie Holmes and Dwight White patrolled the interior with savage speed and power.

Quests

At first the Steelers were stymied by unfortunate timing that had them rising to a competitive level during the Miami Dolphin's glory years, but the Steeltown maulers were getting better all the time. Then so many key Miami players defected to the newly formed World Football League that the Dolphins fell in the 1974 American Football Conference playoffs while Pittsburgh bludgeoned its way into Super Bowl IX.

The National Football Conference would again be represented by the Minnesota Vikings, who had barely survived their conference title game with the Los Angeles Rams when a potentially game-winning Ram pass from the two-yard line was intercepted in the end zone. It was a gutsy victory, but it would be the Vikings' last one that year.

Despite the blatant, blue-collar power of the truculent Pennsylvanians, nobody questioned the sanity of those who hoped for a Minnesota win. It was the Norsemens' third appearance, and the first for their opponents. No Super Bowl veteran had ever lost to a first-timer. Yet.

New Orleans' Tulane Stadium hosted the game, and at first the Steelers did, in fact, seem afflicted by rookie jitters. In the first half Viking middle linebacker Jeff Sieman adjusted to the Pittsburgh blocking scheme, darting forward to plug the holes opened in his front four. Although Minnesota surrendered a second quarter safety on a fumbled handoff it held the Steeler offense scoreless and the half ended uneventfully, 2-0.

Predictably it was the Pittsburgh defense that got the grudging show started with the safety. It would also hold Minnesota's super quarterback Fran Tarkenton to just 102 aerial yards, and his runners to only seventeen steps (twelve of them on one carry by Chuck Foreman.)

The Viking defense could no more contain hard-charging Harris in this game than it had Larry Csonka the year before. Harris broke Csonka's year-old Super Bowl rushing record by gaining 158 yards through this same leaky opposition. In the third quarter Harris scored the game's first touchdown on a nine-yard sweep for a 9-0 lead.

The Minnesotas did have a fleeting moment of hope in the fourth quarter when linebacker Matt Blair blocked a Bobby Walden punt that was covered in the end zone for a score to cut the difference to 9-6. Minutes later, however, Bradshaw hit tight end Larry Brown with a short touchdown pass to sew up the championship for Mr. Rooney's team, 16-6.

It had taken forty-two years, but was well worth the wait. The Pittsburgh Steelers were far, far from finished.

Worthy of the Name
1975 Pittsburgh Steelers versus Dallas Cowboys

All season long the whole NFL had assumed the Pittsburgh Steelers would waltz to their second straight Super Bowl triumph. When they nosed out the Oakland Raiders in the 1975 AFC championship game, it seemed they already had the hard part behind them. If anything, they were even more powerful than the year before.

That previous season had been unkind to the Dallas Cowboys. Involved in major player turnover due to a rash of retirements, they had failed to qualify for the playoffs for the first time in eight years. Their future was saved by what was perhaps the greatest one-team, one-year rookie crop in league history. Twelve wide-eyed, eager young men joined the club en masse. Dubbed the "Dirty Dozen" by the press, they brought a much-needed, infectious surge of enthusiasm to the remaining, dispirited veterans, and the Cowboys re-entered the playoffs as a second-place, wild-card participant. Quarterback Roger Staubach's storied, fifty-yard "Hail Mary" touchdown pass to wide receiver Drew Pearson in the final seconds of the divisional playoff at Minnesota brought a first-round victory and earned the Pokes passage to Los Angeles to contest for the National Football Conference championship. Dallas smashed the heavily favored Rams 37-7 to be borne by miracles into Miami's Orange Bowl for Super Bowl X.

Their overpowering talent made the Steelers a solid favorite, but they soon noticed the youthful Cowboys did not realize they were supposed to be intimidated, and were not playing for mere respectability. They fully intended to win.

When his team received the opening kickoff, Dallas head coach Tom Landry shocked Pittsburgh by having his return man lateral to a linebacker who ran a long time before he was caught. The lovely return set up a twenty-nine-yard touchdown pass from Staubach to Pearson for the first opening period six-pointer surrendered by the Steelers all year.

A short scoring throw from Pitt quarterback Terry Bradshaw to tight end Randy Grossman soon afterward balanced the ledger, but a second quarter field goal gave the Cowboys a 10-7 lead that lasted until halftime. The second half would be very different.

The Steelers had played sluggishly since scoring their touchdown, allowing Dallas to grab the initiative and control the game's tempo. The easy scoring drive seemed to lull them into assuming the game was to become a rout. They all eased up and waited for somebody else to make the next big play. None did. Also, the Cowboy defense stiffened midway through the first quarter, and even the magnificent runner Franco Harris had great difficulty negotiating the complex "Flex" defense, which Landry had created specifically to combat the running game. Only the performance of young receiver Lynn Swann was up to Pittsburgh standards. Still hurting from a severe concussion suffered against Oakland, Swann earned Most Valuable Player recognition by stretching just four acrobatic receptions to 161 yards.

The Steeler's "Steel Curtain" defense greatly missed the play and leadership of tackle Joe Greene, who was forced out early in the game due to a pinched nerve, but midway through the third quarter the tide began to shift. Middle linebacker Jack Lambert tired of his teammates' lackadaisical attitude and commenced exhorting them with scathing vocalizations while violently assailing any Cowboy who entered his vicinity.

The special teams unit was first to get the message, and rose up and blocked a fourth quarter Dallas punt that rolled out of the back of the end zone for a safety to cut the difference to 10-9. Two quick Roy Gerela field goals gave Pittsburgh a 15-10 lead, and then the graceful Swann became the unquestioned hero.

With three minutes to play, the Steelers faced a third down at their own thirty-six. The Cowboys gambled and sent hard-hitting safety Cliff Harris in on a blitz that forced single coverage on Swann. Under a furious rush, Bradshaw heaved the ball an eyeblink before being powdered by massive defensive tackle Larry Cole. Terry was prone and unconscious when the ball settled into Swann's grasp for a sixty-four-yard scoring play that ran Pittsburgh's advantage to 21-10.

Dallas rookie wideout Percy Howard had not even played football at little Austin Peay College in Clarksville, Tennessee, but concentrated on being a basketball standout. The young athlete became a trivia buff's delight by faking out Steeler cornerback Mel Blount so completely that Blount fell flat, and shagging Staubach's thirty-four-yard touchdown pass to pull his team to within four. It was his only NFL reception. He was cut a few months later to end his football career as the only man whose only pro reception was for a Super Bowl touchdown.

The Cowboys were again threatening at the final gun after Pittsburgh strangely turned the ball over on downs, but safety Glen Edwards intercepted a desperation Staubach Hail Mary attempt in the end zone to quash this gallant team's attempt to snatch one last miracle. The Steelers won, 21-17.

Dallas charged the officials with turning blind eyes to dirty football by the Steeler linebackers and defensive backs. Yet the fearless, determined challengers had won the black-jerseyed champions' respect. Both teams had a great deal of future involving both ecstasy and heartbreak, but on this January afternoon in Florida they had played what truly was a super bowl.

— Raiders on a Rampage —
1976 Oakland Raiders versus Minnesota Vikings

Super Bowl XI was a hard one for journalists. The teams involved were the Oakland Raiders and Minnesota Vikings, and the players had little patience with the media. It was easy to understand why— the reporters kept asking, "Why don't you guys ever win the big one?" Through many seasons they had won everything *except* the big one, and were tired of being reminded of it.

After losing this thing nine years earlier, the Raiders were eliminated in the playoffs by the eventual Super Bowl winner in six of the last eight years. So far, 1976 had been vintage as they posted a 13-1 regular season record, then blitzed defending champion Pittsburgh for the American Football Conference title.

Minnesota, meanwhile, was here for the fourth time. Still seeking their first victory.

Most observers saw the teams as pretty evenly matched, with a slight edge given to Oakland because of the game's being played in their backyard. The site was the Pasadena Rose Bowl, which heretofore had been sacrosanct from professional sports. Close examination would have revealed to those who expected a close contest that the Minnesotas never had learned to defense the run, and on this sunny afternoon they faced one of the best ground attacks ever spawned by the NFL.

Oakland did not immediately get its attack untracked, though, and was forced to punt early in the first quarter. Punter Ray Guy is the only player of his position ever taken as a first-round draft pick. His lengthy, altitudinous kicks took many seconds to drop, and his quick motion launched the ball in a twinkling. Ray had never had a punt blocked. His first kick of this afternoon *was* blocked by Fred McNeill of the Vikings' illustrious special teams. The loose ball was covered on the Raider two-yard line, but it was a sterile opportunity.

On second-and-goal, Minnesota quarterback Fran Tarkenton handed off to running back Brent McCLanahan on a power play up the middle. McClanahan crashed into 6'8 defensive tackle Dave Rowe, and before the play was whistled dead linebacker Phil Villapiano jarred the ball loose. Another linebacker, Willie Hall, grabbed the fumble, and as far as the Vikings went the game was done.

The National Football Conference champs had geared themselves toward halting Oakland's punishing fullback Mark van Eegan. However, the Bucs kept sending tailback Clarence Davis upfield behind his huge offensive line as it worked over Minnesota's aged defensive front four.

The Raiders had several holdovers from their previous Super Bowl. One was goal line specialist Pete Banaszak, who tumbled into the end zone twice after deep completions from quarterback Kenny Stabler to another past participant, wide receiver Fred Bilitnekoff, set Oakland up with optimum field position. Fred, in fact, ended the game as its Most Valuable Player.

Yet another old-timer, cornerback Willie Brown, slammed Minnesota's coffin by intercepting a Tarkenton pass and returning it a Super Bowl-record seventy-five yards. It was his side's final score in a 32-14 triumph.

Some were disappointed by the rout. They had hoped for a replay of the last Super Sunday's rock-gut drama, but Oakland head coach John Madden and the players who carried him off the field had awaited this moment too long to have it any other way.

Besides, the next Supe would have excitement aplenty.

Clash of Emotions
1977 Dallas Cowboys versus Denver Broncos

Super Bowls played in the exotic southern playground of New Orleans cannot help being special if only for their location. Super Bowl XII was played there, and was as memorable as the French Quarter.

The teams contesting for 1977's bragging rights were the Dallas Cowboys and the Denver Broncos. Between them and the swarms of raucous fans who followed them they gave the Crescent City the look of hosting a world's fair.

Everyone expected to see the Cowboys there, this being their fourth time. The fabulous draft of two years earlier was bearing sweet fruit, and had been spiced this season by the addition of Heisman Trophy winner Tony Dorsett. After scoring fifty-nine touchdowns at the University of Pittsburgh, Dorsett now filled the only void in Dallas' already high-octane offense by adding the breakaway ground threat that took the pressure off another Heisman winner, quarterback Roger Staubach.

After pacing the Pitt Panthers to the 1976 NCAA National Championship, Dorsett came to the Cowboys as the second choice in the entire '77 college draft, and was now in a position to become the first player ever to go from the best college team in the nation to the world's finest *professional* roster. It was a heady prospect for a young athlete who had pounded out thirteen touchdowns in the regular season despite only playing part-time the first nine games while he laboriously absorbed head coach Tom Landry's intricate playbook. With enemy defenses now forced to keep a wary eye on the lightning-fast, shifty Dorsett, Staubach found more time to wait for one of his excellent receivers to break free—when he was not handing off to his marvelous new tailback.

Offensive prowess notwithstanding, it was Dallas' storied "Doomsday Defense" that carried the team. Carefully selected athletes of exceeding skill manned every position, eliminating weak spots upon which rival offenses could concentrate. Right tackle Randy White turned twenty-four the day of this game, and had never played tackle before this season. He looked as if he had been doing it more years than he was old as the Pokes destroyed Chicago and Minnesota in the playoffs by a combined score of 60-13. With his sidekick, end Harvey Martin, he would today put on a pass rushing spectacle that made them the only co-MVPs in Super Bowl history. Denver was a different chapter.

Like the Cowboys, the Broncos were defensively oriented. Here the resemblance faded. Injuries to linemen the year before had forced Denver to adopt the 3-4 defense that adds an extra linebacker and employs a three-man line. The alignment was so successful that the team stuck with it the following season. The press dubbed the squad the "Orange Crush" defense in reference to their gaudy orange jerseys and bone-crushing style of play.

Quarterback Craig Morton, who had spent ten years as a Dallas Cowboy, headed the offense. He directed an opportunistic attack. Morton and his mates were constantly being presented with optimum field position by the carnivorous defense, which produced more turnovers than a bakery. Denver did not need to score many points because it was easy to score more than the few it surrendered. The Broncos had a nondescript history, but this year they had knocked off one surprised opponent after another while charging to an early-season divisional lead they never relinquished. Their victory-starved fans responded with a wave of wild enthusiasm that came to be called Broncomania. This intoxicating surge of emotion quickly spread to the players and augmented their considerable physical talents.

It had taken a player revolt to bring rookie head coach Red Miller to Denver, where he found more talent than anyone outside the team realized existed. Personality conflicts and numerous petty complaints had distracted the men and brought on resentment and factions that stifled their ability to win consistently. It led to the mutiny that brought a changing of the guard, opening the door for Miller, who eased the tensions, made friends with his players and saw them respond by showing the rest of the league they were for real.

It was the first indoor Super Bowl, with the Louisiana Superdome as the game site, and it was wide-open from the start. After receiving the opening kickoff the Cowboys tried a reverse on the first play, resulting in a nine-yard loss to set the trend for most of the first half

Quests

as the NFC champs were stymied not only by the adrenalin-pumped Bronco defenders, but also by their own mistakes.

Fortunately for Dallas, their opponents seemed afflicted by the jitters so typical of first-time Super Bowl participants as they were unable to capitalize on the many Cowboy miscues. If the previous Supe was the one in which an offensive line most asserted itself, this one witnessed the greatest-ever dominance by a *defensive* front four. The Denver offensive line was totally overwhelmed by the astounding Dallas lead quartet, which merged strength and speed to a demoralizing extent. This pass rush poured over, around and straight through its would-be blockers, and in upon Morton, who had the painful distinction of throwing a record four interceptions in the first half alone. Although Landry had designed his novel, fishnet-like Flex defense primarily to stop the run, the Bronco *passing* game was the most obvious casualty of the first two quarters.

Despite its many gaffes the Cowboy offense managed to squeeze out a 13-0 halftime advantage. The swarming defenders, who sacked Staubach five times that afternoon, forced a large part of its early woes on it. Lineman Lyle Alzado was particularly troublesome in the first half as he twice trapped the harried Staubach, batted an attempted field goal off course and choked off all attempts to run to his side. Also, Dallas seemed confused by its own intricate offense.

After accepting the second half kickoff the Broncos carried out their longest drive of the day, moving the ball from their own thirty-five-yard-line to the Dallas thirty, where kicker Jim Turner capped the march with a forty-seven-yard field goal to cut the difference to 13-3, but the Pokes were starting to find their rhythm.

Midway through the third period they had the ball on Denver's forty-five, facing a not-too-promising third-and-ten. Hoping to take the defense by surprise, Landry instructed Staubach to go deep to wide receiver Butch Johnson, but as Johnson broke from the line he was blanketed with multiple coverage. Making certain his pass would not be intercepted, Roger threw it far enough to get it over the defenders, and, it looked, out of Johnson's reach as well. The lithe receiver had plans for that descending porker's hide, though, and lunged for it, snaring it while diving horizontally to the artificial turf and giving his team a 20-3 lead.

By then few were giving the underdogs much of a chance—lacking a strong offense they were not known as a catch-up type club, and there was still the bellicose Dallas defense. Yet when return man Rick Upchurch took the ensuing kickoff he ran sixty-seven yards before anyone caught him, and the rabid Denver rooters got a fleeting hope.

With a first-and-ten at the Dallas twenty-six the bruised Morton threw an incompletion and was abruptly benched in favor of the more mobile Norris Weese. Weese guided the offense to an impressively quick touchdown in four plays when fullback Rob Lytle punched it in from one yard out to shave seven more points from the Cowboy lead.

The Dallas offense had perked up, but seemed to sag following the Bronco touchdown, but the defense never let up its savage assault. With seven minutes left in the game it knocked the ball loose from Weese and recovered the fumble on the Denver twenty-nine.

The time had come to seal the victory, so Landry's next play had fullback Robert Newhouse take an ordinary-looking handoff and head to his left. Robert was not known as a passer, and being right-handed would surely have a hard time throwing from his off-side. All this considered, it was surprising the Broncos were again not taken flat-footed when the stocky Newhouse pulled up and fired a perfect pass to wide receiver Golden Richards in the end zone. The Denver coverage again seemed complete, as Richards was encircled, but the Cowboy receivers continued their heroics. Golden pulled the ball from a tangle of orange sleeves for the final score in a 27-10 Dallas victory.

Over the years a reputation for being cold and unfeeling had affixed itself to coach Tom Landry, and had it been deserved it is unlikely his Cowboys could have overcome the emotion-fueled Bronks. It was in his own, *winning* locker room that Landry revealed to the press, "I've never had a team this emotional for a game." On this January afternoon in Louisiana the emotional Dallas Cowboys would have beaten anybody, but an empire was coiling to strike back.

— The Greatest Show on Earth —
1978 Pittsburgh Steelers versus Dallas Cowboys

Super Bowl XIII was the first rematch of the super series as the defending champion Dallas Cowboys met the Pittsburgh Steelers in a sequel to the storied confrontation of three years before. The inspired play of that contest would carry over in even greater proportions.

1978 saw Pittsburgh regain its poise after a two-year injury epidemic. Cruising to a 14-2 regular season the Steelers easily tossed aside their playoff foes to earn passage to Miami as a slight favorite over the glamorous team from North Texas.

Despite being the undisputed rulers of their conference the Cowboys were hard-pressed to repeat their impressive '77 performance as a bad case of complacency saddled them with a non-typical 6-4 late-season record. Then a year-ending surge began in this same Orange Bowl in which the Super Bowl was being played as Dallas caught fire and tore off eight straight victories in convincing fashion, finishing with a 28-0 wipeout of archrival Los Angeles in the National Football Conference title game.

Cowboy quarterback Roger Staubach and the Steelers' Terry Bradshaw had finished as the season's number one- and two-rated passers as they directed attacks that just kept getting better. Both these teams were more powerful than they had been in their previous title meeting, and between them they would erase the annual gripe that one Super Bowl contestant woefully outclassed the other. These were by far the best the league had to offer.

The site reserved an ominous ring for Dallas. Both its previous Super Bowl losses had come in this stadium, and both had been seared with controversy. Unhappily for the Cowboys this trend was unfinished.

After receiving the opening kickoff they drove with ease from their own twenty-eight to the Pittsburgh thirty-four mainly on the legs of

All-Pro tailback Tony Dorsett. After moving this far so smoothly Dallas tried to surprise the Steel Curtain defense with a reverse, but it was fumbled and defensive end John Banaszak recovered the loose ball to scorelessly abort the snappy drive.

For the second straight season Dallas had done what no other team had ever managed once—had both its starting safeties, Cliff Harris and Charlie Waters, make All-Pro. Bradshaw still found holes in the Cowboy secondary on an airborne drive he concluded with a twenty-eight-yard scoring pass to wide receiver John Stallworth. Bradshaw's flying circus again took off after his defense forced a Cowboy punt, moving crisply to the Dallas thirty. Pittsburgh advanced no farther on this drive, however, since its ease apparently lulled Terry into becoming careless. The next play was designed to go to Stallworth, but the bomb-dropping Pitt passer telegraphed the play by looking at the intended receiver all the way. Linebacker D.D. Lewis reacted to Bradshaw's gaze by galloping full-speed for Stallworth as soon as the quarterback's arm was in motion, and making the interception. Had this drive brought another touchdown the game would likely have turned into a rout, but given this reprieve Dallas struck back.

Although the Cowboys got no points out of the interception, late in the first quarter defensive end Harvey Martin jarred the ball loose from Bradshaw and Dallas recovered on the Steeler forty-one. Staubach tied the score three plays later with a thirty-nine-yard throw to wide receiver Tony Hill for the first opening period touchdown allowed by the Steel Curtain all season.

After the kickoff, Pittsburgh faced a third-and-ten at its own forty-eight. The play went haywire from the snap as Bradshaw collided with running back Franco Harris while rolling to his right. Terry dropped the ball, only to have it bounce back into his hands, but before he could regain a firm grip a pair of blitzing linebackers hit him. One of them was Mike Hegman, who snatched the football and carried it in for a Dallas score. 14-7, Cowboys.

It was a fleeting lead. On the next series the Bradshaw-to-Stallworth combo again blasted the Dallasites, this time on a seventy-five-yard pass-run play that knotted the score at fourteen.

Cornerback Mel Blount's interception of a Staubach pass eventually led to a seven-yard touchdown toss from Bradshaw to running back Rocky Bleier to give the Steelers a 21-14 halftime lead that seemed crucial since they would be receiving the second half kickoff, and their high-flying offense could commence the second half with a seven-point head start.

Yet in the early minutes of the third quarter the Cowboy "Doomsday Defense" twice throttled the Pittsburgh attack. After the second Steeler punt, Staubach got his crew rolling on a drive that carried to the ten. It was third-and-three, and the next play would have to be good for the 'Pokes to get back into the affair. Head coach Tom Landry called for a pass to tight end Jackie Smith in the end zone. Middle linebacker Jack Lambert read the play and blitzed, but fullback Scott Laidlaw decked him. Staubach's perfect throw hit Smith in the center of his chest, but the sixteen-year vet became famous in a most left-handed manner when the ball slipped through his hands on what is still called "the drop heard 'round the world." Dallas settled for a field goal.

The muffed pass was the first in a heart-rending string of freakish bad breaks that hit the Cowboys in blitzkrieg fashion late in the game and helped secure an unprecedented third Super Bowl title for Pittsburgh.

Early in the fourth period Bradshaw took his team from its own fifteen to a second-and-eight on his own forty-four. The next call was for a deep heave to wide receiver Lynn Swann down the right sideline. Swann was truly lethal—in the regular season one out of every six of his receptions had gone for a touchdown. On this down, cornerback Benny Barnes stayed with him step-for-step. Under a heavy pass rush, Bradshaw threw while off-balance. Reaching back for the underthrown ball, Swann took his eyes off Barnes, the two men collided and both fell to the turf. The official closest to the play waved it off as an incompletion, but from across the field, field judge Fred Swearingen threw his flag and signaled a tripping penalty on Barnes. The outraged defensive back screamed that it was *he* who had been fouled, and his equally apoplectic teammates vocally agreed. The Cowboy reaction was predictable. Film replays showed how Barnes had had his back turned to Swann and was running full speed *away* from the receiver when the two made contact. After the game, league commissioner Pete Rozelle agreed the call had been wrong, but it was just another disaster the second half sprung on Dallas. Three plays later the trend continued.

Soon after the penalty the Steelers had a third-and-nine at the Dallas twenty-two. Correctly assuming the defense would blitz, Bradshaw sent Harris on a trap play over left tackle. Hard-hitting Waters had a clear angle on Franco, but as he made his move he collided with Swearingen, lost his balance and fell, giving Harris an unobstructed path into the end zone and 28-17 Pittsburgh lead.

The final nail in the Cowboy casket was driven when Steeler kicker Roy Gerela slipped on the ensuing kickoff, sending the ball dribbling to defensive tackle Randy White, who was playing on the return team as a blocker. White had broken his right thumb in the conference title game and could not handle the ball, which he fumbled for a Pittsburgh recovery at the eighteen. On first down Bradshaw hit Swann in the end zone to run the advantage to 35-17.

Against any other team in the league Dallas would likely have won in spite of these miscues, but today's opponent was able to capitalize to an extent beyond the ability of any other group of players. *Nobody* could defeat these Pittsburgh Steelers after handing them so many gifts.

There were only 6:51 remaining when Staubach led his offense onto the field in a legendary attempt to unsew the Steeler victory. Forced to start at his own eleven, Roger engineered the game's longest drive and cut the deficit to 35-24 with a seven-yard shot to tight end Billy Joe Dupree at 2:27 remaining. Dallas rookie Dennis Thurman recovered kicker Rafael Septien's onside kick to give Staubach & Co. another turn. Slinging his bullet passes with sniper's accuracy the desperate, magnificent quarterback refused to surrender the possession, overcoming sacks and once converting on fourth-and-eighteen. He finally connected with wide receiver Butch Johnson on a four-yarder to diminish the difference to 35-31 with twenty-two seconds to play.

Celebrating Pittsburgh players and fans had fallen silent and commenced a mass display of nail biting as their indomitable opponents lined up for their latest onside kick. Despite the paucity of precious seconds it is questionable whether the gasping Steeler defense could have stopped Staubach and his straining-at-the-bit, momentum-pumped offense had they again gotten their hands on the ball, but Bleier flopped onto Septien's slow roller to give the relieved Pittsburgh defenders their salvation.

Roger Staubach had pulled off a masterful showing versus a unit that, at 195, had permitted fewer points than any team in the league that year. He did it without the benefit of lucky breaks.

The Dallas Cowboys continued their tradition of controversial Super Bowl losses in Florida, and the fabulous franchise from Steeltown won a record third Supe. This dynasty was not done yet.

To the Bitter End
1979 Pittsburgh Steelers versus Los Angeles Rams

The fortunes of the 1979 Los Angeles Rams undulated like a stripper's torso. They staggered into the post-season with a 9-7 record. A last-second, fifty-yard touchdown pass from quarterback Vince Ferragamo to wide receiver Billy Waddy stunned the sports world by giving the Rams a 21-19 first-round playoff victory over the heavily favored Dallas Cowboys. There followed a bland, touchdownless 9-0 shutout of Tampa Bay in the NFC title game, giving L.A. its first league championship appearance in twenty-four years.

Events in the American Football Conference were much more predictable as the Pittsburgh Steelers easily earned the privilege of contesting their fourth Super Bowl in six years. This thing was becoming routine to head coach Chuck Noll and his entourage, and the eleven points by which they were favored combined with the chance to do four times now what no other team had done thrice to almost make them forget about their upcoming opponents. Meanwhile, the Rams were concentrating on football.

The Pasadena Rose Bowl teemed with 103,985 fans on game day as Los Angeles had what some considered a home field advantage. They did indeed seem to have something unforeseen going for them early on as they bottled up the Steeler running game and outpointed them 13-10 in a push-and-shove first half that left the throng buzzing at intermission over the pugnacious showing of head coach Ray Malavasi's challengers.

The Pittsburgh offense had undergone some changes the past couple of seasons. The running had slackened off, and quarterback Terry Bradshaw more than once saved the day with his muscular right arm, which sent bombs arcing to the distant mitts of his corps of world-class receivers, but on this day the Steelers were so confident of their ability to manhandle the West Coast team that they took for granted their running game would be sufficient.

Yet with nothing to lose and everything to gain, the Rams would not make it easy for their dynastic foes, and played with a skilled abandon that shut down the Pittsburgh attack through the first two quarters. Despite scoring twice on short plunges the Steelers' great runner Franco Harris (essentially their sole ground threat) picked up just forty-six yards for the game while the team as a whole rushed for only eighty-four steps through the fired-up Ram defense which, like its offense, surprised everyone but themselves by playing strictly to win rather than for mere respectability against the Pennsylvania colossus.

An unexpected hero was Los Angeles tailback Wendell Tyler. He emerged as the game's leading rusher despite a severe stomach virus that often had him heaving on the sideline between plays.

Little changed in the third period, which ended with the sluggish Steelers trailing 19-17, although Bradshaw and his turbocharge showed signs of emerging from their torpor when wide receiver Lynn Swann shagged a forty-seven-yard scoring pass. The Rams answered with a surprise fullback option throw that traveled twenty-four yards from Lawrence McCutcheon to wideout Ron Smith for a TD, but in the fourth quarter Pittsburgh began to crack down on its troublesome adversary.

With a third-and-eight on his own twenty-seven Bradshaw decided to play as he did best and uncorked a towering heave toward wide receiver John Stallworth, who was double-covered by cornerback Rod Perry and safety Dave Elmendorf. With startling precision, Bradshaw dropped the ball to Stallworth in such a way that neither Perry or Elmendorf could touch it. The play went seventy-three yards for a 24-19 Steeler lead.

Los Angeles resolutely came back with a drive that carried to a first down at Pittsburgh's thirty-two. Ferragamo faded, looking for Smith, but middle linebacker Jack Lambert read the play, dropped deep and cut in front of Smith. The ball hit Lambert in the stomach for the game's pivotal turnover.

Bradshaw sewed up the victory with a forty-five-yard completion to Stallworth to set up the clinching TD by Harris in a 31-19 Pittsburgh victory. The prognosticators were vindicated by the AFC champs' late surge that gave the final score the anticipated bulge, but this was misleading.

Despite Bradshaw's connecting on fourteen of twenty-one attempts for 309 yards and two touchdowns, the valiant underdogs from the City of Angeles intercepted him three times, and had been dead serious about winning. Yet in the end it was much-loved Steeler Owner Art Rooney, Sr. who received another gleaming trophy from commissioner Pete Rozelle, who quipped, "We've got to stop meeting like this." Sure enough, the Pittsburgh Steelers of the 1970s were easily the team of the decade.

In the 1980s the balance of power would shift westward.

Earning Their Wings
1980 Oakland Raiders versus Philadelphia Eagles

1960 had been a noteworthy year for the Oakland Raiders and the Philadelphia Eagles. The Raiders had come into existence, and the Eagles won their last league championship at the end of that long-ago season.

The Philadelphia franchise plummeted into a two-decade slump after their bright moment, to re-emerge with the arrival of a hard-working young head coach named Dick Vermiel. Coach Vermiel rebuilt the team from the equipment man on up, using the draft, trades, waiver pickups, free agents and any other sources of talent he could find in his massive renovation

From the Los Angeles Rams came a towering young quarterback named Ron Jaworski, whose right arm had more power than a bazooka. He was called the "Polish Rifle." Jaworski's favorite target was 6'8 wide receiver Harold Carmichael. He was a valuable combination of shifty moves and sticky fingers at the ends of arms long enough to outreach every defensive back in the NFL.

A deal with the Cincinnati Bengals brought seasoned linebacker Bill Bergy, whose leadership was the single previously missing element in an enthusiastic young defense that further overcame its lack of experience through raw athletic talent and emotional support spreading from long-deprived fans whose militant support of their beloved, green-jerseyed heroes was almost as much of a problem to opposing teams as were the again-powerful Eagles themselves.

After winning the 1970 Heisman Trophy and being the first player taken in that year's draft, Stanford University quarterback Jim Plunkett endured years of frustration in New England and San Francisco before being released. Forced to try out as a common free agent in Oakland in 1978 he made the squad as a backup. Two years later starter Dan Pastorini went down with a broken leg and Plunkett, who had just asked to be traded to someplace where he would have a chance to play, stepped in and stunned a league that had forgotten all about him. In 1980 his Raiders' 11-5 record was enough for a wild-card playoff berth that carried them all the way to the New Orleans Superdome to face Philly in Super Bowl XV.

Back in 1974 the Birds had paid three draft choices for Bergy. In the '80 regular season Bill and the unit he led were splendid. They had earned a 10-7 win over these same Raiders, sacking Plunkett eight times that day. The grizzled vets in the Oakland offensive line had not forgotten about or forgiven the upstart Eagle defenders, and came into the Superdome seething with determination to protect their passer and exact a measure of vengeance.

An inkling this game would be different from the first meeting came when linebacker Rod Martin picked off Jaworski's very first pass. Martin would finish the afternoon with a Super Bowl-record three thefts.

Following this interception, Plunkett moved his offense to Philadelphia's two-yard line and was forced to scramble for one of the few times all day. Jim pranced away from the pass rush and drilled wide receiver Cliff Branch in the end zone for the inaugural score.

Later in the first quarter Plunkett was again flushed. He still hit tailback Kenny King on a Super Bowl-record eighty-yard pass/run scoring play that gave the Raiders a 14-0 first quarter lead.

The Eagles had managed an early, forty-two-yard Jaworski pass to tight end Keith Krepfle in the end zone, but this apparent touchdown was negated because Carmichael had started downfield before the snap. Philly was emotionally devastated by losing this sorely needed score, and never regained its poise. Super Bowl veteran Oakland had no such problem.

The only points in the second period came from Philadelphia kicker Tony Franklin's thirty-yard field goal, cutting the deficit to 14-3 at halftime, but in the third quarter Plunkett again took to the air. By this time the Raider line was easily controlling the demoralized rushers, so after driving to the Eagle twenty-nine Plunkett again went to Branch. Big Jim's third touchdown pass put his side up 21-3.

Philadelphia attempts to come back were either too late or not at all as the Oakland defense kept choking off Eagle possessions on third downs or with Martin's intercepts. Although Jaworski squeezed in an eight-yard, fourth-period TD throw to Krepfle, Raider specialist Chris Bahr bracketed this score with two placements for a 27-10 victory.

The game's final statistics revealed the Raider dominance. Eagle runner Wilbert Montgomery led his team in rushing with just forty-four yards. Jaworski completed eighteen of thirty-eight pass attempts for 291 yards and a score, but had those three snatched off by Martin.

It would still be the high point of Vermiel's career with the team. After two more frustrating seasons he became the most noted victim of burnout—the bane of pro coaches of the 1980s. American football can indeed become an obsession to those in its direct employ, and nobody is more directly employed and involved than the head coach. Realizing his fixation on his job was distracting him from everything else in his life, he hung up his headset and retired to the broadcast booth at the tender age of forty-six.

It was a smooth, fulfilling transition for such a versatile man. He was as expert at his new job as he had been at his old. Still, he would have his happy ending on the sideline.

Plunkett earned Most Valuable Player honors with his classy performance. After three teams in nine years, Jim's Cinderella re-emergence was a labor of love, but not the only one.

Vermiels's labor-glutted philosophy had brought the Eagles from the abyss to the brink of league mastery, but had an unfortunate, unforeseen side effect. Exacting such a ponderous workload from his players left them weary and bruised by the end of the sixteen-game regular season, and they had dropped three of their last four games of the 1980 schedule. They were momentarily re-vitalized by the Dallas Cowboys' qualifying for the conference championship game. The chance to advance to the Super Bowl over their long-time nemeses was a tasty opportunity they snatched hungrily, 20-7, but they peaked in this game. They were physically and emotionally spent and somewhat apprehensive as they embarked for New Orleans and an intimidating rendezvous with their first Super Bowl. It was a dazzling, distracting two-weeks, but the waiting, vengeful Raiders were familiar and comfortable with the situation.

These worn-out, dispirited, terribly disappointed young Philadelphians would not recover from the heartbreak of Super Bowl XV. Coaches and players began to drift away to other teams and pursuits. Yet their resurrection of a centuries'-old work ethic and the momentary fruits it bore captured the spirit of their city's heroic, patriotic past.

Gold Rush

1981 San Francisco 49ers versus Cincinnati Bengals

1981 saw the advent of true parity in the National Football League as two teams, the San Francisco 49ers and Cincinnati Bengals, who had possessed dreary 6-10 records a year earlier swept to Super Bowl prominence. Predictably, both squads had chips on their shoulder pads.

San Francisco head coach Bill Walsh's pass-happy offense was among the league's best-ever airborne attacks mainly through necessity. There was no overpowering ground-gainer playing for the 49ers, but in Walsh's system this was not a crippling factor. He had apprenticed as a receiver coach in Cincinnati, and absorbed a predilection for the passing game from legendary head coach Paul Brown.

Quarterback Joe Montana's hair spray ad good looks landed him on the covers of several magazines that year, but it was his right arm rather than his visage that had propelled him to his present, exalted status. In his first year as starting quarterback he guided San Francisco to a 13-3 regular season, throwing to a platoon of brilliant receivers.

The 49ers had a starting defensive lineup with few peers, but it lacked depth. Had one of these marvelous first-stringers gone down with a serious hurt, there would have emerged a glaring weakness at that position. Gentle fortune came through for Frisco as its defense was blessed with a virtually injury-free season, much to the shocked dismay of opponents who had become accustomed to coasting to victory over the 49ers.

In Cincinnati several years of high draft choices finally bore fruit, and with stupefying suddenness as new head coach Forrest Gregg honed his team to the summit of physical and mental preparation in the manner of his former mentors Vince Lombardi and Tom Landry, who had urged the burly Texan to grid performances as an offensive lineman that landed him in the Hall of Fame.

Montana and sharp-shooting Bengal quarterback Kenny Anderson had perhaps the best pair of throwing arms in football as each had led his conference in passing that season. After receiving his law degree from the University of Northern Kentucky the previous July, Anderson may have been the world's most famous attorney, although few of the millions of fans who instantly recognized his name had any idea he was involved in the legal profession. To them he was merely one of the greatest QBs in NFL history. After rebounding from a rotten start, this thirty-two-year-old won Player of the Year honors with a parade of magnificent air shows. Completing 62.6 percent of his attempts for 3754 yards and twenty-nine touchdowns against just ten interceptions his 98.5 quarterback rating topped the league. His squad of pass catchers were among the few that could compare with that of his upcoming opponents', although in piledriving, 250-pound fullback Pete Johnson, who had rushed for twelve touchdowns that year, Cincy had a dimension San Francisco lacked. Johnson would figure significantly in one of the most dramatic series of downs in the history of the championship game.

The Bengals were coming off their infamous 27-7 AFC Championship "Cold

Bowl" victory over the San Diego Chargers when the wind chill dipped to fifty-nine degrees below zero. It was not much warmer in Pontiac, Michigan at kickoff time, but here the cold was forgotten. Super Bowl XVI was the first to be played at a cold weather site as the immense Silverdome held out the frigid elements and hosted 81,270 fans who fused into a single, sprawling entity of pulsating enthusiasm.

After winning the coin toss, the 49ers sent their flashy returner Amos Lawrence back to accept the opening kick. Lawrence uncharacteristically fumbled, and John Simmons recovered for Cincinnati at Frisco's twenty-six. The Bengals had a Christmas opportunity to cash in on the miscue for a promising early lead, but six plays later safety Dwight Hicks intercepted Anderson, setting off a seventy-three-yard scoring drive by Montana and his poised offense for a 7-0 first quarter lead.

Gregg's greatest concern before the game was whether his inexperienced secondary could contain San Francisco's intricate passing game. It never occurred to him that his offense, which had surrendered the fewest turnovers of any in the NFL that year, would fall victim to its own mistakes. In the first half the 49ers took the ball away thrice, and capitalized each time en route to a 20-0 lead at intermission.

Desperation, pride and resolve set in on Cincinnati at the beginning of the second half, jarring Frisco into realization of its opponent's ability. Anderson scrambled five yards for his side's first score, and later in the third quarter directed a drive to a first-and-goal at the three-yard line. History was made here as the 49ers put on a game-saving stand, stacking up Johnson on fourth down at the six-inch line. It was San Francisco's sole bright spot in the third period, but it was enough.

Bengal tight end Dan Ross set a Super Bowl record by catching eleven footballs within the miserly 49er secondary. Early in the fourth quarter, Anderson drilled a four-yarder to Ross in the end zone to cut the difference to a seemingly manageable 20-14.

Later in the period Anderson again found Ross on a short touchdown shot, but by then San Francisco kicker Ray Wershing had connected on his third and fourth field goals to ease the contest out of the Bengals' reach. Afterward, Anderson felt small solace in being only the third 300-yard passer in Super Bowl history, for National Football Conference representative Frisco won 26-21.

For the Niners the success was made yet more savory by its being truly unexpected. Four months earlier few had dared hope for even a wild card berth, but their rapture would soon be shoved aside by political turmoil within the league.

The Capital Connection
1982 Washington Redskins versus Miami Dolphins

It could never happen anywhere except in a land that takes its sports as seriously as does America. Two games into the 1982 season the NFL had its schedule interrupted when the disgruntled members of the National Football League Players Association called a strike that gutted seven prime weeks from the heart of the regular season. Two months later play resumed and the top teams were unceremoniously shoved aside by an outfit that had sunk to also-ran status the past couple of years—the Washington Redskins.

Washington won with a defense as powerful as any champion's, but its ball-control offense was the talk of the league. Former kick returner Joe Theisman quarterbacked a turbocharge that allowed the 'Skins' defense to spend long stretches cheering on the sideline. Every part of this attack had a cute nickname. The diminutive but mercurial wide receivers were called the Smurfs, while the heart of the squad, the bulldozing, corpulent offensive line, was dubbed the Hogs by line coach Joe Bugel. Honorary Hog, fullback John Riggins, ran behind this wall of pork for more yardage in the playoffs than he had in the nine-game regular season. With twenty-six free agents on the roster, the Redskins possessed an against-all-odds-type of togetherness that supplied a seemingly unending flow of adrenalin-charged momentum that carried them to a berth in Super Bowl XVII.

In contrast to Washington's quiet young head coach Joe Gibbs, the Miami Dolphins' top honcho Don Shula was the ideal of a sidelines warrior, whose vitriolic vocabulary was ever-ready to scorch to the skull the ears of any player or official whose performance he found wanting. Long recognized as one of the most brilliant technical minds in football, Shula was returning for only the second Super Bowl rematch ever as he faced the same franchise he had defeated in this game ten years earlier.

Quests

Pro football's annual classic returned to Pasadena's Rose Bowl with more at stake that ever. Motivation was boosted by awarding each member of the winning team $36,000.00, while the losers would receive $18,000.00 apiece.

In the game's opening moments, and from deep in his own territory, twenty-four-year-old Miami quarterback David Woodley spied wide receiver Jimmy Cefalo open and nailed him with a risky flat pass that Cefalo carried all the way on a seventy-six-yard pass-run scoring play that gave the American Conference champs a quick 7-0 lead.

After an exchange of field goals, Theisman directed a typical, inexorable drive ending with a four-yard touchdown shot to wideout Alvin Garrett and very short-lived tie at ten. Miami instantly resumed its spectacular style seconds later when Fulton Walker fielded the kickoff on his own two-yard line and did not stop until he ran out of field on a ninety-eight-yard return and 17-10 advantage that lasted until halftime.

After the game, Gibbs stated that at intermission, despite the first half lightning strikes of the potent Dolphins, he had a "good feeling" about the coming two quarters. It was pure clairvoyance.

After Redskin kicker Mark Mosley cut the difference to 17-13 early in the third period, and his defense forced a punt on the next series, Theisman made the type of game-saving play normally reserved for defensive backs. Fielding the snap on his own eighteen, Joe faded to pass, but had his throw slapped back toward him by defensive right end Kim Bokamper. On a dead run for Washington's end zone, Bokamper eagerly reached for the fluttering pigskin, but at the last instant there was Theisman lunging desperately for the ball and knocking it from Bokamper's grasp. Had the 'Skins gone down 24-13 this late in the contest they would have been forced out of their usual ball-control style of offense, and had to take to the air—an unfamiliar departure from their norm. They were unaccustomed to late-game, pressure-packed, catch-up situations, and thanks to Theisman's precision ball batting they were not in one now. They still had plenty of time to overcome a difference of four (not eleven) points.

This reprieve enabled Washington to implement the kind of attack that had brought it this far as Riggins and his fellow porkers ground out yardage and wore down Miami's "Killer Bee" defense. Yet early in the final quarter the Redskins found themselves stymied with a fourth-and-one at the Dolphin forty-three. Just out of range of Mosely's bionic leg, and with Riggins getting stronger with every carry, Gibbs spurned the punt and sent his fullback around left end while the defense clogged the center of the line. Shaking off a would-be tackler like a horse fly, Big John displayed his surprising speed all the way to the end zone to give the Redskins their first lead.

Miami's defense virtually evaporated through sheer exhaustion late in the fourth period as another short touchdown pass by Theisman sewed up the ballgame 27-17 and gave Washington its first league title in forty years.

The volcanic crescendo of sound from 103,667 fans gave no clue that this was the close of a season scarred by labor difficulties. Some might have expected a sullen handful of resentful former partisans after so many sterile, footballess Sabbaths, but this happened in America, where the National Football League is loved to the point that its adoring patrons viewed it as a prodigal son whose wandering sojourn was ended. For every unforgiving older brother there were a thousand joyous fathers who screamed with delight as the ultimate annual trophy came fittingly to the nation's capital.

Most Valuable Player John Riggins, speaking of President Ronald Reagan, succinctly stated, "At least for tonight Ron may be president, but I'm still the king!" Across the country relieved fans were glad John's kingdom was back in business.

A year later the American Football Conference would have its last reason to smile for many, many seasons.

Buccaneer's Bonanza
1983 Los Angeles Raiders versus Washington Redskins

When the Los Angeles Raiders met the defending champion Washington Redskins in Super Bowl XVIII in Tampa Florida the television networks' glee knew scant bounds. Sponsors Phillips' Petroleum, Budweiser, and Gillette shelled out $480,000.00 for each thirty-second slot during which they peddled their wares. Advertiser willingness to pay for the telecast stemmed from expectations of a tension-stuffed barn-burner that would keep every one of the usual hundred million-plus TV viewers rooted in front of their sets from the coin toss to the postgame interviews—not even leaving their roosts during commercials. Ratings-conscious CBS was also delighted.

Predictions for a cliffhanger sprang from memory of a regular-season contest at Washington. The Redskins had pulled off a couple of late touchdown drives to snatch a 37-35 win over Los Angeles. The analysts managed to overlook a couple of factors that would make this rematch something different.

First, the Raiders' impeccable young tailback Marcus Allen had been injured and missed the first game. Also, L.A. did not acquire cornerback Mike Haynes from New England until after the first D.C. contest.

In the 1983 season the Redskins amassed a league-record 541 points with an offense so powerful it needed no deception. Quarterback Joe Theisman simply handed off to his overpowering fullback John Riggins, whose path was cleared by the biggest, best offensive line in the business. This set up the second-and-short situations that were so much more productive than trying to convert on third-and-long. The huge linemen were semi-affectionately called the Hogs, and it was a vanishingly rare defensive line that could handle the Hogs and Riggins without help from linebackers. Yet opposing linebackers were always pitifully overworked as they raced desperately after the lethal receiving corps of Charlie Brown, Alvin Garrett, Art Monk and tight end Don Warren. The Skins had dropped both their Monday night appearances by one point apiece, winning every other game that regular season. It was an attack without an obvious weak spot, but when Los Angeles head coach Tom Flores saw what a gem he had in newcomer Haynes, he commenced devising strategy that no other team in the league dared try.

Flores reasoned that by coupling Haynes with similarly skilled Lester Hayes his four defensive backs might be able to cover the Washington receivers man-for-man with minimal help from linebackers. This would free the 'backers to assist their linemen in containing Riggins. He instructed his linebackers to line up immediately behind the front four, filling the gaps behind the linemen. The Redskins would face what was essentially a seven-man defensive line the Raiders were able to maintain throughout the game without freeing the receivers. The results swamped the defending champs.

After the novel defensive alignment stifled the Redskins on their first possession, punter Jeff Hayes' protection broke down. Reserve tight end Derrick Jensen charged in to block the kick and fall on it in the end zone for a quick 7-0 L.A. lead.

Following a short TD pass from Raider quarterback Jim Plunkett to wide receiver Cliff Branch early in the second period the challengers landed a demoralizing haymaker seconds before halftime with a play that surprised everyone except the Los Angeles defense. Trailing 14-3, Washington head coach Joe Gibbs may have sensed that to have any chance of making the contest competitive he would have to try something uncharacteristically deceptive, so he called for a play titled "Rocker Screen." Three wide receivers lined up to the right and fled deep while tailback Joe Washington tried to slip unnoticed out of the backfield to the left, catch Theisman's pass in the flat and run as far as he could. The play had worked well in the earlier game with the Raiders—who remembered. As Washington headed out, lineman Lyle Alzado spied him and put on one of the best of his thousands of fierce pass rushes. Leaping high he obstructed Theisman's view and forced him to throw early and off-target. Linebacker Jack Squirek jumped in front of Washington at the five-yard line, stole away the ball and stepped into the end zone for a cozy 21-3 lead at intermission.

Most teams would have folded after such a nightmarish half, but the Redskins came out in the third quarter and in sheer desperation ground out one of their familiar drives that Riggins ended with a standard one-yard plunge. Yet there was not enough time left in the game for this brand of clock-consuming football. There was still a twelve-point imbalance, and the bay brigands knew better than to sit on their lead. When one of those omnipresent L.A. linebackers, six-foot, eight-inch Ted Hendricks, blocked the extra point attempt the Washingtons started to lose hope.

Late in the quarter the Raiders held Riggins for no gain on fourth-and-one at the Los Angeles twenty-six, and on the period's last down Marcus Allen made sports history. On a play calling for him to sweep left, Allen ran into a mob of defenders, so he reversed his field. Following Branch's shield block of cornerback Anthony Washington, Marcus wove seventy-four yards for the coup de grace and left the Redskins yearning for the final gun.

Battling the kind of steamroller momentum he was accustomed to meting out, Theisman was powerless to break the stranglehold on his offense as his team was humbled 38-9. None had ever lost a Super Bowl with such totality.

Allen broke Riggins' year-old rushing record by picking up 191 yards through what had been the league's best defense versus the run, and his seventy-four-yard jaunt was the longest-ever Super Bowl run from scrimmage. No one questioned the youngster's unanimous election as Most Valuable Player—not even his linebacking teammates. Especially not be the losers. Not by the television sponsors either. They knew just how the Redskins felt.

The West Coast had yet more glory coming.

The Wild West

1984 San Francisco 49ers versus Miami Dolphins

When twenty-three-year-old quarterback Dan Marino almost ran out of passing records to break during his second season with the Miami Dolphins, and San Francisco quarterback Joe Montana became the NFL's top-rated passer in its sixty-five-year history, 1984 seemed to have brought the Super Bowl an armada of aerial offense. With a combined single-season won-lost tally of 33-3, Super Bowl XIX's contestants had the best mutual record of any teams who had ever played this game, and throughout its two-week buildup the press could extrapolate on little except the coming face-off between the 49ers' marvelous defense and Marino's flying circus. Most managed to overlook Montana and *his* turbocharge.

Three years earlier San Francisco had won this thing almost exclusively off Montana's arm. This strategy was spawned of necessity because of the 49ers' lack of a strong running game, but since then head coach/general manager Bill Walsh had acquired veteran tailback Wendell Tyler from the L.A. Rams, and by drafting versatile fullback Roger Craig he filled the only void in an otherwise demoralizingly potent offense.

It had been a notorious year for injuries throughout the league, yet the San Francisco defense had managed to stay healthy and stingy, and the media fascination with its coming clash with the Miami offense was predictable. It nevertheless raised the ire of Montana and his offensive mates. "We got tired of hearing about how great the *Miami* offense was," crowed the handsome young signal-caller after the game.

Dolphin head coach Don Shula was making a record sixth Super Bowl appearance, and a victory would make him only the second coach to ever with this game more than twice. It was a heady prospect, and the early minutes of competition gave him much cause for optimism.

Quests

Although the game site was Stanford Stadium in Stanford, California, the coin toss happened 3000 miles away, in Washington, D.C. President Ronald Reagan flipped the piece that came up tails and gave the 49ers first possession.

Miami kicker Uwe von Schamann shanked his kickoff and sent the ball careening toward the left sideline where it would have gone out of bounds had not returner Derrick Harmon tried too hard to field it. He did so on a dead run, his forward momentum carrying him out of bounds at the six. After producing two first downs, San Francisco was forced to punt.

A Super Bowl truism states that the team to score first will win, and when the Dolphins drove to a field goal on their opening possession their hopes rose a little too high. Montana responded quickly with a thirty-three-yard scoring pass to Carl Monroe.

Marino wasted no time regaining the lead. He fashioned a brief drive that featured no huddles. The young passing whiz lined up his offense as soon as the preceding down ended, called the play at the line and deprived the 49er secondary of time to make the necessary substitutions to counteract such tactics. At the two-yard line he flipped the ball to tight end Dan Johnson to give the Dolphins, at 10-7, their last lead.

San Francisco responded to the Miami touchdown drive by using its pass prevent defense on every play. Walsh and his assistants knew their linemen were powerful enough to shut down the Dolphin running game without help from their linebackers and defensive backs, as well as put considerable pressure on Marino when his offensive line began to tire. This strategy broke Shula's heart.

The second period belonged to the 49ers as Montana threw an eight-yard touchdown pass to Craig, ran for one himself, and handed off to Craig for another. When its offense was not lighting up the scoreboard the Frisco defense was harassing Marino into ineffectiveness—sacking him four times, intercepting him twice, and hurrying him into incompletions on third downs.

Miami did not score in the second half as the Bay Juggernaut rolled to the final difference of 38-16. Only a late goal line stand by the weary but proud Dolphin defenders kept the score from getting even more out of hand.

Montana broke Super Bowl records for passing yardage and rushing yardage for a quarterback. Despite the brilliant performance of Craig, it was quarterback of the decade Montana who was named Most Valuable Player even before the game ended.

Stanford Stadium is just a few minutes' drive from the 49ers' practice facilities, and the crowd was loudly biased in their favor as it deafeningly honored a team that made winning a gloriously monotonous habit.

The following season an old, old dynasty would briefly emerge from hibernation.

Valley Forge Revisited
1985 Chicago Bears versus New England Patriots

Super Bowl XX was one of those rare ones in which neither team had ever been there before. 1985's finalists were the Chicago Bears and New England Patriots—neither of which had played for a league championship since the pre-Super Bowl year of 1963.

The Bears team that won that long-ago title had included a magnificent tight end named Mike Ditka. Many would later declare it was Ditka who had essentially created the modern tight end position, transforming it from just another offensive line blocking post to that of an integral pass-catching spot that many teams made their primary threat. After finishing his playing career in Dallas, Iron Mike served there as an assistant until he fulfilled his dream by securing the head coaching job in Chicago.

He returned to the Windy City determined to win a title for his ex-mentor, Bears owner George Halas. Halas had ushered the young Ditka into the National Football League, taught him how to play on its level, and now gave him an opportunity to share that knowledge with a new generation. Halas had almost single-handedly built the NFL, and for forty seasons coached his Bears, winning six interdivisional championships and developing and directing a cavalcade of some of the greatest players ever to pass through the league, and whose careers he molded into successful futures in professional football.

Mike Ditka figured George Halas deserved at least one more view from the top, but it was too late. Papa Bear died October 31, 1983 at the age of eighty-eight, before Ditka and his staff had time to mold the Bears into the champions they had been so many years earlier. Yet the death of the patriarch only hastened the return of the Monsters of the Midway.

"Play like he would have wanted you to play," was the message Ditka now used to inspire his men. It worked. After several highly successful drafts, Chicago was ready to make a run for the Super Bowl.

These Bears were young, averaging just twenty-five years old, and possessed the enthusiasm of talented, youthful aspirants to glory. As a junior at Brigham Young University, quarterback Jim McMahon had thrown forty-seven touchdown passes during a twelve-game schedule, and eighty-four overall during his collegiate career. Now leading the Chicago offense he was described by Ditka as having "...the guts of a burglar."

Sharing the backfield was tailback Walter Payton, one of the team's few long-term veterans. The previous year Payton had broken Jimmy Brown's league record for career rushing yardage, but at the end of that season, mainly because of a dearth of healthy quarterbacks, the Bears fell in the playoffs. This year, though, McMahon and his mates were hale enough to post a 15-1 regular season record. They won eight games versus teams that finished 10-6 or better, outscoring them 245-40. Chicago made history by *shutting out* both its pre-Super Bowl playoff foes, giving clue to its real strength. Defense.

Bear defensive coordinator Buddy Ryan had assembled, taught and unleashed a unit so powerful that observers could not think of any squad, past or present, with which to compare it. 6'2, 300-pound defensive tackle William Perry was called "Refrigerator," and became something of a folk hero via his team's novel goal line *offensive* alignment in which he played fullback. Denying this onrushing behemoth a mere yard or two was more than most defensive outfits could manage.

In New England the early days of the season had gone according to recent, dismal precedent as the Patriots lost three of their first five games. Then something subtle and never-quite-understood commenced at midseason as they made the sneaky but decisive turnaround they and their fans had awaited so long.

Like Ditka, New England head coach Raymond Berry was a former tight end, having been Hall of Fame quarterback Johnny Unitas' favorite target on two league champion Baltimore Colt teams. He too had spent time as an assistant in Dallas, learning from the Cowboys' legendary head coach Tom Landry. After spending some time out of football, Berry took over the Patriots and discovered they were a much better team than they and the rest of the league realized.

Youngsters led the way as fullback Craig James, wide receiver Irving Fryer and quarterback Tony Eason sparked New England to a wild card playoff berth. Like the Bears, the Patriots made history in the playoffs. They were the first-ever team to win three straight playoff games on the road. The final one was the American Football Conference title test in Miami, where the Pats had not won in nineteen years. Skipping 31-14 past the flabbergasted Dolphins (the only team to beat Chicago that season) the Patriots embarked for New Orleans to face the heavily favored Bears in the cavernous Superdome.

Chicago received the opening kickoff, but Payton fumbled the ball away at the nineteen to give New England a shot at a promising early lead. Known as a primarily running team the Patriots tried to cross up the Bear defense by coming out throwing. Eason got off three straight incompletions. On first down his splendid tight end Lin Dawson grievously injured a knee when he landed awkwardly while diving for a sideline pass. No defender had touched Dawson, and as his teammates watched him being carried off on a stretcher they may have seen it as an ill omen.

Although Patriot kicker Tony Franklin salvaged the possession with a thirty-six-yard field goal 1:19 into the first quarter for the quickest-ever score in a Super Bowl, it was a record soon forgotten. Two Keith Butler placements gave the Chicagoans a 6-3 lead midway through the first period, and then one of a half-dozen AFC turnovers set up fullback Matt Suhey's eleven-yard touchdown run and touched off an avalanche.

The Patriot passing game was hampered by Eason's slow release, which needed more time than the Bear offensive line would allow. Eason was also playing below par physically because of a severe stomach virus that had tormented him the last days before the game.

Steve Grogan had quarterbacked the team to six consecutive victories before a leg injury sidelined him six weeks before this game. Grogan was rusty, but late in the second quarter an already-desperate Berry benched the ineffective Eason and inserted his veteran. Grogan tried hard, but as so many had learned that season, this Bruin defense was impregnable. Although Steve managed to complete seventeen of thirty aerials for 177 yards and one touchdown, two were intercepted. Defensive back Reggie Phillips returned one theft twenty-eight yards for a third quarter touchdown.

The Bears earned twenty-one points in the third quarter, and their defense fittingly closed out the scoring by smearing Grogan for a fourth quarter safety in a 46-10 mauling. No Super Bowl had ever been more one-sided.

A look at the final statistics reveals Chicago's defensive orientation. Despite amassing forty-six points (eight by the defense,) the Bear offensive stats were not that impressive. Although McMahon connected for an above-average 256 yards, he threw for no touchdowns. Walter Payton led all rushers with just sixty-one steps and no scores. The defense repeatedly set up points by forcing turnovers and shoving New England's offense backward, sacking its quarterbacks seven times for sixty-one lost yards and *holding the Pats to minus yardage until eight minutes into the third quarter.*

Defensive end Richard Dent was elected Most Valuable Player. Along with every man on his team he had played the way Papa would have wanted him to play.

New York, New York

1986 New York Giants versus Denver Broncos

When Super Bowl XXI was called to order the nation dared to hope for a welcome end to the dreary blowouts typical of the past few season-enders. After all, back in October the New York Mets had staged a gut-grabbing turnaround to capture the World Series crown. Now the New York *Giants* were in their first Super Bowl.

After dropping a dramatic season-opener to Dallas, 31-28, the Giants dumped seventeen of their next eighteen opponents, often by clawing from behind in closing moments. The New Yorkers' opponents in the title match-up were the Denver Broncos, who had played them a razor-thin regular season contest, losing 19-16 on a last-second field goal. Although the Giants had crushed their playoff foes by a combined score of 66-3, and Denver had had to pull out two gutsy post-season cliffhangers to reach Super Sunday in Pasadena's Rose Bowl, memory of the previous, close contest led many to expect an overdue end to the sedate, over-before-halftime championship games that had become standard. There was no harm hoping.

Denver head coach Danny Reeves was no stranger to Super Bowls. He had rings from his days as a player and assistant coach in Dallas, but during his first five years in Denver his teams had not won a single post-season game. After going into overtime in Cleveland to win the 1986 American Football Conference title, the Broncos believed they had finally put a few old ghosts to flight. The can't-win-the-big-one tag seemed on the verge of dropping off, but there was still one more game to play.

New York had gone through many chapters in the thirty years since its last NFL championship. By the early 1980s the team had matured into a title contender, but gained a reputation for committing just enough crucial errors at critical moments to stifle its grand potential. Quarterback Phil Simms habitually hung up spectacular statistics, but during the past few seasons injuries repeatedly struck him down when his team needed him most. This year the Giants finally went through a campaign with healthy key players. The offense was finally physically able to achieve balance between passing and running. Diminutive running back Joe Morris rushed for handsome season totals of 1516 yards and fourteen touchdowns.

It seemed that the Giants' magnificent defense was not quite enough to win it all on its own. Simms, his backfield and receivers were needed at their healthy best to lead a potent attack in order for the team to live up to its name. In '86 the golden-haired quarterback directed a season-long highlights film, and NY head coach Bill Parcells may have sensed the Super Bowl would disappoint more than Bronco fans. There was little drama in store.

Still, John Elway and *his* offense had already shown that they could deliver a blue-chip performance under pressure. In the AFC title game in Cleveland they drove ninety-eight yards through the frantic Browns defense and a howling polar gale in fifteen plays to set up the winning field goal in overtime.

The Super Bowl started in seesaw fashion with the eight-point underdog Broncos driving for a field goal that the Giants answered with a seventy-nine-yard touchdown drive. Denver came back with a sustained possession that for a moment appeared stalled at the New York four-yard line, but Elway surprised the Giants with a designed, third-down quarterback sneak up the middle to retake the lead, 10-7.

The offenses controlled the opening period. Neither QB threw an interception, and early in the second quarter Elway directed his squad to a first-and-goal on the N.Y. one-yard line. Had they given up another touchdown here the Giants would have been in for an unexpected dogfight, but their defense rose to its reputation. The Broncos lost three yards on the next three downs, and when the field goal attempt sailed wide New York got another shot at dominance.

Elway came into the game with a sore ankle that hampered his mobility. Three minutes before halftime he was unable to escape defensive lineman George Martin who smothered him for a safety that cut Denver's lead to one point.

The Bronco defense managed to force the Giants to punt 1:05 before intermission to give Elway and his offense a final chance to salvage some momentum for the second half, but when kicker Rich Karlis missed a thirty-four-yard field goal try the men from the Rockies trudged to their locker room discouraged and apprehensive. A long couple of quarters were coming.

After accepting the second half kickoff New York bogged down with a fourth-and-one at its own forty-six. Parcells' faith in his defense inspired him to call the play that blew the game open. Sending in his punting unit he furtively inserted reserve quarterback Jeff Rutledge in the upback position. At the snap, Rutledge stepped in front of punter Sean Landeta, caught the ball and burrowed for the yard that kept the Giant drive going. Five plays later Simms passed to tight end Mark Bavaro for a lead that grew with great speed.

The frenzied Broncos discarded their running game in the third quarter, but were still outgained in total yardage that period by 163-2. A one-yard plunge into the end zone by Morris gave New York a 17-0 scoring advantage for the quarter, and the game would become even less interesting.

Early in the fourth the Giants scored yet again on a bizarre play when, from the six, Simms aimed a pass at Bavaro in the end zone. Mark tripped, the ball hit his helmet and caroomed into the arms of alert wide receiver Phil McConky.

It seemed somehow fated that the New Yorkers would benefit from such a freakish lucky bounce during a game in which they did not need luck in order to win. Now that they were untracked they overpowered the Bronks offensively and defensively.

Former St. Louis superstar Ottis Anderson scored the Giants' last touchdown in a 39-20 savaging of Denver. New York amassed a record thirty points in the second half while matching their town's baseball team's triumph.

Completing twenty-two of twenty-five passes for 268 yards and three TDs made Simms the obvious choice for MVP. In the madcap Giant locker room his face was straight as he told reporters, "I was close to perfect." None argued.

For Denver, the NFC Eastern Division was becoming a recurring nightmare.

Kings of the East
1987 Washington Redskins versus Denver Broncos

The Washington Redskins won a slew of close games in 1987, repeatedly nosing out their opponents by a thin sliver. After nipping their playoff foes the scrappy 'Skins headed for San Diego's Jack Murphy Stadium to represent the National Football Conference in Super Bowl XXII.

Meandering through a confusing season of blowouts and cliffhangers the Denver Broncos found the road to the Super Bowl more complex than ever as league parity made forecasting a champion well-nigh impossible except in hindsight, but they at least earned the right to be in the game. It was Denver's third Super Bowl, and their third against a team from the NFC's Eastern Division. The earlier trouncings by the Dallas Cowboys and New York Giants made many feel the mountaineers were due for a win in this thing.

True, the Bronks' competitive image had been tarnished a bit two weeks earlier when they blew a 28-0 lead in the AFC title game. They held on to win 38-33 when the Cleveland Browns fumbled away what should have been a game-winning drive at Denver's two-yard line in the closing moments. Still, the prognosticators installed them as 3 ½-point favorites mainly because of the overall prowess of cannon-armed quarterback John Elway.

In the early seconds of the contest Elway performed up to expectations as he hurled a fifty-five-yard touchdown pass to his team's number one draft pick that year, wide receiver Ricky Nattiel. John then *caught* a tailback option throw to set up a field goal and 10-0 Bronco lead.

In the first quarter the Washington defenders had trouble keeping their feet under them on the spongy, rain-dampened playing surface, but between periods they changed to longer cleats. This was all they needed.

Quests

On offense, Redskin quarterback Doug Williams endured a frustrating opening period, watching his nervous young receivers drop passes while he scrambled away from the aggressive Denver defenders. Seconds before the quarter ended he was forced to temporarily leave the game because of a leg injury.

The Broncos had meticulously prepared for Washington running back George Rogers, but Rogers nursed an assortment of nagging injuries and was used sparingly. He had an able replacement.

Before draft day the Buffalo Bills had traded a fifth-round selection to the Redskins. They used it on an obscure Texas Tech running back named Timmy Smith whose college career was noteworthy mainly for the spate of injuries that virtually wiped out his junior and senior seasons. His primary bane was a grievously hurt knee that drydocked him almost three years. Today he would show tens of millions that his surgery-ravaged joint had healed.

It was time for The Quarter.

The storied second quarter of Super Bowl XXII, to be precise. The Washington offense finally got untracked early in the period when Williams drilled wide receiver Ricky Sanders with an eighty-yard scoring pass on Doug's first play back after his injury. Minutes later they went ahead to stay on a twenty-seven-yard heave to wideout Gary Clark on third-and-one.

It was the most spectacular fifteen minutes in championship history as Williams threw four touchdown passes and handed off to Smith for another en route to outscoring the reeling Denvers 35-0 in the quarter. The Borncos were the only team in the league Redskin head coach Joe Gibbs had never defeated. On this afternoon his men made all their past victims grateful *they* were not facing this turbocharge as it crucified its unfortunate foes 42-10.

Statisticians were hard-pressed to keep track of all the offensive records tossed aside by the winners. Smith kept charging through the left side of his line for hefty chunks of yardage. He became not only the first rookie to surpass 100 yards in a Super Bowl, but the first player ever to exceed 200 as he picked up 204 yards and two touchdowns on just twenty-two carries.

Sanders' 193 yards and two touchdowns broke the game's twelve-year-old record for receiving, but in spite of these glittering achievements by Smith and Sanders, the main attraction was Williams. The gimpy-legged vet earned Most Valuable Player recognition by showering the hapless mountain men with sniper-accurate throws, eclipsing all records with his 340 yards and four touchdowns. The 'Skins' 602 total yards were yet another new mark.

This one afternoon gave Doug Williams more highlights than his entire previous career. Unremarkable seasons in Tampa Bay and the recently defunct United States Football League (USFL) had saddled him with the reputation of being something of a loser, and left him with little apparent market value. Washington was the only team to offer him a job when he was cast adrift upon the USFL's collapse, leaving quite a few general managers red-faced following this afternoon. The one-sidedness of Super Bowl XXII moved one morose Denver fan to lament, "The feeling around here is, 'Wait until year after next!'"

Indeed, Bronco head coach Danny Reeves, who had spent sixteen years in Dallas as a player and assistant coach, may have wished he had never left the NFC East. Yet the following year would belong to the West Coast.

What a Way to Go!
1988 San Francisco 49ers versus Cincinnati Bengals

In 1988 the city of Cincinnati, Ohio celebrated its bicentennial by watching with much delight as its Bengals rebounded from a 4-12 '87 campaign. The Cats landed in Super Bowl XXIII along with a San Francisco 49er outfit that had squeezed them out 20-17 in a regular season barn-burner. It had been a much-needed victory for the 'Niners as they clawed their way back from a 6-5 late-season record to land in their third 1980s Super Bowl.

Twenty years earlier Cincinnati head coach Sam Wyche had been an obscure free agent quarterback with the Bengals during their first-ever season. His coaching career was now bringing him much more success than his playing days. He was also well acquainted with the San Francisco system, having been an assistant to Frisco head coach Bill Walsh in the 49er-Bengal Super Bowl of seven years before.

These teams came into this rematch with San Francisco ranked number one in the league offensively, and Cincinnati ranked number two. On the basis of its more experienced defense, Frisco was installed as a seven-point favorite.

Pounding, pregame rainfall left Miami's Joe Robbie Stadium's playing surface soupy and treacherous, and this unstable footing became a factor early in the game as 49er offensive tackle Steve Wallace and Bengal nose guard Tim Krumrie slipped in the slop and suffered a broken leg apiece within minutes of each other. Neither man would go to the local hospital, but remained in their locker rooms to watch the game on television. Otherwise, little of note happened in the first half. It ended in a 3-3 tie that greatly surprised the crowd, which had come expecting fireworks from these offensive powerhouses.

Upon close inspection the stalled attacks were not difficult to fathom. Cincinnati's youthful quarterback Boomer Esiason was playing in his first Super Bowl, and like most young men in this whirlwind for the first time he was jittery and often off-target with his throws. Frisco was exploiting his inexperience by switching linebacker/defensive end Charles Haley from one side of the line to the other in a fashion most bewildering to the green signal-caller. The NFC champs were also using a seven-man defensive line, and were throwing off his receivers' timing by using the extra linemen to bump his pass catchers a split second after each snap.

Although the 49ers consistently moved the ball throughout the first three quarters, the inspired Bengal defense rose to each occasion. Steaming under their tiger-striped helmets they held San Francisco quarterback Joe Montana to just four completions in thirteen third down pass attempts.

As a matter of record, no Super Bowl was ever touchdownless so long. 44:26 elapsed before Cincy returner Stanford Jennings woke everybody with a thrilling ninety-three-yard kickoff return and sudden 13-6 lead.

This abrupt strike seemed to fire up both offenses, and Montana unlimbered his passing on a rapid drive consuming just 1:31 and ending with a fourteen-yard scoring toss to busy wide receiver Jerry Rice to re-tie the score. A bad ankle had kept Rice out of practice the past few days, but today's performance gave no hint.

After Cincinnati kicker Jim Breech connected on his third placement attempt to retake the lead 16-13, an infraction on the ensuing kickoff set the 49ers back to their own eight-yard line. From this point, with only 3:20 remaining in the game, Montana directed the winning drive. Rice caught for fifty-one yards on this one series of downs.

After the game 'Niner center Randy Cross informed the press, "As the drive went on, you could see Montana's eyes light up. Halfway through we knew we were going to score."

Montana's confidence was not limited to his eyes—it surrounded him and infected his teammates. With thirty-nine seconds left he had his crew on the Bengals' ten-yard line. He called timeout and huddled with Walsh.

After this consultation Montana returned to the field and took his last snap of the game. While the Cincinnati secondary desperately chased Rice and sure-handed running back Roger Craig the frosty-cool quarterback drilled seldom-used, wide-open receiver John Taylor for the touchdown that gave the 49ers a 20-16 victory.

The heroics of Rice and Montana dominated the fourth quarter. They shone brightest in the eighty-five- and ninety-two-yard touchdown drives that together consumed a total of just 4:17.

Rice's eleven catches for a score and Super Bowl-record 215 yards made him a cinch for Most Valuable Player. Yet his defensive mates glowed almost as brightly as they stifled Esiason throughout the contest. The youthful southpaw came into the game as the league's top-rated passer, but the San Francisco defenders limited him to just eleven completions in twenty-five attempts for 144 yards, no scores, a crucial interception, and sacked him five times while Montana was overcoming early inconsistency en route to a Super Bowl-record 357 passing yards.

With this third title the 49ers were proclaimed the team of the decade. Walsh went out on top when he retired a few days later as the first head coach whose last win was a Super Bowl. When he had taken over what looked like a hopeless case ten years earlier he could never have imagined it would be such a short decade.

It was not over yet.

San Francisco Quake
1989 San Francisco 49ers versus Denver Broncos

Before the 1989 season started many had said the era of the super team was over, that the talent was spread too thinly among the NFL's twenty-eight franchises for one to dominate its peers season after season. No team had captured back-to-back Super Bowl titles during the 1980s, so when San Francisco barely squeezed out victory on the previous Super Sunday, and its cerebral head coach Bill Walsh retired after that day, most figured Frisco's halcyon days were history. However the toasts of the coast had no intention of living off their past glory.

The Niners' new head coach, George Seifert, knew what a still-potent inheritance he had, and wisely made few alterations. He retained Walsh's philosophy, players and strategy, and a bitterly disappointed succession of opponents saw San Francisco's dynasty easily survive the coaching change.

It was Super Bowl number eight for Denver Bronco head coach Danny Reeves. He had gone through them as a player, player-coach, full-time assistant and head coach over the last twenty seasons, and his team this year earned its berth in Super Bowl XXIV through a gritty determination that peaked in the playoffs. Reeves had helped the Dallas Cowboys to a pair of super titles here in New Orleans. Hoping for a third ring he was as anxious for the game to start as was the teeming Superdome audience.

After the Broncos won the coin toss their opening possession brought back
unhappy memories as they gained just two yards in three stabs at the line. They punted then watched San Francisco casually drive sixty-six yards for the first of a caboodle of touchdowns.

When things started going wrong early, Denver panicked and made errors that led to big plays for their steamrolling opponents. The 49ers

Quests

wound up controlling the ball 39:31 of the game's sixty minutes, and turned each of the four Bronco turnovers into touchdowns.

Denver quarterback John Elway was forgivably rattled at his line's inability to prevent his being sacked six times. He was hurried many more times, and when he did manage to get off passes his nervous receivers kept dropping them.

The game was still not quite decided late in the second quarter when, trailing 20-3, Elway and his offense still nursed a faint hope of scoring and picking up some momentum going into halftime, but their last drive of the first half was another bust and ended with a punt. San Francisco had the ball at its own forty-one with 1:38 until intermission.

49er quarterback Joe Montana used all but :34 driving to the Bronco thirty-eight. At the next snap wide receiver Jerry Rice hurtled straight ahead through Denver's zone defense. When strong safety Dennis Smith froze in confusion at the unexpectedly simple maneuver, Rice cut behind him and snared the pass to give Frisco a hefty 27-3 halftime advantage.

The 49er offensive line had not turned in a banner season, and was regarded as the team's sole weak spot. Today these athletes gave Montana so much time that he broke seven individual records for Super Bowl quarterbacks. The unit tied or exceeded fourteen team offensive marks for this game, which Frisco won easier than anyone had ever won it.

On Denver's first possession of the second half, linebacker Mike Walter intercepted Elway. On the next play Montana hit Rice for a twenty-eight-yard touchdown. The third period was just getting started, and the Broncos were already longing for the final gun.

After piling the score up to 55-10 just 1:13 into the fourth quarter San Francisco eased up and sat on this lead that became the final score and made it the first team to retain its title following a coaching change.

With his five scoring passes on this one Crescent City afternoon Montana was the first man to win a third Super Bowl Most Valuable Player award. His knack for reserving the best of his habitually brilliant performances for January earned him recognition as the best-ever big-game quarterback.

Bart Starr had quarterbacked coach Vince Lombardi's storied Green Bay Packers to five league championships and won MVP honors in the first two Super Bowls. Yet after this game Starr himself dispelled any questions about who was better. "I've known a lot of great quarterbacks, but never anybody better in big games than Joe Montana."

In the National Football League Bart Starr's verdict is seldom questioned, especially when backed by such lovely statistics. In his four Super Bowls, Montana threw 122 passes, completing eighty-three for 1142 yards, eleven touchdowns and no interceptions. All records.

Montana was not the only superstar at today's contest, however. The Bronco's thirty-five-year-old tailback Tony Dorsett concluded his career that day hobbled by a leg injury. He ended his last season as he had his first—in the Super Bowl. He was on the roster of the franchise he had, as a Dallas Cowboy, helped defeat in this game twelve years earlier. It was a fitting location for a player of his standing. Despite being much smaller than Jimmy Brown, Franco Harris, Larry Csonka, John Riggins and Jimmy Taylor, Dorsett had gained more career yardage than these greats.

Although the score was inappropriate, being part of a title test *was* for a man who pound-for-pound may have been the best running back the game had ever seen. Regardless of the outcome of the twenty-fourth Super Bowl, Tony Dorsett was always a champion whose class and enduring athletic prowess were unsurpassable.

— Start Spreadin' the Word —
1990 New York Giants versus Buffalo Bills

Watching this game made one wonder how anybody could manage to lose it. Apart from a few dropped passes in the early minutes, no one would make a mistake. Nobody threw an interception. Nobody lost a fumble. It was as if both sides wanted to make the silver anniversary Super Bowl the best ever played.

It was a game the country needed badly. It was diversion from the Iraqi war, and it kept the fans in Tampa Stadium so entranced they hardly noticed the hordes of security men protecting them from the specter of foreign terrorists who would have loved to target this exuberant mass of Americana.

The 1990 season produced the first inter-state Super Sunday as the New York Giants and Buffalo Bills used sparkling execution throughout the schedule to earn Florida passage for Super Bowl XXV. This game's splendid prosecution of play was next to no one's.

The fourteen turnovers the Giants had committed that year were the smallest season total in league history. In the coming game head coach Bill Parcells planned to take few chances. He hoped to have reliable, thirty-three-year-old running back Ottis Anderson tote the ball twenty-five to thirty times in a conservative, ball-control game plan. Anderson would take just twenty-one handoffs, but earn Most Valuable Player honors by stretching them to 102 yards.

Despite their Super Bowl inexperience odds makers who were impressed by the ninety-five points they had scored in their two playoff games installed the Bills as one-touchdown favorites. These tallies were only the most recent in this season in which they had amassed 523 points while compiling a 15-3 record. With third-year runner Thurman Thomas collecting 1552 yards and fourteen touchdowns the American Football Conference champions' attack was fearsome.

By employing a no-huddle offense Buffalo gave defenses little time to make substitutions. Quarterback Jim Kelly lined up his men, called the play over center, and then directed error-bereft execution.

Five weeks earlier the Bills had squeezed out a 17-13 decision at Giants Stadium, and benched quarterback Phil Simms with a foot injury. The New Yorkers had a crucial knack for adjusting to familiar opponents, which Buffalo now was. The game plan called for now-starting quarterback Jeff Hostetler to expend every second, in the huddle and at the line, that the rules allowed. He would concentrate on keeping his deadly offensive counterparts on the sideline as much as possible. After spending virtually his entire seven-year career as a backup, Hostetler would not play today like a man who had won his job by default.

Both teams were wary in the first quarter, and did little beside trade field goals. Early in the second the New York defense got too aggressive, and end Wilbur Marshall drew a roughing-the passer infraction that set the ball ahead to his own four-yard line. Two plays later Donnie Smith had his sole carry of the day and scored the game's first touchdown, raising the Bills to a 10-3 lead.

Things quickly got freakishly worse for the Giants. Hostetler retreated into his own end zone to pass, but tripped over the otherwise heroic Anderson to be buried for a safety by a pack of defenders led by lineman/Defensive Player of the Year Bruce Smith. It could have become grim for New York after the two-pointer, but the last two times Buffalo got the ball before intermission it was stacked up by a defense wholly aware of the dire implications of allowing another score before the half ended.

With 3:49 remaining in the second period the already-battered Hostetler took a whiff of smelling salts then led his offense eighty-seven yards to the game's only touchdown pass. It was a fourteen-yarder to diminutive wide receiver Steve Baker with thirty seconds remaining, and crucially narrowed the Bill lead to 12-10.

In the third quarter the Giants did just what they needed to do—they severely wore down the Buffalo defense with the most time-consuming drive in Super Bowl history. The fourteen plays covered seventy-five yards and used up 9:29, ending with Anderson's one-yard run for his side's first lead.

Early in the fourth the Bills made certain nothing was settled. After Kelly led his crew to the New York thirty-one he surprised the defenders with a power play straight up the middle. Thomas pounded all the way to the end zone through the embarrassed Giants, who had not expected such an old-fashioned stratagem from the fast-paced upstaters.

Trailing 19-17 the Giants fought back with two- and three-tight end formations as Hostetler expertly mixed passes and runs. Tight end Mark Bavaro made critical receptions of seventeen and nineteen yards as the advance worked its way to the four, where linebacker Cornelius Bennet batted down a third down pass. On the next play Matt Bahr's twenty-one-yard placement set the scene for the most hand-wringing, marvelous finish in Super Bowl history.

During the season no team in the league had scored as many points in any period as Buffalo had scored in its fourth quarters. On this final drive any score would have sufficed, and from his own nineteen Kelly again caught the defense looking for something else when he sent Thomas straight ahead on a delayed handoff. The big, speedy runner quickly outpaced all pursuers except tenth-year cornerback Everson Walls. For many seasons Walls had been labeled a sure-handed pass interceptor, but a tentative, timid tackler. Yet on this play nobody had ever been more sure of himself as he went for the big man's ankles and decisively dropped him at the Bills' forty-one.

There was no way Kelly would let the drive end here, so Buffalo bulled to a fourth down at the New York thirty, where its field goal unit lined up with eight seconds remaining in the game. For the Giants it was a familiar tableau. A week earlier they had knelt on the sideline and prayed as Matt Bahr's fifth three-pointer gave them a 15-13 win over San Francisco for the conference championship. This time they would not be imploring the Almighty for a man's aim to be true.

On this play somebody finally made a mistake. Bill kicker Scott Norwood was unaccustomed to the stadium's grass playing surface, and he was one of millions of silent onlookers who watched his field goal attempt sail wide to the right. A 20-19 New York Giant victory was preserved.

The Giants had stuck faithfully to their game plan by holding possession 40:33 of the game's sixty minutes, denying the lethal Buffalo offense enough time to work its wiles. None was more aware of this than Bill head coach Marv Levy, who later remarked with much woe,

"It's hard to beat a team when you don't have the ball any more than we did."

The time of possession inequity was indeed the greatest the Super Bowl had ever seen. It was still barely enough to produce the series' first one-point outcome—a testament to Buffalo's prowess.

In total yards the Bills were outgained only 386 to 371. New York's ball-hogging approach was an errant field goal away from being offset by a fast-moving, big-play attack, but Kelly's air show was for the most part frustrated by the Giants' novel alignment of just two down linemen, three or four linebackers, and as many as six defensive backs. One point was enough.

On the other side of the world American soldiers sat up until almost dawn in the cold, rain-swept Mideastern desert to watch this game that did not kick off until after 2:00 a.m. their time, but they would not have missed it for anything. Even a war.

Corporal Pierre Thibodeaux of San Antonio summed it up best: "This may sound corny, but you couldn't make it no better." Especially after the previous year's record blowout this entertaining nerve-scraper was the best support America could possibly send her servicemen.

Meanwhile, in this time of war, the nation's capital was coiling to strike.

Way of the Warrior
1991 Washington Redskins versus Buffalo Bills

Throughout the 1991 regular season the Buffalo Bills were carried by a thoroughbred attack that averaged a league-leading 448 yards per game. The defense statistically ranked twenty-seventh in the twenty-eight-team National Football League, but in a very surprising AFL title matchup Buffalo locked with Denver in a grinding defensive battle, winning 10-7 on linebacker Carlton Baily's touchdown on an eleven-yard interception return. It was this unexpected defensive emergence that prompted odds makers to favor the Washington Redskins by a mere one touchdown in Super Bowl XXVI.

The Detroit Lions had tried hard in their first conference championship appearance in thirty-four years, but could not avert the inevitable as they were upended 41-10 in Washington. The NFC champs' crushing, balanced attack produced a 14-2 regular season.

During the two weeks leading up to the Super Bowl Redskin head coach Joe Gibbs used a stop watch to time drills in which he had his defenders practice substitutions at top speed to counter Buffalo's speedy no-huddle offense. Word was that giving a teacher as brilliant as Gibbs two whole weeks to get ready was something of an unfair advantage. This rumor started in the Bills' locker room after the game.

Five years earlier Washington had used a fifth-round draft pick on a muscular quarterback named Mark Rypien who spent the next few seasons fumbling, throwing interceptions and getting injured. In the summer of '91 he decided to give football one last try and signed a fleeting, one-year contract. Suddenly, Mark Rypine could do no wrong on the playing field, and the January title trial in Minneapolis' Hubert Horatio Humphrey Metrodome was his showcase. In the days before the game he kept a low profile that together with his nondescript past lulled Buffalo into forgetting to prepare for him.

There were too many preparations for the Bills to make anyway as the Redskins took full advantage of five turnovers to pile up an early lead that forced Buffalo to forsake its ball-control game plan. Trying to use the strategy that had nosed them out the year before would have been sound had it not been for the "Skins' first half scoring spree. Fullback Thurman Thomas' time-consuming, grind-it-out running style is not suitable for a team trailing by thirteen points, and between the score and the belligerent Washington defenders this great runner picked up just thirteen yards on ten carries.

Buffalo head coach Marv Levy was compelled to abandon his game plan to the point that his quarterback Jim Kelly not only tied a Super Bowl record by throwing four interceptions, but set a new one by attempting *fifty-eight passes* in his frantic efforts to catch up. While his no-huddle offense's timing was being disrupted by blitzing linebackers that Gibbs was able to rotate into the game faster than the Bills had thought possible, Rypien spent brief intervals on the sideline. After every turnover or punt he re-entered play and effortlessly dissected the Bill secondary, completing eighteen of thirty-three pass attempts for 292 yards and two touchdowns. His wide receivers Art Monk and Gary Clark collected over 100 yards apiece.

The Redskins also dominated on defense. During the off-season safeties Alvoid Mays and Brad Edwards and linemen Jason Buck and Jumpy Geathers were cut by other teams. Their careers were saved when they joined Washington via the Plan B free agency system, and in this Super Bowl these grateful young men eagerly stifled Buffalo's feared attack. Edwards, with two interceptions and five knocked-down passes, drew the only two Most Valuable Player votes to not go to Rypien.

Two of the main reasons for the Bills' strong defensive showing in the AFC championship game were strong safety Leonard Smith and linebacker Cornelius Bennet. In the Super Bowl, Bennet made an early exit because of a sprained knee ligament, while Smith, with a staph-infected knee, did not play at all. Six minutes into the game the knee injury bugaboo struck yet again and sent linebacker Shane Conlan hobbling to the bench, leaving a skeleton of the cast that had stifled Denver.

Late in the second quarter Buffalo, after having early scoring opportunities ruined by hard-charging defenders and a series of dropped passes, managed to reach the Washington twenty-yard line on what would be the game's most critical drive. Here, for the Bills, things went irretrievably haywire.

On first down linebacker Wilbur Marshall dropped Kelly for an eight-yard loss. On second down he threw an incompletion. On the pivotal third-and-long wide receiver Andre Reed, furious over no flag being thrown on what most observers agreed was an obvious pass interference penalty, slammed his helmet to the turf, drawing a fifteen-yard personal foul that pushed his crew out of range of even a consolation field goal.

Despite having an apparent touchdown nullified by the instant replay official, Washington led 17-0 at the half. It also owned a 266 to seventy-eight advantage in total yardage.

The Bills did manage to score ten points in the third quarter. This raised some hope among the heavily pro-Buffalo crowd, but the 'Skins quickly stomped out this flicker with the surprise introduction of their own no-huddle and had the matter pretty much determined by the end of the period despite the Bills' scoring a touchdown then using a successful onsides kickoff to score again near the end for a misleadingly close final of 37-24.

Somewhere in the process of enduring five sacks Kelly had sustained a concussion, leaving him with mercifully few memories of the lengthy afternoon. "The part I remember I don't like," he unhappily slurred afterward.

The Washington Redskins had performed their complex game plan expertly. In their madcap postgame locker room Gibbs explained, "We wanted to do as much as we could to confuse them and not give them the same look two times in a row." Giving this intellectual two weeks to prepare was indeed unfair.

The dominance of the NFC Eastern Division was far from over.

Shuffle off to...Pasadena
1992 Dallas Cowboys versus Buffalo Bills

The teams who played the first Super Bowl, the Green Bay Packers and Kansas City Chiefs, had won their respective conference title games on the road. Green Bay won in Dallas. Kansas City won in Buffalo. Twenty-six seasons passed before two road teams again met in the finale, and they were that first year's losers. In 1992 the Dallas Cowboys and Buffalo Bills both had quite a bit to prove.

After the glory of the 1970s the Cowboys entered a decade of steady decline with a series of demoralizing playoff losses that ended after a few years because the franchise stopped making it to the postseason. In 1989 Arkansas oilman Jerry Jones purchased the team and immediately hired his old college dorm roommate Jimmy Johnson as head coach. Johnson was fresh from guiding the University of Miami Hurricanes to the 1988 NCAA National Championship, and he would put to flight the truism that college coaches are incapable of success in the big league without first serving a lengthy apprenticeship as assistants to established pro head coaches. Using his first-ever draft choice on UCLA's dazzling quarterback Troy Aikman, Johnson started well in his top-to-bottom rebuilding blitz. With his untouched set of assistant coaches he engineered one of the fastest turnarounds in sports history as the 'Boys hardly broke a sweat through their 13-3 1992 regular season, and were still gaining momentum as they blew into the Pasadena Rose Bowl for Super Bowl XXVII.

During the three-year overhaul the new Dallas organization ignored conventional dogma that decrees an effective defense is constructed through the draft, and takes several years to develop. Johnson and his brilliant defensive coordinator Dave Wannstedt had nothing against drafting, but also employed free agents, trades and the waiver list in assembling 1992's number one-ranked defense.

Quests

After the Cowboys defeated long-time nemesis San Francisco for the NFC title, free safety James Washington described his unit as "...a melting pot defense. We've got high picks, and we've got low picks. We've got Plan-B guys, and we've got guys that teams were trying to dump on us in trades. The key is every guy's willing to accept his role. Maybe no one knows who James Washington is, but I'm part of the number one defense in the league, and I'm in the Super Bowl. That's how I feel."

It was a heady time for young men like Tony Casillas and Charles Haley. Casillas, the second player taken in the entire 1986 draft, had never been able to see eye-to-eye with the Atlanta Falcons. In the summer of 1991 Johnson bought Tony wholesale for low second- and eighth-round draft picks. Pass rushing specialist Haley was rescued from a similarly soured relationship with the just-beaten 49ers to become an integral part of a line that regularly stopped cold surprise running plays even when the secondary behind it was arrayed in pass-prevent.

Finding further unsung bonuses in the in the lower rounds of the draft, Wannstedt assembled an unselfish cast of such depth that he was able to rotate his men according to all situations, keeping everybody rested with no drop-off in talent. Mysteriously, not one member of this best-in-the-league defense was voted to the Pro Bowl.

Dallas running back Emmitt Smith was in his third season, and had led the league in rushing the last two, making him the first rushing champion to play in a Super Bowl. It was just one more departure from convention for this brash young franchise whose re-emergence into greatness was at hand.

Unlike most teams possessing a superstar running back the Cowboys did not have a one-dimensional attack. Despite gaining 1713 steps in the regular season Smith was part of a carefully *balanced* offense whose passing was as great a part as the running, as multitudes of delighted Texans had noted.

A new breed of fan followed these reborn Pokes. When the team went into its late '80s slide the wealthy, reserved adherents of the first golden age, people who took winning for granted and were spectators rather than rooters, allowed their season tickets to expire, making room for a new cast of enthusiastic, working class partisans who deafeningly brought Texas Stadium alive with a wave of passion such as the place had never seen or heard. These new, blue-collar Cowboys not only won more games than any in franchise history had in one season, but with an average age of just twenty-six were the youngest team in the league. A gilded future was presaged, but first, the Bills.

Buffalo Bills quarterback Jim Kelly was very, very good, and played behind the American Conference's best offensive line as far as sack prevention went, but the hits he *had* taken had been hard. His damaged right knee idled him much of the regular season and playoffs. Happily for the team it had in Frank Reich the best reserve quarterback to be found.

As a wild-card participant, Buffalo worked hard in the playoffs, spotting Houston a thirty-two-point third quarter advantage before stampeding back for professional football's greatest-ever comeback. Inspired by this epic the Bills went on to pulverize Pittsburgh and Miami by a combined score of 53-13. It was magnificent melodrama by a gritty, talent-glutted crew playing in its third straight Super Bowl, and haunted by the heartbreak of the first two. Yet the past month's killing, intense pace was something they could not ignore. They were tired and they hurt and would receive little quarter from the latest juggernaut to come charging out of the National Football Conference's overpowering Eastern Division.

The opening minutes of the game gave Buffalo some cause for hope as the first two Dallas possessions came up dry. Aikman was having difficulty reading the complex Bill defense, and later admitted, "I was having trouble getting into the feel of the game."

These first-Super Bowl jitters looked significant as wide receiver Steve Tasker blocked a Cowboy punt to set up a touchdown and 7-0 first quarter lead. Earlier in the week Tasker had prophesied, "If you block a punt for a touchdown you'll win the game eighty percent of the time." The world would soon see that other twenty percent.

Starting late in the opening period the Dallas defense thrust a succession of mishaps upon Buffalo and destroyed its dreams of third time charm.

Hopeful of their quick lead, and in the midst of a promising drive with five minutes left in the first quarter, Kelly had his crew camped at midfield with a first-and-ten. So far his no-huddle advance had had fair success, but it seems this was due to the teams being almost total strangers. It had taken Wannstedt and his wranglers this long to decipher the unfamiliar Bill offense. From this point nothing would be the same.

Fading to pass, Kelly was forced to throw ahead of schedule because of nickleback Kenneth Gant's blitz. Washington intercepted the hurried toss, setting up a forty-seven-yard march that Aikman ended with a twenty-three-yard scoring throw to tight end Jay Novacek.

On the next series Haley outmaneuvered 325-pound tackle Howard Ballard and creamed Kelly on his own two. When the ball popped loose defensive tackle Jimmie Jones grabbed it and stepped into the end zone for a lead that would widen mercilessly.

Wannstedt had figured out a solution to the no-huddle. He would leave in a group of defenders until a series of downs ended or there was a break in the action such as a measurement or time out, and then exploit his squad's marvelous depth by replacing nearly every man on the field. Buffalo head coach Marv Levy's usual tactic of wearing down defenses with his fast-moving, potent offense was ineffective against this rotating, continually rested lineup. Eventually the Bill attack was worn down in the same way it had exhausted so many defenses during the regular season, but first there was a moment of armrest-gripping drama when Buffalo almost managed to keep things interesting.

Still trailing by just seven it moved to a first-and-goal at the Cowboy four early in the second quarter. On first down fullback Carwell Gardner gained three yards up the middle. On second down Thurman Thomas was decked at the line of scrimmage. Kelly next sent Kenneth Davis around left end, but linebacker Kenny Norton spilled him for no gain.

After three futile charges by three capable Bills, and no sign of a field goal unit the Pokes figured a *pass* might be coming even if this was a goal-line play, and Kelly did indeed drop back on the next snap. Surprised by the pass rushers crashing in around him he tried to connect with tight end Pete Metzelaars, but safety Thomas Everett stole the ball away in the crowded end zone, robbing Buffalo of momentum and sorely needed points.

So far a two-defensive back, deep zone had shut down the Dallas wide receivers. Aikman adjusted with short passes down the middle to Smith and Novacek, loosening the defense and opening up his passing game. Aided by another turnover, Aikman and wide receiver Michael Irvin hooked up for two second period touchdowns in a span of eighteen seconds

Not even the stingy Bill defense could contain such a multi-warhead assault. Every time it doubled up on the wideouts, Smith would come thundering down the sparsely manned middle. Up in the press box offensive coordinator Norv Turner overlooked nothing as Buffalo was overmatched on the sidelines as well as between them.

Second quarters had not been kind to AFC Super Bowl representatives in recent years. During this game's lively fifteen minutes Kelly's right knee again blew out, leaving him a crutches-bound spectator for the rest of the game.

When super sub Reich entered the contest his teammates and fans could not help remembering the miracle he had conjured against Houston a month earlier. However, Reich and his rooters quickly learned the Cowboy defense had little in common with that of its South Texas colleagues. His passes, too, kept thumping into the wrong-colored jerseys. Despite wide receiver Andre Reed's five catches for 124 yards in the first half alone, Buffalo trailed 28-10 at intermission.

Aikman's passing had been aided by his team's first defensive touchdown, which seemed to panic Buffalo into using drastic defense tactics prematurely. After Jones' score the Bills suddenly began blitzing, forcing single coverage on Irvin and his sidekick Alvin Harper. The small Buffalo cornerbacks, who also had to keep an eye on Smith, were unable to cover the towering, leaping Dallas wideouts.

On the other side Kelly, Reich and their normally free-scoring offense had never encountered such a fast, aggressive and large pack of defenders. This new Doomsday Defense kept shutting down plays as they were developing. Swift, husky linebackers would dart through gaps an instant before they closed, and show up unexpectedly in the Bill backfield. It was an almost-perfect game plan that forced turnovers in bunches.

The Pokes mopped up in the second half, collecting more gifts and pressing their advantage to a 52-17 final score. Aikman finished with twenty-two completions in thirty attempts for 273 yards and four touchdowns. He reserved his best for last in a string of sparkling post-season performances during which he threw eighty-nine balls for eight touchdowns and no interceptions. It was a sweet homecoming for this young winner and Super Bowl Most Valuable Player on what had been his college field. He had never led UCLA to a Rose Bowl, but this was forgotten and forgiven after today.

With nine takeaways the Dallasites broke a fifteen-year-old Super Bowl record set by an earlier generation of Cowboys. Previously unheralded youngsters like Everett (who intercepted two passes) would never be obscure again. Five of these turnovers set up touchdowns for the new champs, and the sixty-nine total points made it the highest-scoring Super Bowl ever played.

Thurman Thomas had led the league in combined rushing and receiving yardage four straight seasons. This miserly defense held him to nineteen yards on eleven carries and no receptions.

With 108 yards on twenty-two totes Smith was the first runner all year to pass the century mark versus the Buffalo defense. In three playoff wins the Bill defense had collected fifteen quarterback sacks, but only reached Aikman once.

At the game's emotional finale the Dallas defenders bade their beloved teacher farewell. Wannstedt had finalized arrangements for taking over as head coach of the Chicago Bears.

The heartbroken Bills shuffled off for home. A year later they would again stare bleakly into the eyes of Texas.

Play it Again, Emmitt
1993 Dallas Cowboys versus Buffalo Bills

It was the year of the true sports hero in Dallas. Fourth-year running back Emmitt Smith was 1993's rushing champion despite not even playing a full schedule. Idled by a contract dispute he sat out all of training camp, pre-season and the first two regular season games, both of which the defending champion Cowboys lost. One of these defeats was a 13-10 decision to their upcoming Super Bowl XXVIII opponents, the Buffalo Bills. Shocked by this 0-2 outset, management threw up trembling hands and wrote the superstar the lucrative contract he desired. It was a great bargain—despite still being paid less than one or two of the NFL's big names, Smith led the league in running and was voted its Most Valuable Player despite missing the season's first two games. He had yet another Most Valuable award coming.

The season-opening losses compelled Dallas to whip the New York Giants on the road in the season finale to win the National Football Conference's Eastern Division title and earn a two-week rest before playing their first post-season match. The bye was crucial because Smith slightly separated his right shoulder in the first half of the Giant game, but returned for the second half and led the way to a 16-13 overtime victory. The pain-wracked young man picked up 168 yards that dreary afternoon to finish his partial year with 1486 yards, nine touchdowns and a gaudy 5.5-yard average per carry.

After the sorely needed break the rested Cowboys defeated Green Bay and San Francisco in the playoffs before packing for the next, Super game. Although he had little to say on the matter it was obvious that Smith (who had been mysteriously passed over by sixteen teams in the 1990 draft) was worth at least the $13.6 million paid him by his new contract.

Before the game, Buffalo head coach Marv Levy (a former Cowboys assistant coach) mentioned a favorite saying of his: "Football doesn't build character. Football *shows* character." His teams had displayed enough character, guts, determination and skill over the past four years to deserve infinitely more respect than was being shown them by a sports world blind to everything except their three consecutive Super Bowl losses. They had made it this far four straight times while their American Football Conference colleagues sat home.

By now the Bills had become a defensively oriented club. They brandished a defense that collected forty-seven turnovers and scored four touchdowns in '93. All this gift-giving to the offense was a great help to quarterback Jim Kelly as he peaked in the playoffs, completing forty-four of sixty-four attempts for 447 yards while knocking off the Kansas City Chiefs and Los Angeles Raiders.

Rival offenses still found it risky to key on Kelly because of the menace of runner Thurman Thomas (who had been recruited for Oklahoma State University by now-Dallas head coach Jimmy Johnson.) Thomas ground out 183 yards in the Kansas City game, and was eager for a major statistical matchup with Smith in the looming title trial.

Some things had not changed from the previous Super Sunday. Dallas wide receivers Michael Irvin and Alvin Harper were still 6'2 and 6'3 respectively, and the 5'9 defensive back duo of Nate Odoms and Mickey Washington knew they would still be stargazing.

The gracile Cowboy defense had 4.5-in-the-forty linebackers Kenny Norton, Darrin Smith and Dixon Edwards behind a continually rotating line whose depth allowed its coaches to constantly alternate refreshed players into the game without suffering any drop-off in talent, but even with so many positive considerations, Dallas' winning of Joe Namath's pregame coin toss would be one of its few first half causes for celebration.

With their nineteen free agents the Pokes were thought to be immune to the traditional champion's bane of complacency because of the chip-on-the-shoulder pads attitude this situation is thought to breed. There was also the early-season scare, but in the first half the Texans did indeed look like a bunch taking for granted its record seventh Super Bowl appearance.

Cowboy quarterback Troy Aikman had recovered swiftly and completely from June back surgery, but early in this test Buffalo's well-executed zone pass defense stymied his attack, which was geared almost exclusively to passing. This odd neglect of one of the best running backs in history led to a meager pair of field goals and 13-6 Bill halftime lead.

As they returned for the third quarter Irvin told Smith, "You've got to run the ball!" He had done little of it so far, but after a dismal, forty-one-yard first half the unassuming young millionaire would end up with 132 steps and two touchdowns on thirty carries to become the first-ever player to earn both league and Super Bowl MVP honors in the same season.

Those most knowledgeable have long considered the early minutes of a tight game's third quarter its most telling. This one's were very, very telling, and it would not be tight much longer.

After receiving the second half kickoff, Kelly promisingly captained his offense to the Cowboy forty-three, where tackle Leon Lett tore the ball from Thomas' grasp. Free agent, reserve defensive back James Washington snatched the prize and wove forty-six yards to the tying score.

Defensive tackle Charles Haley later summed up the implications of this play: "They seemed to panic after that, and he (Kelly) started to go downfield, and that opened up our pass rush." It was the hard-working Dallas defense, so overshadowed by a glittering, big-name offense, saving the day.

At this point Smith approached offensive coordinator Norv Turner and politicked, "Coach, get me the ball some kind of way!" It seemed a good idea to Turner (who was directing his last Big D game before departing for the head coaching job in Washington,) so when the defense stomped out the ensuing Buffalo possession, he oversaw an eight-play, sixty-four-yard drive featuring Emmitt on all but one play. Smith punctuated the possession with a fifteen-yard scamper through the pass defense-specializing Bills. The Pokes led for the first time, 20-13.

Most disheartening for the upstate New Yorkers was how casually Smith had shucked off 275-pound tackle Jeff Wright behind the line of scrimmage before charging downfield. The defenders had read the play well enough, but seemed powerless to stop it.

Buffalo's two-back zone was incapable of containing the brutally powerful right-handed rushing assault belatedly unleashed by its now-focused opponents. His massive offensive line ripped gaping holes through which Smith pounded with demoralizing ease as the 'Boys struck for twenty-four unanswered second half points.

In a postgame interview Bill linebacker Darryl Talley summed up: "It wasn't that we didn't make an adjustment. We just didn't make the tackles. We were reaching for him instead of going through him." Emmitt did plenty of going through the best defense in the AFC as he sealed his hero's status.

Besides sacking Kelly three times in the second half, Dallas' defensive dominance was typified by the wrap on Bill receiver Andre Reed. It was his fourth Super Bowl, and he finished it as the Super series' top career receiver. However, all six of his catches and seventy-five yards came in the first half. Past intermission Andre Reed was as invisible as the rest of his offense.

With the Buffalo defense now forced to concentrate on the eventful middle of the field, the Cowboy passing game also began to stir. Aikman hooked up with Harper on a sixteen-yard fourth quarter scoring toss to boost the difference to 27-13 en route to the team's eighth consecutive win.

After kicker Eddie Murray's third placement, a fourth quarter twenty-yarder, put Dallas up by a final score of 30-13 another NFC-dominated Super Sunday wound down. The winners picked up $38,000.00 per man, and a savory consolation of $23,500.00 apiece went to the runners-up.

In the delirium of the Cowboys' postgame locker room offensive lineman Kevin Gogan caught the essence of his team, remarking how "...you might stop us early, but you won't ever stop us in the end."

Even after their team's back-to-back league championships Texans were soon distracted from dynasty talk. Following the close of this contest head coach Jimmy Johnson remarked, "I'm not much of a historian. I just know we've won two Super Bowls in a row!" For not being much of a historian this dynamic young coach was certainly one for *making* history. In five years he had taken the Dallas Cowboys from a 1-15 first season to consecutive league titles, but it was time to move on. He had never spent more than five years in any one coaching job, and this had been his fifth season in North Texas. After a final off-season clash with owner Jerry Jones, he would appease his wanderlust and step down to take an analyst position with the league's new broadcasting company—the Fox Television Network.

It had been a thrilling half-decade in Big D as its team scaled the distance from doormat to dominance. America's team had become just that for a fourth time, and even as millions of heartbroken fans took leave of their beloved resurrector they continued to look eagerly to the future--as he had taught them.

— An Empire Strikes Back —
1994 San Francisco 49ers versus San Diego Chargers

The San Francisco 49er dynasty of the 1980s had lain dormant and angry the past four years, watching the National Football Conference's Eastern Division monopolize the Super Bowl. There were those who printed and postulated that head coach George Siefert would never match the accomplishments of predecessor Bill Walsh, and that quarterback Steve Young, now thirty-three, could not emerge from the shadow of his Hall of Fame-bound forerunner Joe Montana. There was no questioning the ability of both men and the team they served, but they had assumed their positions at a time when the NFL's balance of power was shifting far to the east of the Bay area. Now, following a quartet of homebound Januarys, 49er owner Eddie DeBartolo, Jr. decided the New York Giants, Washington Redskins and Dallas Cowboys had had enough fun. He took out his checkbook and hired the best crop of free agents anyone had ever seen. Young men whose contracts with other teams had expired flocked to California in a latter-day gold rush. It was not long before a new cast of 'Niners was advancing through the post-season.

When DeBartolo's father died on the eve of the playoffs the franchise was infused with yet more incentive to win it all for themselves and their late patriarch, and prove to the National Football League that their Super Bowl-winning days were not ended. Led by a grim Young, Frisco cruised to a 13-3 regular season and emotionally bypassed Dallas in the 1994 conference title game on its way to Super Bowl XXIX in Miami's Joe Robbie Stadium.

The American Football Conference was sending the San Diego Chargers, who were not unfamiliar with the 49ers. Counting an exhibition game the Chargers had already faced off twice with San Francisco that year. Both times San Diego got a bloody nose from its

California cousin. Few expected this would change just because this time they would play in the unfriendly East.

With an 11-5 regular season record the Chargers had shown their own brand of gritty determination in topping their conference despite a pass defense that gave up twelve touchdowns in the six games leading up to the Super Bowl. Still, with underrated quarterback Stan Humphries and power runner Natron Means skillfully spearheading the offense the Chargers had a knack for falling behind early, but winning anyway. Ten times that year they had rebounded from deficits to win games. Analysts noted that they had not done it versus San Francisco (nor had anyone else,) and installed them as eighteen-point underdogs. Few teams had ever been so expected to lose a title game.

This one proffered few surprises as the 49ers immediately set the trend by winning the opening coin toss. On his side's first three possessions Young heaved scoring passes to three separate receivers. San Diego did manage a slow drive that used up almost half of the first quarter and that Means ended with a one-yard dive, but by halftime the overmatched Chargers, wide-eyed and befuddled in their first Super Bowl, trailed 28-10 with a pitiless second half coming.

Before the game San Francisco wide receiver Jerry Rice was tormented by a respiratory infection so severe that he had to be hooked up to an IV bottle two hours before kickoff. Yet the veteran receiver set a record for the quickest-ever Super Bowl touchdown by picking off the first of his three scoring receptions just ninety-four seconds into the opening period. Finishing with ten catches for 149 yards he encapsulated his side's dominance.

Young completed touchdown passes on four of Frisco's first five possessions. His sole failure to pierce the Charger end zone during this stretch came when Rice missed a series of downs because of a minor shoulder injury.

It was fitting work from a QB who had achieved a record regular season passing rating of 112.8, throwing thirty-five touchdown passes and completing 70.2 percent of his attempts. Yet for a moment just before halftime San Diego seemed about to add some seasoning to the unfolding rout.

After guiding his squad to the enemy thirteen-yard line Humphries watched his receivers drop perfectly thrown passes on back-to-back downs, forcing the Chargers to settle for a field goal. They got the ball back minutes later when San Francisco missed a placement attempt. The underdogs moved with rare authority down the field as they tried heartily to establish a precedent for the second half, but Humphries underthrew wide receiver Tony Martin, giving cornerback Eric Davis an easy interception in the end zone. For the first time all year the comeback kids were losing hope.

Even now San Diego possessed a prayer of sparking a turnaround. It received the second half kickoff, and might have done something constructive enough to pull within a couple of touchdowns, but an illegal block on the return set the Chargers back to their ten-yard line. Three plays later a critical third down pass was dropped, forcing them to punt. This set up a long 49er drive that running back Ricky Watters ended with San Francisco's sole rushing touchdown of the day as he pounded in from nine yards.

Late in the third quarter San Diego return man Andre Coleman livened things up with his ninety-eight-yard kickoff runback for a score, but this followed the second Young-to-Rice end zone connection. Minutes later the Charger defense managed to force a punt, but the offense stalled with a fourth-and-one at its own thirty-seven. Means charged fearlessly into the pack of defenders, to be hurled backward four yards. Young and his crew now had their shortest payoff drive of the day.

Steve ended it with a seven-yarder to Rice. It was the sixth TD pass that afternoon for Young, and the third such catch for his favorite target. So complete was San Francisco's aerial superiority that quarterback Young's forty-nine steps led all rushers.

The final was 49-26 as the 49ers collected their record fifth Vince Lombardi trophy. It was the type of bracing performance they had made commonplace during the previous decade.

Although it was true when Charger head coach Bobby Ross remarked in his silent postgame locker room that his troops "...did not play well," they could have played considerably better that afternoon and still lost. Dallas would regain the mastery the following season, but never had the oft-decorated San Francisco 49ers been more determined. Or better.

Duel in the Desert
1995 Dallas Cowboys versus Pittsburgh Steelers

There were those who were surprised to see the Dallas Cowboys in Super Bowl XXX. Even though this was the blue and silver-clad wranglers' third appearance in the last four years so much had changed in the last two that the odds seemed favorable that all the recent distractions would have derailed them.

The latest franchise reconstruction began with immensely popular head coach Jimmy Johnson quitting early in 1994 after one too many spats with owner Jerry Jones, who then hired former University of Oklahoma head coach Barry Switzer. When the San Francisco 49ers nosed Dallas out for the 1994 National Football Conference championship, sideways glances quickly started turning toward Switzer. Nowhere but in Dallas would a head coach be *expected* to win a title his first season, but this town was accustomed to football greatness, and demanded it from its athletes and their mentors every year.

Careful to maintain the system used so successfully by Johnson, Switzer achieved more success his first two regular seasons than some had expected, but he still had not won a Super Bowl. Until he earned the Vince Lombardi Trophy the buzzards would keep circling. Besides, he was not the only newcomer.

Although it was just two years since the Cowboys had last been in this game, they had twenty-seven players on their roster who had never before played in a Super Bowl. Barry Switzer was far too preoccupied with readying his surprisingly inexperienced men for the big game to worry about anybody's lack of faith in his ability.

Via untouched skill and execution the Cowboys' still-young veteran core carried the team through 1995. Quarterback Troy Aikman finished the playoffs as the league's all-time leader in postseason completion percentage (68.5) and yards per attempt (8.62.) His 104.0 quarterback rating stood second only to former Green Bay Packer luminary Bart

Starr's 104.8. With perennial rushing and receiving standouts Emmitt Smith and Michael Irvin keeping defenses loose and off-balance the Dallas offense was already potent as diamondback venom, but this year there was even more.

Before each season Aikman would sit down for a man-to-man consultation with the Dallas Cowboys' former super-quarterback Roger Staubach. They would discuss whatever matters that seemed most mutually beneficial to them at those moments, but predictably it was football that dominated their conversations.

In the summer of '95 Staubach told Aikman that once the team reached the post-season the physical aspects of the game would largely take care of themselves. As starting quarterback what he most needed to do was to prepare himself mentally and emotionally for the less-tangible hurdles the playoffs toss into the path of every young man trying to guide his team through the stressful Wild Card, divisional and conference title matchups. As the latest rounds of January professional football shook many a chilly stadium, Aikman was careful to concentrate on his execution, to keep his wits, and to expect the unexpected, as Staubach had advised.

This tutoring rescued the team in the conference championship test in Texas Stadium. The Green Bay Packers owned a 27-24 mid-fourth quarter lead, but Troy refused to be rattled. He lined up behind his huge offensive line and directed two late touchdown drives for a 38-27 win in a fashion that looked very familiar. Long-time Dallas partisans had seen Staubach do it many times.

Jones managed to hire cornerback/wide receiver Deieon Sanders from San Francisco during the off-season. Sanders' two-way contributions coupled with diminutive wide receiver Kevin Williams' season-ending emergence as a deep threat to re-instill a fear of Dallas upon a league that had lost it on Johnson's departure, but stinging regular season losses to Philadelphia, San Francisco and Washington spawned finger-pointing. Few seemed to consider that the mass turnover in players and coaches might have *temporarily* steered Dallas off the yellow brick gridiron. Sure enough, the revamped Cowboys meshed into a smoothly operating football machine just in time. In the regular season finale in the coming Super Bowl site of Tempe, Arizona's Sun Devil Stadium the Pokes mashed the Arizona Cardinals 37-13. With offensive and defensive lines that could stop wars the 'Boys overpowered Philadelphia and Green Bay in the playoffs to merit a rematch with a long-ago bane.

Following the 1975 and 1978 seasons Dallas had absorbed heart-wrenching, controversial Super Bowl losses to the Pittsburgh Steelers. As the decade waned the Steelers slipped into a long sabbatical from the championship as players and coaches from the dynasty era aged and retired, but when owner Dan Rooney hired a bubbly, brainy young head coach named Bill Cowher patient, still-devout Pittsburgh fans emerged deafeningly from their long torpor as what they were suddenly seeing on the field looked delightfully déjà vu. Thanks mainly to their strapping running game the Steelers overcame a 3-4 start to win ten of their last eleven games. This Pittsburgh team was not that exciting to watch, and did not have to be. Every man knew his responsibilities intimately, and carried them out in very above-average fashion. It was a well-jelled outfit with no use for oversized egos or need for a handful of superstars to pull it over the top each week. It won strictly as a team. It would almost be enough.

After Dallas won the pregame coin toss it seemed headed for a victory at least as one-sided as the Las Vegas odds makers had predicted when they installed the Cowboys as two-touchdown favorites. A couple of early drives brought a field goal by kicker Chris Boniol and a three-yard touchdown throw from Aikman to tight end Jay Novacek.

In the second period Dallas moved to a third-and-one at the Steeler fifteen. The conventional course would have been for Aikman to hand off to best-in-the-business running back Emmitt Smith straight up the middle, but so far Pittsburgh had effectively stifled this ground threat. Offensive coordinator Ernie Zampese may have been reflecting on how Smith to this point had only been averaging about a yard per carry. He called for an end sweep. Emmitt grabbed the handoff and headed east, but linebacker Levon Kirkland spilled him for a three-yard loss. Had the Texans picked up another seven points here the pummeling Las Vegas had predicted would likely have commenced, but with the Cowboys forced to settle for a field goal there was still hope for a dogfight.

As they had frequently done during the regular season the Steelmen picked up momentum late in the second quarter. On their last drive of the first half they drove from their own forty-six to a third-and-thirteen at the Dallas twenty-three. On the next two plays quarterback Neal

O'Donnel connected for a seventeen-yard gain to wide receiver Ernie Mills, then a six-yard scoring bullet to wideout Yancy Thigpen.

The taut 13-7 halftime score jolted the Cowboys from the strutting overconfidence so many of them had given in to the past couple weeks. It was clear their opponents had not come to Arizona to make anything easy for them. The Pokes would have to fight for this victory.

Boniol's second half kickoff bounced out of bounds, giving Pittsburgh possession at its own forty and a glittering chance for a momentum-building quick score to perhaps establish them as the final quarters' dominant team. However the Steelers quickly learned the Dallas defense already had the message—shaken from any lingering complacency it doggedly stanched Pittsburgh's opening drive. The Cowboy offense was another story.

After taking their first possession Aikman and his platoon appeared uncertain and bewildered. Following three downs in which Smith lost several more yards they were forced to punt, and the defense had to return to action before it was rested.

Versus these weary defenders the Steelers marched to their own forty-seven, where the promising-looking drive went drastically awry. O'Donnell was expecting the next play to be a deep pass to Mills down the right sideline, but Ernie had misunderstood the call in the huddle. A couple of seconds after the snap O'Donnell arced a perfect spiral far downfield, then watched in horror as his receiver, who thought the play was a slant, suddenly cut to the left and away from the ball. There was no one within ten yards of him when Dallas cornerback Larry Brown cradled the interception and lit out down the sideline all the way to Pittsburgh's eighteen.

On first down Aikman hit wide receiver Michael Irvin at the one-yard line, and on the next play Smith squirmed into the end zone for a 20-7 lead. This score lasted until the end of the third quarter, but the Steelers were still not quite ready to be conquered.

The Cowboys continued having difficulty with the stingy Pittsburgh defense as the fourth quarter started, and had to punt away their first possession. O'Donnell and his crew had been moving the ball well enough through the Dallas defense, but kept coming up dry, not scoring at all in the third quarter.

They did manage to reach the Cowboy twenty-nine early in the last period, when kicker Norm Johnson made a field goal and Cowher got a great idea. The Dallas return team were taken utterly unaware when Johnson tapped an onside kick downfield, where cornerback Deon Figures fell on the ball at his own forty-eight. This time the grim Steelers would not be deflected from the end zone. Confidently firing his passes, O'Donnell moved his offense to a first-and-goal at the five-yard-line. From here it took three violent charges by fullback Bam Morris to score and narrow the difference to 20-17. 6:36 remained in regulation time, and Dallas was staggered.

The Cowboy offense went nowhere on its next possession, and quickly had to punt. The Steelers took over at their own thirty-two, and the game seemed headed for the most dramatic comeback in Super Bowl history, but O'Donnell went astray.

The belatedly productive quarterback had completed eleven of his last twelve attempts, and would likely have further padded his stats had he squeezed the ball a little harder on second down. At the snap wide receiver Corey Holliday darted downfield a few yards and looked back for the short pass that was supposed to come his way. O'Donnell had ample time as he set up and threw, but the ball slipped from his fingers an instant too soon. It sailed over Holliday and straight to Brown. Larry again followed up his pickoff with a scintillating runback, reaching the Pittsburgh six before he was shoved out of bounds. Moments later Smith produced his second short touchdown run to give his team the final edge of 27-17 despite the Pokes having been dominated statistically.

The Pittsburgh coaching staff had painstakingly prepared for the marquee big guns of the Dallas Cowboys, only to be hamstrung by an unheralded fifth-year defensive back they had scarcely heard of before today. Coming out of Texas Christian University as a twelfth-round choice in 1991 Brown had not been expected to start, and only became a slender draft possibility when his MVP performance in the '91 Blue-Gray Game gave him some exposure. He figured to spend 1995 on the bench, but when number one draft pick Kevin Smith went down with a torn Achilles tendon in the season opener Larry Brown took over at cornerback. His six pickoffs tied for the team lead, and he returned two of his intercepts for touchdowns.

It was a soul-warming performance for a young man with a heavy heart. His prematurely born infant son Christopher had died in October, but on the evening of January 28, 1996, as Larry Brown became only the second defensive back ever named Super Bowl Most

Valuable Player (and the first one in twenty-three years,) he was finally able to smile again. Twice he had resisted the temptation to desert his position and follow the flow of the play, and both times he saved the Dallas Cowboys from likely defeat in this last game he would play in a blue-starred helmet. His contract was expired, and the following spring the Oakland Raiders purchased his services for the hefty sum he had made it clear they were worth by helping his team make history.

For the first time an NFL franchise had won Super Bowls under three separate head coaches, and this last one was under the tutelage of the most maligned teacher ever to lead a team to the summit. As Barry Switzer gazed down from it he knew he owed his redemption to an underrated young player named Larry Brown who would be terribly missed by the throngs of Cowboy players, fans and sundry supporters now involved in the most emotional postgame celebration this game had ever seen.

Meanwhile, a long-ago empire was stirring.

Green and Gold Bowl
1996 Green Bay Packers versus New England Patriots

Wisconsin lived off past glory for almost thirty years. Memory of the long-ago Packer dynasty was their sole link to the greatness that once warmed their frosty corner of the NFL. When the regime of coaching legend Vince Lombardi ended, and the players who had upheld his towering standards drifted into retirement, the Green Bay franchise sank into a torturous era of mediocrity. Even when the team returned to a competitive level in the early 1990s it could only hammer in futile frustration on the Dallas palisades as it dropped a string of playoff games to this superpower.

In 1996 the angry Packers bludgeoned their way to a defense-dominated 13-3 regular season, then knocked off a pair of frostbitten playoff opponents to earn a trip to Super Bowl XXXI in distant New Orleans. The New England Patriots also had plane fare.

This game was new to the players on both sides, but the Patriots were not as nervous as most newcomers. Head coach Bill Parcells had brought the New York Giants here twice, and won twice. His high-speed receivers had him, his men and hundreds of thousands of supporters hoping they had enough velocity to outrun Green Bay's best-in-the-business defense. Later, many would suggest New England put too much emphasis on air power.

The Packers were not particularly jittery either, but they were getting fed up with Parcells' media monopoly in the days preceding the game. These NFC champs were tense and eager to get started.

As Super Sunday loomed the Packers were irritated by how Parcells expertly courted a press corps that duly depicted him as football's Einstein. When the Green Bays heard that he had bragged to his players that he would, "Show you what to do," *after* reaching the Super Bowl they got so mad they almost lost their focus, but head coach Mike Holmgren pulled them back onto the straight and narrow.

"I don't have to show you how to win this game," Holgrem told his men in the pre-game locker room. "I've already showed you how to win. You don't need me to hold your hands. Now go out and do it." They wasted no time.

For the second straight year Packer quarterback Brett Favre had been voted league Most Valuable Player despite working for a defensively oriented team. He had a wide receiver named Andre Rison who was released and re-signed twice in '96 after some questioned his ability. Some were silenced with 11:28 remaining in the first quarter when he snared a Favre pass and went fifty-four yards for a speedy 7-0 lead.

Less than two minutes later Holmgren's offense was presented with lovely field position after an interception off Patriot quarterback Drew Bledsoe. Specialist Chris Jacke's thirty-seven-yard placement gave the Pack a 10-0 blowout indicator with the opening period less than half elapsed.

Parcells managed to calm his players enough for them to implement the clever game plan he had devised. Assailing the Green Bay defense with a complex cocktail of rollouts, screens and play-actions his offense drove to a pair of late first quarter scores with Bledsoe tossing two short touchdown passes. It was the highest-scoring opening period in Super Bowl history, and left the heavily pro-Green Bay crowd much more subdued from a few minutes earlier.

After the game Packer strong safety LeRoy Butler remarked, "We were completely baffled. We were missing tackles, they were flying right past us, and they were pushing us around. No one had pushed us around all year, and they were killing us, doing stuff we hadn't seen before. It was a great game plan."

During that stretch Bledsoe completed six of nine throws for 108 yards and one- and four-yard touchdown passes to fullback Keith Byars and tight end Ben Coates. Between quarters Green Bay defensive coordinator Fritz Shurmer called his squad together for some verbal abuse. "Enough is enough!," he bellowed. "Go do what you're supposed to do!" He ordered Butler to commence blitzing Bledsoe from the blind side so the quarterback would start looking over his shoulder, giving the Packer pass rushers an extra instant to reach him.

Shurmer also began inserting five and six defensive backs to offset New England's long-range passing. The biggest risk was that Parcells might counter by sending powerful running back Curtis Martin into the thinned-out Green Bay interior. If the powerful Patriot offensive line could open a crack for Martin in the row of front-line green jerseys he could bolt through into a linebackerless backfield and have his wide receivers to run interference as he plowed through the safeties and cornerbacks.

Parcels had used this tactic effectively in his Super Bowl win over Buffalo six years earlier, but Bledsoe's first quarter air show apparently convinced him this was the only way to fly. He stuck with the aerial strategy even after the Pack adjusted to it. He allowed Martin to carry the ball just eleven times.

By the third period the Packers had seen enough Patriot play-action, and they stopped biting on the fakes. Still, Parcells did not run the ball. In the first half he had called thirty passes to only seven runs. By intermission Favre and his offense had regained their poise.

This magnificent quarterback from nearby Kiln, Mississippi had spent the last days before Sunday miserably sick with the flu. He lost lots of weight that week, but woke up game day feeling much better. Then he thought about the dimensions of the game he was about to play, and got sick all over again. Fortunately for Wisconsin his stomach was empty, and although he dry-heaved throughout the evening he was able to stay on the field.

Lining up on his own nineteen-yard-line one minute into the second quarter Favre was surprised to see the New England defense arrayed in what looked to him like a blitzing formation that left his three-wide receiver set with single coverage. With the Packers so deep in their own territory the Pats were expecting a short- safe quick-out pass to tight end Mark Chmura. Receiver Antonio Freeman also noticed the unwise set-up, and was listening carefully when Favre audibled to a play called "74 Razor." Freeman flew past strong safety Lawyer Malloy and late-arriving free safety Willie Clay as his quarterback uncorked a towering rainbow over the helmets of blitzing linebackers. The defenders had mistakenly assumed the crowd of pass-catchers was a ruse, so Freeman was long gone when the ball reached him. His eighty-one-yard score was the longest touchdown from scrimmage ever seen in a Super Bowl, and Green Bay would not trail again.

A few minutes after Jacke converted a thirty-one-yarder his defense forced a punt, and Favre led a march to the Patriot two-yard line. Seconds before intermission Brett snatched a snap and went loping to his left, and seeing nothing but covered receivers he decided to do it himself. Lunging for the goal line he thrust the ball forward and just inside the pylon for a 27-14 halftime lead.

Besides Favre and the strapping Green Bay defense New England was bedeviled by a kick returner who before this season was little known except to college football fans. In 1991 University of Michigan senior Desmond Howard won the Heisman Trophy, but did little to excite the Washington Redskins and Jacksonville Jaguars his first four seasons in the league. After these teams discarded him the Packers looked at him warily, but gave him a tryout. After he was almost cut a third time Howard convinced his newest franchise he was in fact a professional by returning three punts for touchdowns during the regular season, and another against San Francisco in the divisional playoff. Prior to Sunday the Patriots made an enemy of him.

The New Englanders kept talking about how they intended to aim all their kicks at Howard, and were not worried about it. Early in the game they jeered at him, "Nothing for you today, baby. We're going to shut you down." Desmond returned his first punt thirty-two yards to crucially shorten the opening scoring drive, and he would come through again at his team's moment of greatest need.

Smoke from the halftime fireworks show still hung thick under the Superdome ceiling when Martin finally got the chance to flash his skill as he capped a seven-play, fifty-three-yard drive with his eighteen-yard scoring run to slice the difference to 27-21. This got the Patriots to thinking seriously about an upset in the Crescent City, but unhappily for the again-hopeful Pats they now had to kick off to Howard.

Holgrem was aware that New England kicker Adam Vinatieri tended to slice his kickoffs to the right, so for the first time all year Howard lined up on this side. He squinted through the smoke until he locked onto the tumbling ball, took a step forward and caught it. Taking the shortest route he pelted down the middle at such a clip that he bypassed the bulk of the coverage team before it had time to converge. He sloughed off Hason Graham at the thirty, cut away from Vinatieri, then ran and ran and ran. The angry young man made it look absurdly easy as he broke yet another Super Bowl record with his ninety-nine-yard return to become the first-ever player to return both a punt and a kickoff for scores in the same postseason.

When Favre pitched a two-point conversion to Chmura there were still three minutes left in the third period, and the Packers were ahead by the fourteen points the experts had foreseen. It was time to protect an acceptable lead.

As Holmgren's offense took no chances, and Shurmer's defense was careful to not displease him again the fourth quarter was scoreless but entertaining as the Pack picked off two more Bledsoe passes and twice slammed him to the plastic turf. A thirty-five-year-old Baptist preacher/defensive lineman named Reggie White pulled Bledsoe down three times after the scoring ended and stoked his defense's smothering late momentum, protecting the final score of 35-21, Packers.

Never before had a special teams man been acclaimed Most Valuable Player in a Super Bowl, and although Howard tried to give all the credit to Favre, his own 244 return yards and touchdown elected him by a landslide. The last time Patriot punter Tom Tupa kicked the ball he made sure it stayed out of Desmond's hands. He booted it out of bounds.

The Green Bay Packers had conjured recall of their glittering past as banners in the smoky stadium proclaimed, "VINCE IS SMILING!" Indeed, somewhere the late coaching paladin of long ago was very, very pleased.

Resurrection
1997 Denver Broncos versus Green Bay Packers

It had been thirteen years since the Super Bowl was last predictable. The National Football Conference had dominated the American Football Conference with monotonous totality. During that stretch the Nationals outscored the Americans 483-219, and even those rare games that were competitive saw the NFC beat the clock with a late scoring drive, or the AFC miss a last-second field goal attempt. The Denver Broncos, New England Patriots and Buffalo Bills had suffered miserably through this era—one man in particular.

The last year that the American Conference had won a Super Bowl the hottest prospect to leave college for the pro wars was a bionic-armed rookie named John Elway. He wanted to play on the Pacific coast, and made it clear to the Baltimore Colts that he would not respond to their advances. When they drafted him anyway he threatened to quit football and instead play in the New York Yankee outfield. The Colts cut a deal with the Broncos, and Big John decided Denver was far enough west. Still, his happy ending was somewhere far beyond the Rockies.

By the end of 1997 Elway had finished his fifteenth season in the mile-high city, but his bushels of heroics in regular seasons and playoffs shriveled in significance before his lack of the ultimate talisman of pro football greatness—a Super Bowl ring. Over the past two decades the Bronks had fallen four times to a succession of too-powerful foes from the rival conference, and John had quarterbacked the last three of these humiliations. His untouched ability and determination were never enough to pull his teams up to his level of superstardom, and he spent his prime bruising himself against the NFL's dominant conference. He was now old and tired, but his heart pumped as strongly as ever as he and his latest brood of Broncos approached what they all felt might be his final chance at a ring and a trophy. Nearly all onlookers forecast a sad ending to this quest.

Elway had won more games than any quarterback in league history, but none was a Super Bowl. It was eight years since he had even played in the thing, and most of his '97 teammates had still been in high school or college at the time of that 55-10 Waterloo. The cast of players now surrounding him had not been around long enough to develop an inferiority complex.

There were those who had thought Elway's career ended back in the pre-season when he tore his right bicep muscle. Not only did his thirty-seven-year-old pitching arm heal without surgery, but it completed a career-high twenty-seven touchdown passes that year. Few oddsmakers considered these data. All they noted was the opposition.

Led by three-time league Most Valuable Player Brett Favre the Green Bay Packers cruised into San Diego's QualComm Stadium riding a seven-game winning streak. They had carried the previous Super Sunday rather decisively, and it had been fourteen years since a defending NFL champ had lost a title test. That was also the last time an American Football Conference team had emerged victorious. Like many others, the Packers were overlooking the fact that they had won the year-ago Super Bowl mainly on the big-play heroics of a now-departed kick returner. It was a contest they could easily have lost. Yet now it never occurred to them they might lose to any AFC team, much less one that made it to this Super Bowl XXXII as a lowly wild card playoff entry. Furthermore, in the previous year's regular season Green Bay had blitzed Denver 41-6.

Between the established tradition of NFC superiority and the Packers' fine showing in their 23-10 conference championship game trouncing of San Francisco it seemed sealed that the league mastery had been decided in that game. Green Bay thought so, and the National League would field a dangerously overconfident Super Bowl representative.

The young men wearing their gaudy new Bronco uniforms were much more sure of themselves than anyone outside the team realized. They saw no reason to take seriously the thirteen points by which the Packers were favored. In fact, they felt rather insulted by the lop-sided betting line.

Green Bay head coach Mike Holmgren believes in creating strategy that will work against any team. Denver's Mike Shanahan, however, prefers tactics that exploit opponents' specific weaknesses. He detected a Packer overdependence on strong safety LeRoy Butler, and with it a glittering opportunity.

Holmgren and his defensive coordinator Fritz Shurmer relied on Butler to not only cover deep receivers, but also to help contain running backs, watch for screen passes, and keep quarterbacks honest via his dreaded blitzes. Shanahan brewed up a novel blocking set-up in which an offensive tackle would sometimes leave the end in front of him to the tight end on power running plays, then slam into Butler before he could react. On tailback sweeps fullback Howard Griffith might turn over his usual blocking assignment, the outside linebacker, to a wide receiver then go after Butler. On weakside runs the Bronks would bolster the small blocking element with an unexpected wide receiver whose mission would be to shield LeRoy off the runner.

This Butler-blocking had to be done fast, for as tackle Tony Jones later explained, "You have to get on him quickly, or he'll ole you and you'll be blocking air." Such speedy takeouts were generally successful regardless of which defender was targeted. Averaging 289 pounds per man, Denver's offensive line was the smallest in the NFL, but the men were cat-quick, Sumo-strong, and hard as tombstones. They handled the huge, aging Packer front four throughout the afternoon.

Apart from the complex blocking scheme, the Broncos spent the day sending their running plays out of passing formations. Two wideouts would line up on one end of the line, and tight end Shannon Sharpe on the opposite side. This had always been an exclusively aerial alignment, and the Green Bays could not bring themselves to believe running plays could spring from it. They never adjusted.

Every time Shurmer's defense saw Elway position his squad in this formation, it would drop into pass-prevent. At the snap the tiny terrors in front of the quarterback would crack open clear lanes for tailback Terrell Davis, who kept popping through into a secondary whose cornerbacks and safeties were far downfield. He would run quite a ways before encountering any defenders. Despite missing the second quarter because of a concussion, Davis finished with 157 yards, three touchdowns, and Most Valuable Player status. It was a royal performance not only by him, but also by linemen who were outweighed thirty pounds apiece by the defenders they were pushing around. In the first quarter alone, Davis carried the ball nine times for sixty-four yards and a touchdown.

Also in the first period Favre threw an unwise pass that strong safety Tyrone Braxton intercepted. Minutes earlier tight end Mark Chmura had beaten Braxton for a touchdown. The pickoff set up Davis' first score. In the second quarter free safety Steve Atwater achieved the game's only sack of Favre. The surprised signal caller coughed up the ball for a Denver recovery that led to a field goal and 17-7 Bronco lead.

The back-to-back turnovers and ten-point difference shocked millions, but late in the second quarter things seemed to be turning in the expected direction. Favre directed a ninety-five-yard, seventeen-play drive capped by his six-yard touchdown toss to Chmura. After a still-dizzy Davis fumbled the ball away on the Bronks' first offensive play of the second half the Packers tied the game on Bryan Longwell's twenty-seven-yard field goal, and masses of Las Vegas bettors and Green Bay rooters began to relax. Too soon.

Late in the third quarter Elway and his offense faced a crucial third-and-six at the Packer twelve-yard line. Fading to throw, John spied no uncovered receivers, so he pulled down the ball and scurried up the middle. As he neared the first down marker, Butler fought clear of his blocker and aimed the top of his helmet at the undaunted ball carrier. Instead of safely flopping flat Elway met Butler head-on and spun propeller-like to the turf just far enough downfield to move the sticks. He sprang to his feet, jubilantly pumping his fist with the exuberance of a rookie. His teammates were instantly infected with an adrenalin high that carried them into the end zone and buoyed them for the rest of the game. From this point they were as fresh as at the opening kickoff.

Despite Davis' heroics it was much-older Elway who set the pace and radiated the poise, confidence and morale that kept his men focused and momentum-charged. Green Bay was, however, simply too powerful to make it easy even for such a champion. Aided by a twenty-five-yard pass interference penalty Favre moved his unit eighty-five yards in just ninety seconds to re-tie the score. The final quarter was Shakespearian.

With less than five minutes to play and the game still even the Packers had a yummy chance to drive slowly downfield, deplete the clock and score last. Then rookie left tackle Ross Verba was caught holding, and moments later he jumped offsides. These misdemeanors pushed the Pack fifteen yards in the wrong direction, and a pitiful Craig

Quests

Hentrich punt set the Broncos up on the Green Bay forty-nine. Denver won the championship on the next series of downs.

As Elway led his men onto the field for the last time third-string quarterback Jeff Lewis noted a tangible aura of confident determination. "You could see it in his eyes; he was ready. It was one of those times you just have to stop and watch the best quarterback ever do his thing."

A face mask-grabbing call on cornerback Darius Holland gave Denver fifteen quick, cheap yards. Elway then completed a twenty-three-yard screen to Griffith for a first-and-goal on the Packer eight at the two-minute warning. On first down Sharpe drew a ten-yard holding penalty. On the replayed first down Davis swept left all the way to the one-yard line before being knocked out of bounds, and the Bronks called time out to discuss tactics.

At this point Holmgren became confused. Forgetting that the holding call had moved the offense back ten yards, but allowed it to run first down a second time he erroneously concluded, after Davis' seventeen-yard run, that it was first down rather than the actual second-and-goal. Fearing Elway would snap the ball three times, run down the clock then watch as kicker Jason Elam booted a chip-shot field goal with too little time left for Green Bay to respond, Holmgren had his defenders stand aside and allow Davis to trot untouched into the end zone with 1:45 to play. All four Denver touchdowns came on one-yard runs.

Holmgren had figured regaining possession was more important than spending precious seconds trying to prevent an almost certain three-pointer. Perhaps Favre could use the remaining time to drive for a speedy touchdown and go on to win in overtime.

Mysteriously, nobody on the field, sideline or upstairs coaches' box informed Holmgren that the Broncos had one down fewer than he thought. With two times out remaining, his chances might have been better had he allowed the Bronks to run a couple more plays, stop the clock after each one, concede Denver a placement and have over a minute left to try for a touchdown or field goal of his own. Considering how the Pack finished the day with 104 yards in kickoff returns this late drive could well have been a short one. However, no one told Holmgren it was second down, and his team fell behind 31-24 instead of 27-24.

On the next series Favre pumped completions of twenty-two and thirteen yards to receiver Dorsey Levins for a first down at the Denver thirty-five with a full minute remaining. The next play was a quick flip Levins carried out of bounds at the thirty-one, stopping the clock. With still enough time and downs to move yet deeper into field goal range the significance of Holmgren's error became terribly apparent. Now there was nothing Longwell could do. Favre had to go for the end zone.

On second-and-six he zipped one to Antonio Freeman on the fifteen, but Tony dropped the hard-thrown football. Favre's third-down pass to Robert Brooks on the ten was off-target and fell incomplete. On fourth down eight Broncos pass-rushed. Brett managed to heave the pigskin toward Chmura, but one of the only three defenders who had not blitzed, linebacker John Mobley, slapped the ball off-target to give Denver its first Super Bowl success in five tries.

The Broncos had come into existence in 1960, which was also the first (and only) year Vince Lombardi's Packers lost a league championship match. For the AFC it seemed that long since it had won the trophy named for Coach Lombardi. Holmgren, Favre and Wisconsin did not appreciate the irony.

MVP Davis was not only the first man to ever rush for three touchdowns in a Super Bowl, but the first to play the game in his hometown. On the previous Tuesday his high school jersey was formally retired at nearby Lincoln High. Now he accepted not only the accolades always accorded a Super Bowl hero, but a spot in the record book as the first player to score eight touchdowns in a single post-season.

In the winners' postgame locker room Sharpe sang out, "We came in here and shocked the world, but we didn't shock the Denver Broncos!" Unlike a generation of preceding AFC victims the Broncos had, at 3-2, won the turnover battle. They had played the kind of hard-charging, power-running game teams from the NFC's feared Eastern Division had used to win eight Super Bowls during the 80s and 90s. Instead of employing the AFC's previously typical tentative, pray-for-a-Hail Mary-type offense, the Denvers simply lined up and ploughed through their overconfident, overweight, out-coached foes. The American Conference had finally learned the lesson of all those heartbreaking Januarys. Defensively as well.

Although Favre completed twenty-five of forty-two attempts for 256 yards and three touchdowns, he was constantly distracted by the blitzing linebackers Denver defensive coordinator Greg Robinson kept throwing at him. Apart from the two first half turnovers, in the second half Brett twice missed wide-open receivers on throws he sorely needed to complete. On third downs his offense was 0-7 in the final two quarters.

The Denver Broncos had been in a position not only to be the first team to lose five Super Bowls, but to lose them to five separate teams. Instead the quest was theirs to savor. For John Elway, the loving Denver fans, and all the players present and past who spent almost four decades aching with frustration and fear that their dream was an impossible one, the moment was superbly worth the wait.

Next year, too.

King of Hearts
1998 Denver Broncos versus Atlanta Falcons

For the first thirty-three years of their existence the Atlanta Falcons got little respect. Generations of opponents greedily rubbed their hands together and reached for easy victories over one of the league's traditional patsies. Playing in the same division with the ever-powerful San Francisco 49ers did little to ease the burden of this obscure franchise that always seemed such an ideal stepping stone for powerhouses with an eye on the postseason.

In 1997 the Falcons got an ailing new head coach when Danny Reeves moved in from New York. Before guiding the Giants, Reeves had coached the Denver Broncos to three fruitless Super Bowls during the long, long era of National Football Conference dominance. In his first year in the Deep South Danny Boy was too busy re-building his new team to worry about posting a winning record, but that first, 7-9 season was all it took.

Even as its crew commenced a dramatic turnaround in 1998, Atlantean fandom was so accustomed to mediocrity that many rooters overlooked the emerging contender en route to its first divisional title since 1980. Just three home games sold out as the Birds fought to a 14-2 record and outgutted heavily favored Minnesota 30-27 in an NFC title test overtime thriller far to the north of friendly confines.

Coach Reeves was the inspiration as he did not allow mid-December quadruple heart bypass surgery to drydock him for the playoffs. He is like that. He refuses to let problems make a difference. He either cures them or gets rid of them whether they be physical or temperamental. Players who will not strive for the team's best interests soon find themselves at bus stops. Cornerback Ray Buchanan explains: "There were cancers on the team, guys who weren't ready to perform. Dan Reeves cleaned all that up."

Quests

The post-operative coach showed his men the essence of overcoming adversity. With his doctors hovering anxiously near him on the sidelines he steered his team through the playoff stretch and postseason to Miami's Pro Player Stadium to play underdog to his former team just forty-eight days after his operation. As much to celebrate their coach's survival as their abrupt success the players punctuated each win with their delightfully rhythmless "Dirty Bird" celebratory dance.

With many whispering that the Denver Bronco's win in the previous Super Bowl was something of a fluke versus an overconfident foe the mountain men were almost *too* eager to capture their second straight championship. They had considerable difficulty early in the American Football Conference title game as the error-plagued New York Jets held them scoreless in the first half. At the start of the third quarter tight end Shannon Sharpe stomped into the Denver huddle and bellowed, "Here we go! It's time! This is for all the mini-camps, for all the weights we lifted, for all the sprints we ran! We're better than this!" His determined but so-far-unfocused teammates caught on, stopped playing down to the level of their opponents and left a 10-0 deficit far behind on their way to a 23-10 win.

Denver was head coached by Mike Shanahan, a fearless young man who loved fast cars, faster motorcycles, hang gliding, bungee jumping and white water rafting. Following charges of insubordination in 1991, Reeves had fired him as the Bronks' offensive coordinator. A year later disaffection between Reeves and future Hall of Fame quarterback John Elway led to Reeves' ouster, and two years after that Shanahan was summoned to take the reins as head mentor.

His boundless courage aside, Mike seemed to have little to fear anyway coming into Super Bowl XXXIII. *He* knew the previous year's had been nothing less than an earned victory. He had detected a weakness in the favored Packers' run defense and exploited it via hard running by tailback Terrell Davis. Even if some did think Green Bay should have won that game, Denver's Super Bowl experience and their having won a league-record forty-six games over the past three years led the odds makers to install them as seven-point favorites.

Now that the thirty-eight-year-old Elway was no longer a great player surrounded by a fair team, but one superstar among many after a four-year talent-gathering and training crusade by his coaches and scouts these odds may have been conservative. Unlike during the previous decade Elway, now quarterbacking a record fifth Super Bowl, no longer had to carry his cast through regular seasons and playoffs only to be demolished by National Conference powerhouses in the final confrontation. Elway even missed four '98 games with nagging injuries, and his team still won. Ten years earlier Denver could not have reached the Super Bowl without him in for virtually every snap. In fact, the Broncos had won their first thirteen straight games of the regular season.

In Davis, Denver had one of the finest ball carriers ever to tear turf. He personified the team's move toward a multi-weaponed attack by gaining over 2000 yards that year and making it possible to win despite Elway's having just two 300-yard passing games. With Atlanta gearing itself to stop this fearsome sixth-round draft pick, Elway would play younger than ever, not at all like a man starting his 252nd game, 162 of which had been victories.

As if this dazzling extravaganza of which they were a part and the highly publicized enmity between their head coach and his counterpart were not already too much distraction for the wide-eyed Falcons, their veteran team captain, cornerback Eugene Robinson, was arrested the night before the game on a charge of soliciting sex from an undercover policewoman in Miami's red-light district. Whereas the Broncos regained their focus in their conference championship game, the Birds lost theirs in this pregame chaos. 74,802 attended, and as a falcon mascot was released for a flyover of the stadium all eyes watched as the raptor ignored its trainer and soared off into the gathering twilight. As the Atlantas saw their mascot abandon them they wondered what else was about to go wrong.

Although Falcon quarterback Chris Chandler had played for six teams during his nine years in the league he had never seen anything like the defensive formations thrown at him that night. In the six games prior to the Super Bowl Chandler's quarterback rating was a whopping 125%, but on Sunday he was lost as Denver defensive coordinator Greg Robinson blitzed with plays he called Venus, Inverted Double-Double, and Two-Deep Squeeze. "We used ten different blitzes, two of which we've never shown before," said Robinson after the game. His recently suspect secondary had begun to shine at the start of the playoffs, which it finished after giving up just thirty-two points (including only two offensive touchdowns) to three opponents.

Chandler's blockers were as befuddled as he was by the magnificently peculiar alignments facing them. The Broncos repeatedly showed deep zone coverage, and then came with blitzes that either sacked Chandler or forced him to throw before he was ready. Cornerback Darrien Gordon picked off two errant pitches and returned them a total of 108 yards, aborting drives and setting up his own offense with optimum field position.

Denver's run defense also sparkled as its linemen easily read Chandler's pulling guards' body language as they set up for a critical second quarter fourth-and-one. It was at the Bronks' twenty-seven, and Keith Traylor dropped Jamal Anderson for a two-yard loss. Even finishing the day with ninety-six yards on eighteen carries for a gaudy average of 5.3-yards-per-carry was little solace to Anderson as the scrappy Bronco defenders shut him out of the end zone.

Chandler came into the game as the league's top-rated red zone quarterback, but in this contest he repeatedly moved his squad downfield with deceptive ease only to have the Ponies stiffen deep in their own territory. Six times Atlanta penetrated Denver's thirty-yard line in the first three quarters, to come away with but a pair of field goals. In the second half a worried Chandler began trying too hard, and threw three interceptions.

On defense the Falcons were praying Elway was no longer the threat he once was, and hoped to get away with keying on Davis. They crowded the line to stifle running plays, but Elway took advantage of this weak pass rush and paucity of backs covering his receivers. In a postgame interview Bronco center Tom Nalen commented in wonderment on Atlanta's defensive strategy: "They took Terrell out of the game and dared John to beat 'em. Well, John beat 'em. It was weird. Even the defensive backs weren't respecting him. I'd never seen that."

Neither had Elway. His pride aroused, he picked the Falcon secondary to pieces while seldom throwing to the same receiver twice in a row. The five-receiver sets he kept using against the run-oriented defense made this easy even though Sharpe injured his left knee in the first quarter and missed the rest of the game.

When Elway did use the run he made it as damaging as his passing. Throughout the game he and his runners were supported by a line that pass-blocked and run-blocked with equal ardor. On short-yardage downs he would fake a handoff to Davis, spin and give the ball to seldom-used fullback Howard Griffith, who scored twice on one-yard power plays.

Elway was careful to not try and force the ball to his Pro Bowl wide receiver Ed McCaffrey. He instead looked to the other side of the field where unheralded wideout Ron Smith played. Smith carried a wrinkled, one-dollar food stamp in his wallet to remind him of his humble roots. He had joined the club in 1994 as a practice squad target. Even after earning starting status he toiled uncomplainingly in McCaffrey's shadow...until this Super Bowl.

Shanahan had a play in his book he called "Fake 19 Handoff QB Keep Right X Post." He had not used the alignment for two months prior to Super Sunday. Correctly assuming the Falcons would not have prepared for it he watched for a suitable situation to exploit the Atlanta safeties' tendency to bite on play fakes to Davis and leave Smith with single coverage. With five minutes remaining in the first half the Falcons' Morten Anderson missed a twenty-six-yard field goal attempt, preserving a 10-3 Bronco lead. As his offense took over on its own twenty Shanahan felt the time was right.

At the snap Elway froze the safeties with the fake to Davis, set up and fired a lovely spiral toward Smith. The anonymous young pass catcher shot past distracted, thirty-five-year-old Robinson, snared the perfect throw on his forty-three and raced untouched to the clinching score. Atlanta never threatened the Denver lead after this point.

By the time the beleaguered Birds managed to get their offense in gear and started scoring points it was early in the fourth quarter and they were behind 31-6. A couple of too-late scores (one of them a spectacular ninety-four-yard kickoff return by swift Tim Dwight) kept the waning moments interesting as the Denver Broncos became the sixth team to win back-to-back Super Bowls, 34-19.

With eighteen completions on twenty-nine attempts for 336 yards and a touchdown in this last game of his career, Elway finished with the third-highest one-game yardage total of any Super Bowl quarterback, and became the oldest man ever named Super Bowl Most Valuable Player, *and* the first *unanimously* elected MVP. Even before this supernova performance his lofty status was entrenched. After arriving at the Miami hotel where he and his team bivouacked before the game Elway had signed the register "John Wayne." Room service never had to be told which suite was his.

In the next Super Bowl ancient history would be repeated.

One for the New Age

1999 St. Louis Rams versus Tennessee Titans

The L.A. Rams had only topped the league once. They were still new to the West Coast in 1951 when they upset defending champion Cleveland via a legendary seventy-three-yard rainbow from Norm van Brocklin to Tom Fears. They had not won the title since. Forsaking apathetic Los Angeles in 1997, they filled a pro football void in St. Louis and tried to start over.

Things did not straighten out too quickly, though. In 1998 they hobbled to a 3-13 regular season. Head-shaking Missourians labeled them the "Lambs" and growled "Show me!," when the team vowed better days to come. The players were humiliated, angry and very, very close. This family found a favorite son in an obscure young man whose roots were as humble as his personality.

Twenty-eight-year-old quarterback Kurt Warner placed his faith in God five years before the 1999 National Football League season. He was earning a living by sacking groceries in an all-night supermarket. His devotion and prayers were rewarded as he worked hard in the semi-pro football circuit. He managed to earn a reserve spot with the Rams, but was so unheralded that his head coach Dick Vermiel left him unprotected in the expansion draft. Fortunately for St. Louis the rest of the league was as oblivious to him as was his own franchise. Then, four months before Super Bowl XXXIV, starting signal-caller Trent Green limped onto the injured reserve list.

Warner's emergence was truly divine as he won All-Pro status while guiding his team to a 13-3 regular season record. With forty-one, he had the most productive touchdown pass-producing season in National Football Conference history, and was voted the league's Most Valuable Player. He was still gaining momentum as he and his mates winged their way to Atlanta to face another cast of carpetbaggers.

For their first thirty-eight seasons the Tennessee Titans had been the Houston Oilers. Their decades in Texas never saw them survive the playoffs, and when they packed and headed east few expected this to change. The year before the team's Super Bowl run quite a few Volunteers had their hopes exceeded when the newcomers finished 8-8.

1999 brought eruptions of joy from mobs of NFL fans in parts of the country where no such sounds had ever been heard. Highways running to Atlanta from Missouri and Tennessee were crowded the last week in January. The new millennium would arrive in the Deep South with more fireworks than anywhere else on Earth. The game was played on a rainy night in Georgia, but inside the Georgia Dome only palms were wet.

St. Louis offensive coordinator Mike Martz had been studying the pass-happy West Coast-style offense since his high school days in San Diego. At first he had a hard time selling his liberal ideas to the staid Vermiel. Then Dick examined statistics from the 1998 playoff teams. He learned that two of the four teams that had played in the conference championships spent more time passing than running in first quarters. So had six of the other eight post-season teams. Said Vermiel to Martz, "Go run your offense!" By the end of the Super Bowl the Rams had run forty-five passing downs to just thirteen on the ground.

The Titans were also 13-3, and knew how to beat the Rams—they had done it 24-21 on Halloween. Yet as the Super Bowl's first half played out, it seemed that the NFC champs had learned more from their defeat than had their rivals. All season the Tennessee pass defense had allowed an average of 231 yards per game, but behind chalkboard-ideal blocking Warner drilled completions in bunches as he amassed 277 aerial yards by *halftime.* Yet something was wrong.

On each of its first five possessions St. Louis pierced the Titan twenty-yard line, but for all this easy movement the Rams came away with just three field goals and a 9-0 halftime lead. As the second quarter ended, Warner momentarily went down with bruised ribs and millions of onlookers within and without the arena suspected Tennessee was still very much in business. After all, this team had come from behind to win all three of its playoff games.

The scene did not immediately improve for the Titans in the second half, however. With 8:24 left in the third quarter strong safety Blaine

Bishop was felled by a scary neck injury that left most of both teams kneeling on the field, praying for his well-being. Tennessee's secondary was already thin from injuries suffered in the playoffs, and sure enough rookie wide receiver Torry Holt scored the game's first touchdown three plays later on a nine-yard bullet from Warner.

Trailing 16-0, quarterback Steve McNair hurriedly found his groove. He directed a sixty-six-yard drive he ended by handing off to running back Eddie George on the one-yard line with fourteen seconds remaining in the third.

Eager to get its offense back on the field the Titan defense stomped out a feeble St. Louis possession on the next three downs. McNair again rushed his squad downfield, bulling the ball in himself from two yards out.

The score was suddenly 16-13, and the Tennessee defenders again throttled Warner's flying circus. McNair's next series reinforced his reputation for shining late in hard-fought contests. He punched deeply enough into Ram territory for kicker Al Del Greco to drill a perfect, forty-three-yard placement with 2:12 remaining. With the score even these unheralded teams of destiny were bound for a climax that was truly a religious experience.

Vermiel had already lost one Super Bowl, nineteen years earlier. At sixty-three he was now the oldest man to coach a team to this game. He had been around long enough to realize his panting, perspiring defenders needed to spend some time on the sideline. Yet his quarterback and offensive coordinator were not planning to waste any seconds.

Both men knew the Titans would be watching for short, outside pass routes designed to work the ball steadily downfield and use up as many seconds as possible. This was too obvious.

After St. Louis ran the kickoff out to its twenty-seven, Martz sent Warner a play called "999 H-Balloon." In this setup Holt lined up wide to the left. Three wideouts crouched to the line's right. Inside man Ricky Proehl ran a deep route while middle receiver Az-Zahir Hakim and outside catcher Isaac Bruce took shallower patterns. As Warner bent over center he noticed Bruce was single covered by cornerback Denard Walker. Tennessee did not have enough healthy defensive backs to adequately chaperone all the men in this receiver-glutted alignment, and Bruce is very, very good at what he does.

At the snap he galloped for his assigned spot downfield, but Warner was under a withering pass rush by defensive end Jevon Kearse. Pressured into throwing earlier than he would have liked, his heave was a couple of yards short. Skidding to a halt, Bruce reached back and snagged the ball at his own forty-three. He then voodooed every defender who reached for him as he wove a crooked path to the end zone. Just like forty-eight years earlier, the winning pass covered seventy-three yards.

After the most tumultuous two-minute warning in history, McNair arranged his players around him and directed a desperate drive that carried to the Ram twenty-six with twenty-two seconds remaining. He then faded and looked for a receiver. Ten yards behind the line of scrimmage he ripped from the clutches of defensive linemen Jay Williams and Kevin Carter before winging a perfect dart to Kevin Dyson, who was pulled down on the ten. There was time for one more play.

Hoping to lure a couple of coverage men to the wrong sector, McNair sent tight end Frank Wycheck into the end zone while Dyson tried to slip unnoticed into the center of the field and catch the ball just shy of the goal line and with no one near him. The only problem with the stratagem was that linebacker Mike Jones *did* spot the speedy receiver moving laterally as McNair cocked to throw.

Jones later said, "I couldn't see McNair throw the ball, but I could feel it." He felt much less than Dyson did. An instant after he cradled the reception at the five, Jones slammed into him and held on like a squid. Time expired with Dyson in the linebacker's grasp at the two, his arm fully extended as he tried to thrust the ball into the end zone. He could only reach the one-yard-line.

As Titan head coach Jeff Fisher whispered words of consolation to McNair, players and fans shook off their exhaustion to celebrate and mourn with equal abandon. The dramatic ending and 23-16 final score reinforced the notion that these two casts of unknowns were the most evenly matched to ever play this game.

Winning a world title is a luscious, heady blast for any sports team, but despite their glittering 1999 performance the Rams had the worst cumulative record of any NFC team over the preceding ten years. Yet as the decade expired they earned respect and silence from generations of critics who had derided them through a half-century of falling short. Their quarterback set the pace.

Warner had cracked an eleven-year-old Super Bowl record by passing for 414 yards and two touchdowns. It was his first-ever 400-yard game, and his right arm had been pretty much the whole offense. With just twenty-nine steps, no team had ever won this test with so little rushing. His offense did not turn the ball over once.

In the riotous postgame locker room Warner had his Bible in one hand and the Vince Lombardi trophy in the other when told of his selection as the game's Most Valuable Player. Although he was MVP for both the season and the Super Bowl he was not overwhelmed by his honors. When someone asked him how he felt about his accomplishments he mildly replied, "How can you be in awe of something you expect yourself to do?" His faith had led to anticipation.

Warner was not the only unsurprised Ram. Speaking of Vermeil, Carter said, "He told us from the day he got here that we were going to win. He didn't say when, but he was right."

Even if no one else on Earth had believed in them a few months earlier, the St. Louis Rams had had faith in themselves. It was all they needed as they ushered in a new millennium with a performance that rose above a worldwide storm of celebration. It was as if Someone had planned it that way.

— Nice Guys Finish Second —
2000 Baltimore Ravens versus New York Giants

When Cleveland Browns owner Art Modell moved his franchise to Baltimore in 1996 he broke millions of Ohio's hearts. Cleveland soon got another NFL team called the Browns, but Modell and his club still trailed a bunch of hard feelings. For folks in Maryland, however, Art filled an aching void.

When the Colts had forsaken Baltimore they left the fans there with nothing. No professionals. No major collegiate team. Nada. Then Model arrived with a cast he renamed the Ravens, and from him on down everyone in the organization set about giving their new rooters as much to yell about as this town had had in the dim past. At the turn of the millennium word was that the Baltimore Ravens had a defense that could stop a locomotive, and an offense that was much better than its statistics indicated. As the 2000 season waned few were willing to argue that the Ravens were stronger than they had to be.

The previous year Baltimore had staggered to an 8-8 record, so head coach Brian Billick decided to become less fixated on running his offense and become more of a general overseer of the entire team. He wisely stressed unity, which saved the season at the midway point. The evolving, not-yet-jelled offense derailed and went twenty-one straight quarters without scoring a touchdown as the club dropped to 5-4. Billick installed former Tampa Bay Buccaneer Trent Dilfer at quarterback, and the men began to gain momentum as the new signal-caller's brazen attitude and magnetic presence and performance won games and teammates. By season's end the Ravens had scored twice as many points as they had surrendered. Still, defense was the basic story.

Baltimore's undisputed on-the-field leader was linebacker Ray Lewis, who had a reputation as a man to be avoided whether or not he was in uniform. A year earlier Lewis had been involved in a barroom brawl that left two young men dead. After pleading guilty to a minor charge of obstructing justice, Lewis commenced redirecting his aggression strictly into a savage championship effort that set an example his teammates had to emulate. It worked, as Lewis was chosen NFL Defensive Player of the Year. No prideful man could share a gridiron with a comrade so blatantly willing to spill his guts on the turf if it took that to bring his side in first, without giving the same effort himself.

The Ravens were arrogant and boastful the weeks leading up to Super Bowl XXXV versus the New York Giants, even speculating about being the first SB contestant to shut out its opponent. After all, they had not lost a game since October, winning eleven straight. The Baltimores cared little about whom they offended or put off those two weeks in Florida. They figured they had earned the right to say whatever they thought, but it would take the game itself to prove how correct they were.

The Giants had some kind of set-up themselves. After pulverizing Minnesota 41-0 in the National Football Conference title game, they had many looking for a replay of the previous year's nail-chewing stage drama. Some even predicted a New York win considering how the NFC's Eastern Division always contributed heavily to Super Bowl representation and had not lost one of these games in seventeen years.

Those who expected a close game did indeed have some statistics on their side. Most of the league's best quarterbacks had not faced the Ravens that year. In the playoffs the player many considered to be the American Football Conference's best passer, Denver's Brian Griese, was on injured reserve and missed his date with Baltimore.

Like the Birds, the Giants had dramatically reversed their previous year's performance, rebounding from 7-9. They played hard but clean and classy, seldom berating their many defeated opponents or crowing over their accomplishments. With a roster largely staffed by athletes discarded by other teams they built a defense that stayed modest despite ranking fifth overall out of thirty-one teams.

Back in November the New Yorkers had just finished several dismally played games and seemed poised for collapse when head coach Jim Fassel rocked the league (and his team) by *guaranteeing* a playoff appearance. The Giants were as honest as their coach, looking better every week. They peaked in the conference championship as quarterback Kerry Collins tossed for 385 yards and five touchdowns, leading his offense to all forty-one of its points despite mercifully and humbly shutting down voluntarily early in the third quarter.

It was too impressive a turbocharge for many experts to believe it could be dominated. Most figured even the rabid Raven defense would have its paws full. "We'll show 'em," growled Billick fifteen minutes before kickoff.

The Baltimore defense showed New York, 3300 attending journalists, 71,921 paying spectators in Tampa's Raymond James Stadium, and most of the world. With 6:57 remaining in a still-scoreless first quarter second-year reserve wide receiver Brandon Stokely out of little Louisiana-Lafayette College lined up across from All-Pro cornerback Jason Sehorn. Stokely had caught just eleven passes that season, and only four in the three playoff games, so what happened next was unexpected front-page photography. He and his offense were on the Giant thirty-eight, and the play was titled "Scat-left, Double-pump." Blessed with blistering speed, Stokely clutched Dilfer's lovely throw on the ten-yard line, and then dragged an anguished Sehorn into the end zone.

Just before halftime Dilfer found wideout Qadry Ismail for a forty-four-yard gainer that set up a forty-seven-yard Matt Stover field goal. The Ravens rubbed their hands together at the 10-0 intermission lead.

Although New York could not help but remember how it trailed in both of its previous Super Bowls before coming back to win, by now Baltimore knew it owned the crown. Over the past two years the Ravens were 15-0 in games in which they scored at least ten points. It was all they ever needed. Their defense had set a league record in 2000 by permitting just 165 points over a sixteen-game schedule, and only sixteen combined to their three playoff opponents. When Baltimore's great but underrated defensive end Rob Burnett was at a restaurant the Wednesday before the game he predicted the Giants would score, "Zip, zero. Stingy with dinero," and he had history to back him up. The coming contest would be the thirty-sixth straight in which his unit would not allow a 100-yard rusher.

New York had sixteen possessions this evening. A Super Bowl-record eleven of them ended in punts, four were aborted by interceptions, and the last was foundering when the final gun sounded. While running like a hare from mad dogs in his own backfield, Collins threw his record-tying four interceptions to four separate defenders.

Quests

Ray Lewis was in the thick of this flock of Hitchcock's birds, knocking down four passes and deflecting a fifth into the hands of teammate Jamie Sharper in the second quarter. Being on probation did not seem to distract him at all as he also made five tackles on his way to becoming only the seventh defender voted Super Bowl Most Valuable Player. He was just the second linebacker (and the first in thirty years) to earn this honor.

After romping through the Minnesota defense two weeks earlier Giant wide receivers Amani Toomer and Ike Hilliard managed only five catches between them for fifty-four yards against the Ravens. After the game Hilliard, grimacing as his team doctor examined his bruised ribs, groaned to reporters, "Even though I face a great defense in practice every day, I have to tip my hat to the Ravens—especially the way I feel."

The Lewises ripped into New York from every direction. Ray hounded its offense into impotence, defensive coordinator Marvin Lewis diagramed the Great Wall from the sideline, and rookie runner Jamal Lewis galloped through what had been a prime unit itself, picking up 102 yards and a touchdown.

The game did become briefly interesting in the third quarter as cornerback Duane Sparks intercepted a hurried Collins pass and returned it forty-nine yards for a touchdown. Moments later Giant return man Ron Dixon fielded the kickoff on his own three-yard line and charged right down the middle to the end zone to shrink the Baltimore lead back to ten points. New York might have made the game into a dogfight had it not been for what happened next. Yet another Lewis, Jermaine, grabbed the latest kickoff and expertly meandered down the sideline eighty-four yards for the backbreaker. Three touchdowns within thirty-six seconds provided the rout with a sorely needed dose of excitement, but did little for the NFC cause.

Ten more points in the third quarter completed the blowout as the Ravens slew their Giants 34-7, scoring by run, pass, defense and special teams, becoming just the third wild-card playoff entry to win a Super Bowl. Burnett's forecast in the eatery had been right. He said his *defense*, not special teams, would pitch a no-hitter, and a kick return was the only way New York was able to crack the goose egg.

The run-oriented Giants were able to rush for just sixty-six steps, and 149 total yards. It was the third-lowest yardage output in SB history. Dixon's kickoff return was the sole time his team crossed midfield in the second half. Still, they had little cause to feel ashamed. *Nobody* had been able to do much all year against this super-defense that allowed just one offensive touchdown through four postseason games.

The Ravens had brought the people of Baltimore their first pro football title in thirty years, and second-year head coach Billick had no misconceptions about how. He had spent the past couple of weeks antagonizing the media, now in the postgame interviews the mood was surprisingly congenial. "For the first time in my life I feel I finally understand the game—I mean really understand it. This is the ultimate about how football is not about the star quarterback, the star running back. It's about team." He might have said *defensive* team, but was too considerate of his own offensive players.

The sages have long preached that offense sells tickets, but defense wins games. Sure enough.

In less than a year the NFL would grimly close ranks with the rest of America.

Shadows of September
2001 New England Patriots versus St. Louis Rams

New Orleans, Louisiana had the look of a massive military encampment as Super Bowl XXXVI approached. American soldiers, heads swiveling, roamed the whole city, but the center of their attention was the Louisiana Superdome. Snipers patrolled the stadium's perimeter and peered down from its roof. The airspace above the enclosed arena was off-limits to aircraft as a security-conscious White House designated the Super Bowl a "National Special Security Event."

New England Patriot fan Tricia McCarthy said before the kickoff, "It's a sign of the times. Whenever you have big crowds somewhere you have to worry about terrorism. It's pretty sad to say." Fans were encouraged to show up a full five hours before kickoff in order to have time to filter through the thick defensive perimeter.

The game was not played until February 3 because back on September 11, 2001 a band of foreign criminals had used hi-jacked jet airliners as weapons to murder thousands of innocent Americans in New York and Washington. Even the National Football League took a week off its schedule as the country picked up smoldering pieces and buried its dead. By the time the shock wore off every American was a patriot. The game was as big a surprise as the terrorist attacks. American Football Conference Eastern Division teams had lost in their last eight straight Super Bowl appearances, and the press treated the Patriots as the "other team" throughout the two-week pregame build-up.

Few took into account how the New England front office had spent the off-season signing more than a dozen free agents to modest contracts. These mens' experience, professionalism and thirst to prove themselves turned the franchise around.

When the Patriots galloped onto the field before the coin toss they eschewed the opposing St. Louis Rams' example of individual player introductions. Instead, resplendent in their red, white and blue uniforms, they pounded out of their locker room en masse to demonstrate their emphasis on teamwork. Later, as they took the field for the game's final possession, this low-paid squad of unknowns would face the greatest test of their union.

The Rams, the fans, the broadcasters and tens of millions of television viewers figured the New England offense would eat the clock and hope for the best in the first-ever Super Bowl overtime. After all, following the Bighorns' last kickoff the Patriots were pinned on their own seventeen-yard-line with just 1:21 on the clock and with no times out. To many, overtime seemed the friendliest option. New England head coach Bill Belichick, however, could not help but note how his opponents' league-leading offense, led by golden-armed quarterback Kurt Warner, had belatedly jelled in the fourth quarter. Giving this suddenly potent turbocharge the ball in overtime seemed too dangerous. Throughout the 2001 season this offense had averaged a whopping 32.6 points per game.

With just those eighty-one seconds to work with, Belichick huddled with offensive coordinator Charlie Weis. Weighing their options and the recent state of the competition they agreed. "OK, let's go for it," said Belichick.

Although surprised by the decision, twenty-four-year-old Patriot quarterback Tom Brady was unperturbed. A sixth-round draft choice in 2000 he was steady, dependable and methodical, playing with poise far beyond his years. He did not win games by being spectacular, but by making virtually no errors. As Belichick explained after the game, "With a quarterback like Brady, going for the win is not that dangerous because he's not going to make a mistake."

Fans of both teams grew wide-eyed and silent as Brady expertly used that little bit of remaining time. Apart from a couple of clock-stopping spikes, he went five-for-six in passing attempts on this drive as he worked his offense fifty-three yards before grinding to a fourth down on the St. Louis thirty. The clock read 0:07 as dependable placement specialist Adam Vinatieri trotted into place behind the ball. While the pigskin traveled those forty-eight yards the clock ran out and the scoreboard announced to an astounded America that the appropriately named Patriots had defeated the St. Louis Rams 20-17 in the biggest Super Bowl upset in over thirty years. Perhaps it should not have been so surprising—all three teams New England beat that postseason

Quests

(Oakland, Pittsburgh and St. Louis) were division champions. With fitting drama the Pats were also the first team to ever win a Super Bowl on its very last play.

Much had changed in the five months since the terrorist attacks, both for a superpower that had never before been assailed on its own soil, and for the team that eventually earned the right to represent the American Football Conference in the Big Easy. America would never again feel complacent and insulated from the worldwide peril. The New England Patriots, meanwhile, simply emerged.

That rueful September saw the Pats tumble to a 1-3 early-season record. The turnaround came grudgingly. In the year's tenth game New England lost to these very Rams and fell to 5-5. They did not lose again, and at 14-2 the Rams amassed the league's best tally.

Americans love underdogs, and in beating supremely confident St. Louis the Patriots, who had lost two previous Super Bowl appearances in New Orleans, completed an amazing, magical journey absolutely no one had seen coming. With the chant "USA" drowning the cheering in the Superdome, New England staged a seminar in colonial values of teamwork, refusing to be predictable, bucking odds, and meeting a challenge head-on.

St. Louis was led by quarterback Kurt Warner, who had thrown for thirty-six touchdowns and 4830 yards in 2001, and by running back Marshall Faulk, who led the league in scoring that year with 128 points. They were the National Football League's brightest supernovas, and their side did indeed outgain the Patriots this evening by 160 yards. This was unsurprising, for these Rams had now done three years in a row what no other team had ever managed twice straight—score over 500 points. Yet the no-name Pats won by outhitting, outcoaching and outhustling despite allowing a generous 427 total yards. On offense and defense they came through when the outcome was at stake.

What Vinatieri's right leg finished had started in the pre-season. "We play together," said cornerback Ty Law before the game. "All year we've had a lot of stuff go down that will either cause you to fold or come together. We've been faced with things that can tear up a team."

They refused to fold when a heart attack killed assistant coach Dick Rehbein during training camp. They kept their focus when one of their few standouts, wide receiver Terry Glenn, was repeatedly suspended because of his disruptive behavior. Nor did they crumble upon losing three of their first four games and seemed headed for a repeat of the previous year's 5-11 finish. By September's end $103 million quarterback Drew Bledsoe was out with a collapsed lung inflicted by the New York Jets. Not to worry. "Whenever we've had out backs to the wall we've responded," said Brady.

Following Bledsoe's injury Brady quarterbacked so well the rest of the season that he made the Pro Bowl, led the team to a divisional title and a gutsy, snowy first-round playoff victory over Oakland. When Brady twisted his ankle midway through the conference championship game with Pittsburgh, Bledsoe came out of the bullpen and directed a 27-17 upset decision. Yet when Brady's ankle healed and Belichick named him the Super Bowl starter, Bledsoe uttered not one word of protest or resentment. As a team New England had truly mastered the concept of unselfish unity. Even though it was a season seared by national tragedy, and they wear red, white and blue, and are called the Patriots, this bunch never wanted to be called a team of destiny. It just turned out that way.

Coach Belichick and his players were perfect for each other. In previous coaching jobs in New York and Cleveland, Belichick had alienated his players by pushing them too hard in practice sessions. No more. Said linebacker Ted Johnson after the game. "Coach Belichick is a mastermind." His new firm but unpretentious style was ideal in guiding his team through a riotous week that was a new experience for them, but not for the Rams. As game time loomed the Patriots stayed focused, undistracted and eager.

Two days before the kickoff Belichick gathered his players to watch a crucial series of films of earlier St. Louis games. The Rams' high-risk passing offense often surrendered turnovers (forty-four in 2001,) but even more often it scored early. The Ram defense was also in the turnover business, forcing bushels of them. Watching these films the Pats saw Ram opponents repeatedly commit turnovers the Bighorns used to build early leads they never relinquished. This included their own 24-17 loss in Foxboro on November 18. The pattern was clear: with their high-speed, league-leading offense St. Louis scored points so fast that their foes could rarely overcome these early deficits. As his men listened closely, Belichick told them, "If you can get through those first few minutes you've got a fighting chance."

On Super Sunday New England used a runner named Antowain Smith, whom the Buffalo Bills had discarded, to keep the Ram defense off-balance. St. Louis managed to overlook how Smith had gained 1157 yards in the regular season. He piled up ninety-two yards on just eighteen carries through the disbelieving NFC champs.

On defense the Patriots shut down Warner's dread aerial attack by packing the secondary with as many as seven defensive backs, and keeping him from adjusting by constantly shifting defensive alignments. While his receivers were being smothered by aggressive multiple coverage, Warner was getting hit more than he was used to getting hit as the fired-up New England pass rushers disrupted his timing. Careful to not play the same kind of game they had in their earlier loss to this bunch, the Pats blitzed infrequently but effectively. This unexpected strategy slowed the Rams' famously speedy offense. Warner was so befuddled by this unpredictable, patternless defense that he held the ball longer than usual, giving rushers more time to reach him.

Belichick later said blitzing the Rams was risky because, "Kurt Warner's throwing off those three-step drops. He gets those racehorses coming out untouched, they catch the ball and they're off and running." In this game, however, Warner was playing with a sore right thumb that gave him problems with his accuracy. Furthermore, his offensive line did not have one of its better days. It blocked consistently poorly for the run, and was erratic with its pass blocking.

New England blended a zone defense with man coverage, both anchored in the aggressive play of cornerbacks Law and Otis Smith. By shuffling players in and out of the game and from position to position, Belichick made it yet more difficult for St. Louis to adjust. Sure enough, the Rams fell to an ancestral shortcoming that had bedeviled them in 1970s post-seasons—turnovers in big games.

After the victory Smith explained, "We call it re-routing. Knock them out of their pattern. Get them out of sync with Warner." The swarming, snapping defensive backs grabbed fumbles and interceptions throughout the game, scoring a touchdown themselves and setting up ten points with turnovers. It was nothing new—three of the six touchdowns the Patriots had scored in the playoffs were made by the defense.

Late in the second quarter St. Louis tried to force New England out of its pass-oriented defense by running Marshall Faulk on four straight downs for thirty yards, but on third down Warner threw an off-target pass that Smith intercepted. This set up a field goal and 17-3 Patriot halftime lead. For the first time all year the Rams were shut out of the end zone throughout a first half.

Another problem solved by Belichick and his gifted young secondary coach Eric Mangini was how to stop Faulk. Mangini later said, "We took turns chipping on him, never giving him a clean release." Also an excellent receiver, Faulk caught just four passes for fifty-four yards and no scores.

The New England strategy started paying off on the scoreboard late in the first half. With St. Louis leading 3-0 with 8:49 left in the second quarter Patriot linebacker Mike Vrable confused the Rams by lining up at left end. Nobody had been assigned to block Vrable at this position, and nobody blocked him. He charged in untouched and hit Warner as he threw. Law intercepted the wobbly pass and returned it forty-seven yards for a touchdown.

Just before intermission the Pats exploited a fumble by wide receiver Ricky Proehl on the St. Louis forty. Brady ended the drive with a lovely eight-yard scoring toss to former Cleveland Brown David Patten for the two-touchdown halftime edge.

The drawback with Belichick's strategy was that all the hustling and hitting by the New England defenders left them exhausted before the game ended, "Actually drained. On the ropes," said Law. Late in the fourth quarter Warner piled up much of his 345 passing yards on this worn-out defense, tying the game 17-17. He scored on a quarterback sneak to end a drive during which weary backs Law and Lawyer Milloy each dropped easy interceptions in their end zone. Warner's two-yard sneak with 9:31 remaining was his first rushing touchdown of the year and narrowed the score to 17-10. After forcing a punt the Rams took over on their own forty-five. Twenty-one seconds later they tied the game on Warner's twenty-six-yard pass to Proehl.

Brady used the last 1:21 of regulation to accumulate the bulk of his own 145 passing yards. He did not even reach the 100-yard mark until this final possession. With his primaries covered he completed three dump-off passes to scatback J.R. Redmond. With his third catch Redmond picked up a priceless first down and stopped the clock by dragging a defender past the marker and out of bounds. Weis later remarked, "Had either of those things not happened we would have

Quests

probably killed the clock." Glancing over at his exhausted defense Brady knew he could not let that happen.

The possession leading to the winning kick was the only Patriot scoring drive of the game that did not follow a St. Louis turnover. After dodging a first-down blitz Brady drilled wideout Troy Brown through a gap in the Rams' zone defense. The Pro Bowl pass catcher ripped all the way to the St. Louis thirty-six. Brady was as cool as the chilled champagne in his locker room as he bent over center for the next-to-last time that season. He found tight end Jermaine Wiggins for six yards, lined up again and stopped the clock by spiking the ball with seven seconds remaining.

Bewhiskered Vinatieri loped onto the field in what had become a familiar situation for him. Four times that year he had won games with last-second field goals. A few seconds later he made it five, this one by a score of 20-17 as his tired defensive teammates (and millions of fans) screamed in delighted relief. These fourteen-point underdogs were the first team all season to hold the Rams under twenty points.

The bedlam of postgame was heavy with the spirit of '76. This was one of the biggest upsets since the American Revolution. It was also the third straight Super Bowl won by a first-time champ.

The aftermath was different from its thirty-five predecessors. Even the losers found themselves smiling and chanting "USA" amid a blizzard of red, white and blue streamers.

Twenty-four-year-old Brady was not only voted Most Valuable Player, but was the youngest quarterback ever to win this game. The closing drive did it for him. Perhaps he should have been named first among equals. He had simply, flawlessly steered his offense with a steady hand and taken advantage of opportunities presented by his defense, special teams and the opposition. He made a special day possible in a special way. His franchise owner Robert Craft said, "The people of New England have been waiting forty-two years for this day." Brady's postgame attitude topped off his classy performance as he told the press, "This whole team, as far as I'm concerned, is MVP."

The Pats had indeed put on a clinic in classic teamwork throughout the contest, and then won as a team versus the league's finest collection of individual superstars. Said Milloy, "We beat all the odds. No one can ever take that away from us."

It was a game their country needed—the inspiration was obvious. Like the fifty states, the New England Patriots are strictly a team, and this is the best way in the world to win...whether against Rams or terrorists.

The following season another traditional underdog would howl.

— Clash of Corsairs —
2002 Tampa Bay Buccaneers versus Oakland Raiders

Tampa Bay Buccaneer head coach John Gruden figured this day would come, but even he could not foresee how soon. The first Super Bowl he recalled watching on television was number four in January 1970. He was six years old. Thirty-three years later he became the youngest man ever to guide a team to the mastery as his bay brigands gutted the venerable winning tradition of the Oakland Raiders in Super Bowl XXXVII. It fit in several ways.

One year earlier Gruden had been head coach of these very Raiders, who were now favored to beat him in this culminating contest of the Year of Our Lord 2002. In the four seasons he coached the Raiders he had raised them from a 4-12 laughingstock to a powerhouse. Gruden's acumen caught the eyes of Buccaneer owner Malcolm Glazer, who set out to purchase the young man's services. Glazer never wavered in his dedication to this end, finally paying eight million dollars, two first-round draft selections, two second-round picks and agreeing to a condition that no Oakland assistant coaches would accompany Gruden to Florida. Until January most believed the Raiders got the best of the deal, but with a rare ability to both coach and motivate brilliantly, Gruden was just what Tampa Bay needed to escape an unwanted tradition.

Joining the league as an expansion franchise in 1976 the Bucs made history by going 0-14 that first year, losing a total of twenty-six straight games before finally outscoring an opponent. The players wore pale orange jerseys with light-colored helmets that made many fans think they looked like animated candy corn. After revamping their wardrobe the Buccaneers started rebuilding in other areas. Things did not get better quickly—the years dragged by slowly. In 1986 the league's top draft choice refused to play for Tampa Bay, opting for baseball instead. From 1983 through 1996 the Bucs were the NFL's least successful franchise, having no winning seasons. They lost ten or more games in thirteen of those fourteen years. The team could not be saved even by a procession of surprisingly skilled players and coaches. It remained obscure and ended most seasons as a doormat. Yet by the end of the millennium Tampa Bay had assembled a collection of talent (particularly on defense) that was capable of great things. Gruden turned out to be the sole missing element. His accomplishments attracted so much attention in '02 that he almost became a distraction to his own team in the days prior to the Super Bowl.

An offensive-minded teacher himself, Gruden was wise enough to not tinker with an already-splendid defense. In fact the Buccaneers had the league's number-one-ranked defensive unit, which was assisted by an almost injury-free season. Hale and heroic, this squad was the first since the 1985 Chicago Bears to lead the NFL both in total defense and in fewest points allowed.

For the first time ever the NFL's number one defense would face a year's number one offense in a Super Bowl, and the teams assembled in San Diego's Qualcomm Stadium. The Raiders' top-seeded turbocharge's collision with the Bucs' Great Wall made most of the 67,603 bleacher-borne fans and 100 million television viewers anticipate the coming contest would be the classic case of irresistible force meeting immovable object, however no low-scoring dogfight was in store. It should not have been a surprise. Even the most explosive offenses have a history of coming unglued in Super Bowls against defenses that do not let them throw the ball.

With fifteen players over thirty, and six key starters aged thirty-five or older, Oakland was hoping for one last hurrah to close out some magnificent careers. The team had shown great poise by keeping its focus despite losing four straight games at mid-season. Then they got distracted just before the Super Bowl when head coach Bill Callahan suspended Pro Bowl center Barret Robbins for truancy. It turned out to be a grave loss as the year's Most Valuable Player, thirty-seven-year-old journeyman quarterback Rich Gannon, was buried by the Tampa Bay pass rush. Gannon had thrown but ten interceptions in 418 regular season attempts, but on Super Sunday he was sacked five times and held to just seventy-two passing yards through the game's first forty minutes as Buc defensive backs kept running back intercepts for touchdowns.

It was Gruden's style of football. As wide receiver Keyshawn Johnson explained *before* the game, "Jon gave us new energy—a charge."

The evening started out like a low-scoring shoving match as the defenses dominated both nervous offenses in the first quarter. Early in the second period the Buccaneers led 6-3. Gannon took a snap just shy of midfield and looked deep toward Hall of Fame-bound wide receiver Jerry Rice. When Gannon pumped his throwing arm without releasing the ball the Tampa Bay defensive backs screamed, "SLUGGO SEAM!" This was the Raiders' most productive big play maneuver. It had helped Gannon set an NFL-record by tossing ten 300-yard passing games that season. Ordinarily, after the fake to Rice sent the defensive backs scurrying in the wrong direction, Gannon would turn and hurl the ball long to wideout Jerry Porter on the other side of the field, but this defense knew what to expect. As the quarterback turned his head to the right, Buc free safety Dexter Jackson reacted, cutting in front of Porter, picking off the pass and returning it twenty-five yards to set up the game's first touchdown.

Tampa Bay had intercepted a league-high thirty-one passes that year. It was Jackson's second theft of this game, and along with his overall flawless performance would make him only the eighth defensive player ever voted Super Bowl Most Valuable Player. His mates followed suit as they snatched off three more Gannon aerials and returned them for touchdowns. The hapless QB was confused by an alternating pass coverage that used cornerback Ronde Barber like a weakside linebacker, making it appear there was room for receivers to maneuver when there was not. By halftime the feared Oakland offense had just sixty-two total yards, while the Buccaneer offense, ranked twenty-four out of thirty-one teams that year, had picked up 198 yards.

Gruden was coaching against the very offense he had directed a few months earlier, and he knew its every nuance. Also his defensive coordinator Monte Kiffen directed his men flawlessly as they shut down an attack that had been averaging 390 yards and twenty-eight points per game, and 5.8 yards per play. Kiffen moved Pro Bowl tackle Warren Sapp up and down the line, exploiting his speed versus the Raiders' ponderous offensive linemen. Averaging 318 pounds per man, these players were not up to chasing *and* blocking the cat-quick and panther-strong Sapp. Oakland's nineteen total yards on the ground were the third-lowest team rushing output in the history of the Super Series.

Tampa Bay was almost as successful on offense, maintaining ideal balance with thirty-three passing plays to thirty-two rushes. The previous spring the team had agreed to pay former Cardinal Michael Pittman $8.75 million to carry the ball. His regular season performance kept him out of the public eye and embarrassed his general manager as he averaged just forty-three steps per game. After being tormented all year by a sore ankle he decided this last game was his best chance for redemption, and he grabbed the opportunity like a handoff. Playing in his home town he ground out 124 yards on twenty-nine carries, helping his side maintain possession for 37:14 of the game's sixty minutes. At the final gun the maligned Buc offense had collected 365 total yards and three touchdowns. Pittman's rushing output was just the second time all season a Tampa Bay runner had a 100-yard day.

During the week leading up to the game Gruden himself played quarterback in drills. Being so intimate with the foe's attack, he ran his practice offense in a style identical to what his men would face. Despite questionable passing ability (wide receiver Reggie Barlow said some of his coach's throws "...looked like kickoffs") he showed his players almost exactly what to expect, even using Raider terminology. In the game Buc defenders were amazed to hear Gannon, when calling audibles, use the same words and phrases Gruden had during practices.

Even though Tampa Bay quarterback Brad Johnson described himself as "...slow and weak-armed" he led the National Football Conference in passer rating with 92.9. He had thrown twenty-two touchdown passes that year against just six interceptions. Although he got off to a shaky start in *this* game, he found his groove and finished with eighteen completions in thirty-four attempts for 215 yards and two touchdowns. He was spared disaster in the first quarter when he slung an off-target pass that hit Oakland safety Rod Woodson in the middle of his chest. There was nothing but well-manicured grass between Woodson and the end zone, and a touchdown would have given the Raiders a 10-3 lead. He dropped the ball.

The Buccaneers mashed Oakland hopes for a comeback on the first possession of the second half when they drove eighty-nine yards on fourteen plays. The drive was sustained by clutch catches by wide receiver Joe Jurevicius, and consumed almost eight minutes en route to the score that gave Tampa Bay a cozy 27-3 lead.

Trailing 34-3 in the third quarter Oakland tried to fight back, scoring on a blocked punt and two Gannon touchdown passes, but failing on three straight two-point conversion attempts. With their lead cut to thirteen points the NFC representatives tightened up on their desperate foes. Predictably, the defense slammed the door.

Forced by the score to take to the air, the Raiders ran just one rushing play the entire second half. It came when Gannon had to scramble away from the pass rush. Tampa Bay strong safety John Lynch later said, "We were very opportunistic, especially in the second half when we knew they weren't going to run, and we could concentrate on stopping the pass."

In the fourth quarter All-Pro linebacker Derrick Brooks intercepted a Gannon pass and ran it forty-four yards for a touchdown. Moments later Buc nickleback Dwight Smith grabbed another errant aerial at midfield and ran it back all the way for the game's final score. For the last ten yards Gruden joyfully galloped along behind him into the end zone. As they crossed the goal line there were only two seconds remaining on the clock—just enough time for the extra point that mercifully finished the rout 48-21.

During a postgame that was madcap even by Super Bowl standards, Gruden exclaimed, "It was a grind of a year, but I'll tell you what—it's been a blast. I'm not philosophical or anything, but this has deep meaning for me!" Of course it did. Any time a franchise that spent so many years in the cellar finally gets to look down from the heights the view is even sweeter than usual.

En route to his victor's television interview this super coach was himself intercepted—by his mother. As she wrapped him in her delighted embrace he could not hear her words because of his fans' chorus of, "WE LOVE YOU, JOHN!," but she was probably saying the same thing anyway.

North and South
2003 New England Patriots versus Carolina Panthers

It was thirty years since the National Football League had allowed Houston to host the Super Bowl. In the distant past the city was the site of Super Bowl VIII, in which the Miami Dolphins dumped the Minnesota Vikings in a 24-7 groaner that was more one-sided than the score. Perhaps hoping for more television-ratings-grabbing drama the league shied away from the Great State for three decades, but now Texas had a lovely new football arena called Reliant Stadium that convinced the paladins of professional football to send to Houston a North versus South matchup that was classic Americana.

With the political and military situation again sizzling in the Middle East the arena was infested with security cameras, guards and snipers, but Super Bowl XXXVIII would not be affected by global unrest. It turned into a football fan's nirvana—as intense, dramatic and entertaining as the town's long-ago predecessor had not been. Ticket prices reflected this. Tickets to the 1974 game had cost $15.00, but admission to the 2004 title test was $600.00.

New England Patriot signal-caller Tom Brady modestly described himself as the "...slowest quarterback in the league," but after shredding the Carolina Panthers' secondary during two spectacular fourth quarter scoring drives he was voted Super Bowl Most Valuable Player for a second time. Only three other men had ever managed this feat before him. Finishing the 2003 campaign with this novel contest that alternated between defensive and offensive domination, Brady completed thirty-one of forty-eight attempts for 354 yards and three touchdowns, breaking more southern hearts than had General Grant.

The Super Bowl-experienced Pats were favored despite spectacular improvement by Carolina over the past three years as they rose from 1-15 in '01 to 7-9 in '02 to 11-5 in '03, and winning the National Football

Conference's new Southern Division. They were fabulous in the clutch, winning four overtime games this season.

Panther quarterback Jake Delhomme was only the second undrafted QB to ever start a Super Bowl, and in this game he earned his status by completing sixteen of thirty-three attempts for 323 yards and three touchdowns. The main quarterbacking difference was Delhomme's being sacked three times while Brady never tasted turf.

The offenses and defenses took turns pushing each other around all day. Although the New Englanders had opened their previous five games with touchdown drives, on this evening the defenses shooed both attacks away from the end zones for the first twenty-seven minutes of play as the game went scoreless longer than any previous Super Bowl. Another factor that delayed scoring was constantly flying penalty flags as officials called twenty infractions, not counting those that were declined.

Both sides suddenly found their groove three minutes before halftime, ripping off twenty-four points in that brief span. After a streaker pranced onto the field during intermission to delay the start of the second half the defenses again closed in, choking off any scoring in the third period. The turbocharges exploded anew in the final quarter, ringing up thirty-seven points.

For the AFC champion Patriots the year was ending as unbelievably as the regular season had been for this remarkable team. Despite Brady being the franchise player, New England was defensively oriented. The Super Bowl was the Pats' fifteenth straight victory despite starters having missed a league-high eighty-seven cumulative games because of injuries. Unheralded young men like linebackers Mike Vrabel, Willie McGinest and safety Rodney Harrison came to the rescue.

Patriot head coach Bill Belichick emphasized the importance of each member of the lineup. "You can rattle off every name on the roster and find someone making a contribution. We finished with two backup safeties. That's the way it's been all year for us." Even Harrison followed the trend as he suffered a broken arm late in the Super Bowl.

Along with being a master defensive tactician, talent scout and expert at game preparation, Belichick was a whiz at motivating. During a team meeting the night before the game he held his players spellbound with his oratory, then brandished the Lombardi Trophy they had won two years earlier and declared, "Only thirty-seven teams can say they've owned this. You guys can be the thirty-eighth." His men believed him.

So meticulous was this head coach in preparing for Super Sunday that after his linebacker Mike Chatham flattened the halftime streaker he answered postgame reporters who asked him if he had been surprised by the flasher's appearance, "I play for Bill Belichick. You don't think I've watched film on that guy all week? I'd seen everything there is to see."

Still, with such opposition nothing would come easily. Carolina had reached this big game by defeating heavily favored opponents, upsetting the Philadelphia Eagles and St. Louis Rams in the playoffs. During the season they shocked the defending Super Bowl champion Tampa Bay Buccaneers. The Panthers were at their best late in games, winning eight times that year on final possessions. They used their hard-hitting defense and bruising ground game to wear down opponents over three quarters, then counted on Delhomme to win with sparkling fourth period performances versus worn-out defenses.

In this their first Super Bowl the Panthers fought like their namesakes. Following New England's first score, Delhomme guided Carolina on a ninety-five-yard scoring drive (tied for second-longest in this game's history) that ended with a thirty-nine-yard touchdown pass to Steve Smith for a 7-7 tie. It was the first time all year anyone had managed a touchdown play of thirty or more yards against this Patriot defense. Panther kicker John Kasay booted a Super Bowl-record fifty-yard field goal to close the first half with his team trailing 14-10.

Behind 21-10 early in the fourth quarter Delhomme directed a six-play, eighty-one-yard drive that running back DeShaun Foster finished with a thirty-three-yard sprint down the left sideline. It cut the difference to 21-16 after a failed two-point conversion attempt.

One of the few problems with Brady's offense that season was that it had had trouble scoring touchdowns from inside the red zone. Today it scored TDs on its first three penetrations of the Carolina twenty. With a five-point advantage Brady was in a position to salt the game away as he drove his squad to the Carolina nine, where he made a rare error. He lobbed a soft, risky pass into the end zone, and cornerback Reggie Howard intercepted it with 7:38 left in the game.

Just three downs later Delhomme uncorked the prettiest pass of the afternoon. Wide receiver Muhsin Muhammad picked off the perfect spiral at his thirty-three and flew into the end zone for a Super Bowl-record eighty-five-yard scoring play. Muhammad was a major reason for his quarterback's gaudy statistics as he stretched just four catches out to 140 yards and a touchdown.

After failing on another two-point conversion attempt Carolina, significantly, led by only 22-21. It was their only lead of the day, and fleeting. New England would withstand Delhomme's magnificent fourth quarter performance.

After pushing his offense to the Carolina one-yard line Brady executed a remarkable play sent in by offensive coordinator Charlie Weis. Vrabel checked into the game at tight end. This linebacking slugger already had two sacks and had jarred a fumble loose from Delhomme. Now he would shine from the other side of the line. The play was called "136 X Cross Z Flag." After faking a handoff Brady saw Vrabel cutting across the middle, scarcely noticed by his brother defenders in different-colored jerseys, and flipped the ball to him in the end zone. A beaming Vrabel later recounted how he gripped the pigskin "...like it was my third child." Running back Kevin Faulk powered up the middle for a two-point conversion and momentary 29-22 Patriot lead.

Delhomme moved his offense eighty yards in the next seven plays. From the twelve he drilled wideout Ricky Proehl for the tying score with 1:08 remaining. Yet Brady was 26-4 as a starter in games played in November or later. Despite facing one of the fiercest pass rushing front fours in the league the New England offensive line was unbreachable, and protected Brady like a newborn. He was not sacked in this game or at all during the '03 post-season, so the finale was no surprise to this twenty-six-year-old passing sensation.

Following the tying score Kasay hooked the kickoff out of bounds at the Patriot forty, giving Brady and his bunch optimum field position from which to start their pivotal drive. He passed his team to the Carolina twenty-three-yard line with four seconds left in regulation. Placekicker Adam Vinatieri jogged onto the field.

Often called the finest clutch kicker of his day, Vinatieri was not overconfident as he lined up for the monumental placement. Earlier in the game he had shocked millions by missing a mere thirty-one-yard attempt. His next try was blocked. Because of a pregame threat of rain Reliant Stadium's retractable roof was closed. Vinatieri had never in his career missed a field goal attempt in an enclosed stadium except for here in Reliant, where he had missed four over the course of his career... so far. He was grim and determined. At halftime he had changed into a different left shoe, one with longer cleats to give a firmer hold for his plant foot. His follow-through was textbook and to his endless relief, "I looked up and it was going down the middle."

The 32-29 decision broke southern hearts and earned the New England Patriots $68,000.00 apiece in winners' bonus money. Meanwhile Delhomme summed up his team's almost-Cinderella season, "It's been a great ride, but it's over." Believing his squad had not lost, but simply run out of time, Carolina head coach John Fox remarked, "I am very, very proud of our football team. New England just got the ball last."

After waiting four decades for their first title, the Pats had earned two in three years. Counting playoff games and Super Bowls their record over that period was 40-14.

With his tally now at 6-0 Brady had never lost a post-season game. As he cuddled with movie starlet girlfriend Bridget Moynahan in the postgame uproar, other franchises began to worry about this posse of young stallions.

Three by Three
2004 New England Patriots versus Philadelphia Eagles

For a quarter century the sages of professional football had preached with the greatest of confidence that the era of the superteam was over. The National Football League had expanded into too many franchises, and the pool of top college talent was now spread too thinly for one team to dominate repeatedly. Yet there were always the annoying exceptions. In the 1980s the San Francisco 49ers held sway. The 1990s belonged mainly to the Dallas Cowboys. Now that a new millennium had dawned the New England Patriots stepped forward to embarrass the experts.

The Patriots did not win their Super Bowls by wide margins. Their titles after the 2001, 2003 and 2004 seasons came by a combined total of just nine points. They never beat the same team twice, so no one could accuse them of having figured out one squad's weaknesses to exploit year after year. They did not win via the heroics of one or two superstars, but were the quintessential *team*. In the Indianapolis Colts and Pittsburgh Steelers the Pats had defeated two marvelous teams in the playoffs. This Sunday would see them win their ninth straight post-season game, equaling the record of coach Vince Lombardi's legendary Packers. Following their latest Super Sabbath triumph the Patriots' eleven-year linebacker Willie McGinest explained his franchise's religious dedication to unselfish cooperation: "You might not call them stars, but they just went out and embarrassed people in the biggest game of their lives, so why wouldn't they be stars? It doesn't matter if we won by three or 103."

As the Patriots and NFC Champion Philadelphia Eagles assembled in Jacksonville, Florida's Alltel Stadium the 78,125 fans and eighty million-plus television viewers sensed they were in for another of the Pats' typical title tests—one heavy with rock-gut drama. Super Bowl XXXIX would be yet another of New England's nail-chewing grid productions. They would win it all for the third time in four years, but even now respect was elusive.

Patriot head coach Bill Belichick came to Florida angrily clutching a copy of an e-mail sent by someone in the Eagles' front office to an employee of the World Series champion Boston Red Sox, asking for advice on how to organize and arrange a victory parade. When Belichick read this missive to the team Sunday morning his men bristled like tomcats in a bag. Yet they relied on much more than their bruised egos to win this game.

Belichick and his defensive coordinator Romeo Crennel were worried about Philadelphia's mobile quarterback Donovan McNabb's scrambling. They replaced their standard 3-4 defense with a 4-3 alignment in which McGinest moved from linebacker to pass-rushing defensive end. With four down linemen instead of the usual three it would be easier to enclose Donovan in a semi-circle of rushers, making it harder for him to run or to throw to the inside. Trying to master this unfamiliar new arrangement in the last few days before the game was a trial, but the New England defenders figured it out sufficiently to make it work.

Coming into the game with thirty-one touchdown passes for the season, and just eight interceptions McNabb was the first Super Bowl quarterback to have thrown for over thirty scores and less than ten intercepts. Although in this contest he managed to complete thirty of fifty-one passes for 357 yards and three touchdowns, he was also intercepted three times and sacked four times. He could not run the ball, either. He carried it just once and was dropped for no gain. This opportunistic defense accomplished just enough to win. It would not come easily, though. With 10:02 to play in the second quarter McNabb flipped a six-yard scoring pass to tight end L.J. Smith. It was only the second time in their past twenty-seven games that the Pats had not scored first.

Also, the Philly defense started the game as if it had been reading the *Patriot's* mail. After shutting down running back Corey Dillon, quarterback Tom Brady and his stable of thoroughbred receivers through the first quarter, the Eagle defenders were making their side's 7-0 lead look promising. By blitzing Brady early in the game Philadelphia knocked his offense off-balance, but early in the second period New England offensive coordinator Charlie Weis got a great idea.

Pat tight end Christian Fauria later described how, "We were playing so tight. We were worrying about their blitz. We couldn't figure out who to block." By this point New England had had four possessions, picked up just thirty-seven total yards, committed two penalties, converted no third downs, and Brady had been sacked once. On their fifth possession they started at their own thirteen-yard line. Weis shocked both teams by sending four wide receivers onto the field. It was an alignment rarely seen in an offense so deep in its own territory. In yet more unorthodoxy, the next two plays Weis called were screen passes out of this deep-pass formation.

The Eagle defense was rocked by these totally unexpected plays, and warily re-assigned the men who had been blitzing to instead guard receivers. By halftime the Patriots had tied the score 7-7, and came out for the second half with renewed confidence. On their next four possessions they scored two more touchdowns and a field goal. High-speed wide receiver Deion Branch became the game's Most Valuable Player by gathering in a Super Bowl record-tying eleven completions while Philly's young cornerbacks could not keep up with him. When he was not spearing Branch, Brady kept sending Dillon and Kevin Faulk up the middle on surprise running plays out of the receiver-loaded sets. Fauria later gave the credit where it was due: "Give Charlie two weeks to prepare and he'll kill people."

After tying the game just before halftime on his four-yard pass to wide receiver David Givens, Brady wasted no time in the second half, driving to the Philadelphia two-yard line and drilling an end zone shot to two-way linebacker Mike Vrabel. By this time nobody was surprised at Vrabel's moonlighting. It was his fifth career reception, and every one had been for a touchdown. Yet the Birds were not grounded.

There were 3:39 remaining in the third quarter when McNabb slung a ten-yard touchdown pass to running back Brian Westbrook to make this the first Super Bowl to have a tied score after three quarters. The numerically superior Eagle fans erupted in a blast of joyful noise that might have fazed some teams, but by then the Patriots were familiar with Super Bowl crowds, and scarcely noticed the deafening sea of green.

Made even more resolute than usual by the death of his beloved, ninety-four-year-old grandmother Margaret days before the game, Brady set his jaw on the next drive and went four for four while leading his offense sixty-six yards. He is brilliant at throwing touchdown passes from inside his opponents' ten-yard lines, so the Eagles were surprised yet again when he *handed* the ball to Dillon, who ran it into the end zone from two yards out.

After his defense forced a punt Brady again drove his teammates downfield, setting up kicker Adam Vinatieri's clinching, twenty-two-yard field goal by whipping a nineteen-yard completion to Branch. Ahead 24-14 with the fourth quarter half over, New England found it was still in a fight.

McNabb passed his unit to the Pats' thirty-six-yard line on a drive he desperately needed to end with a touchdown, but on the next play he made the biggest mistake of the game. Aiming for the end zone he badly underthrew Smith, and Tedy Bruschi intercepted on his own eight. The fourth quarter was half over.

Eagle wide receiver Terrell Owens was not supposed to be a factor. It had only been six and one-half weeks since he had had surgery on his right ankle. He had a metal plate and two screws in his ankle, but the Patriot defenders could not keep him from catching passes. Running like a deer he picked off six of McNabb's throws, gaining 122 yards. Still, time was running out.

Philadelphia head coach Andy Reid confused millions by not installing a time-saving no-huddle offense with only 5:40 remaining in the game and his side trailing by ten. McNabb hit wideout Greg Lewis with a thirty-yard touchdown pass at the end of a seventy-nine-yard drive to cut the Patriot lead to three, but by then there was only a paltry 1:48 on the clock.

When Eagle kicker David Akers nudged an onside kick downfield Fauria eagerly flopped onto it. Intent only on killing the clock, Brady ran three time-consuming running plays to use up all but forty-six seconds. New England punter Josh Miller thumped a towering kick that pinned McNabb and his offense on their own four, and moments later strong safety Rodney Harrison intercepted the last pass of the game, silencing tens of thousands of Philadelphia rooters. The Pats had won their twenty-ninth game out of the last thirty-three they had played.

The twenty-seven-year-old Brady became the youngest quarterback ever to win three Super Bowls. Passing for 236 yards and two touchdowns in this game he ran his total to 9-0 in playoff games—another record.

It was a giddy accomplishment for someone who had been the 199th player taken in the 2000 college draft.

The Patriot minority made up the difference as it exploded into a red-white-blue postgame celebration that was bittersweet as both Weis and Crennel took leave of their much-loved players. Weis was taking over as head coach of the Notre Dame Fighting Irish, and Crennel would be head-coaching the Cleveland Browns the following season. Yet as Belichick and his eighty-six-year-old father Steve shivered under a cascade of iced Gatorade they could not shake off the whirlwind of joy that was centered on them. At 10-1, Belichick's post-season record was the best in history. Weis summed it up with his parting words, "You can be the richest man in the world and not be able to buy moments like this."

— On the Road...Together —
2005 Pittsburgh Steelers versus Seattle Seahawks

In thirty-nine years of Super Bowls no team had ever won the Vince Lombardi trophy exclusively as a road team. Those vanishingly rare squads who made it to the championship contest after winning their two or three playoff games on the road had always lost on Super Sunday. The 2005 Pittsburgh Steelers stumbled and fumbled their way through most of the regular season, dropping the year's twelfth game to the Cincinnati Bengals and falling to 7-5. It was the third straight game they had lost. Fourteen-year head coach Bill Cowher had started the year already fed up with playoff losses, and followed up this uninspired outing with a surprise classroom assignment for his men.

Issuing them grade sheets he had them repeatedly watch films of the Cincinnati game, evaluate their individual performances, then grade themselves on how well they played in their home loss to the Bengals. He later said, "The most important point I wanted to make was that if each guy did just a little bit more and was accountable for his actions we could turn this thing around—together."

The self-evaluating and self-critiquing worked. By repeatedly watching the film Cowher's men sniffed out and corrected numerous of their own faults and bad habits they had been unaware of previously. Thirty-three-year-old running back Jerome "The Bus" Bettis captured the essence of this unorthodox coaching success strategy. "It drove home the message. Before you start to point fingers you've got to look at yourself first." Each Steeler took the responsibility of improving his own performance in the confidence that all his teammates were doing the same thing. Their late-season turnaround was magical as the players unanimously decided to win a title both for the Bus and for Cowher, who was 14th on the league's all-time head coaching win total, but had no champion's ring.

Sweeping its last four regular season opponents Pittsburgh slipped into the playoffs as a sixth-seed (*last* seed) wildcard entry when Dallas pulled out a final-seconds victory over Kansas City on December 11. Ripping off postseason wins in Cincinnati, Indianapolis and Denver the Steelers were careful to keep wearing their "lucky" white road jerseys when they arrived in Detroit for Super Bowl XL even though they were designated the game's home team.

Many of the players on Ford Field that day had not even been born the last time the Steelmen won the mastery, and that 1970s dynasty that sent nineteen players to the NFL Hall of Fame was long dead. Cowher gave no thought to the glories of the golden past, when Pittsburgh had won four Super Bowls in six seasons. Ten years earlier he had made it this far and lost. Now he brought a new cast to the brink, and was still looking upward.

Standing between the Pennsylvanians and their dream were the Seattle Seahawks. This franchise had joined the league as an expansion team back in 1976. After playing their first season in the National Football Conference they switched to the American Football Conference and played many, many years without ringing up much memorable history. Secluded in the faraway Pacific Northwest they had no close neighbors, and were generally thought of as an obscure opponent who rarely bothered anybody and watched the playoffs on television. When the National Football League realigned its divisions the Seahawks returned to the NFC and hired Mike Holmgren as head coach. Holmgren already had a Super Bowl ring from his years as head coach in Green Bay, and the Seahawks had high expectations that he would bring his winning ways to Seattle.

In '05 the formula seemed just right. Holmgren improved morale by dismissing some players whose attitudes had distracted their teammates the previous season. "Chemistry in our locker room enabled us to win a couple of games this year we would've lost last year," he said.

He expertly directed quarterback Matt Hasselbeck and their offense through a field of stunned opponents, amassing a 14-2 record that included a winning streak of eleven straight games and ending the season as the league's top-scoring team with a 28.5 points-per-game average.

Although 23-year-old Pittsburgh quarterback "Big" Ben Roethlisberger had played spectacularly in the playoffs, Holmgren did not consider him a serious offensive threat because he did not feel he had been adequately tested in the playoffs.

"I can't believe how poorly Denver played in the secondary in the [conference] championship game," Holmgren said on Thursday. "Denver, to me, didn't make Roethlisberger think very much. What we can do is give him a lot of different looks."

Seattle would impose this strategy effectively, limiting Roethlisberger to just nine completions in 21 attempts, 123 yards and intercepting him twice. Yet there were other offensive (and defensive) threats in this perfectly jelled *team* Cowher had created.

Holmgren knew the opposing defense would be homing in on his league-leading rusher Shaun Alexander, so he concentrated on his aerial attack early in the contest. During the regular season Alexander earned NFL Most Valuable Player recognition by rushing for 1880 yards and a league-record 28 touchdowns. Although he would gain a respectable 95 yards on Super Sunday, only 31 came in the first half, when the game was still up for grabs.

Two minutes into the Super Bowl the Seahawks were doing as they had done all year—ripping off hefty chunks of yardage as they moved downfield with seemingly unstoppable impetus. Then they met up with their first third-and-long.

Inside linebacker James Farrior departed his standard position and set up on the outside left. Clark Haggans moved to the inside from his usual left outside spot. Charging forward in a blitz Farrior got a step on his surprised, somewhat confused blocker and forced Hasselbeck to step up in the pocket, where the also-blitzing Haggans sacked him and aborted Seattle's snappy opening drive.

Steeler defensive coordinator Dick LeBeau later said, "That play helped our bogus." "Your *what*?," a reporter asked. "Bogus blitz," LeBeau explained. "You show it, then you back off. We were doing it all day. It's what you do against a team that's max protecting."

Max protecting means a team is according maximum protection to its quarterback. This is a favored tactic of Holmgren's, who as a former quarterback coach hates to see his signal caller under pressure. He is therefore quick to leave an extra blocker or two, usually wide receivers, in the backfield to help contain the pass rush. Usually this approach works. During the five games leading up to the Super Bowl Hasselbeck had completed over 70 percent of his attempts for nine touchdowns and no interceptions.

Yet by requiring a consistently sterling performance from the quarterback this system makes an offense vulnerable to LeBeau's Bogus Blitz. Throughout the first half, whenever Seattle found itself in third-and-long, Pittsburgh would employ their specialized tactic, sending in only three pass rushers and dropping the other eight defenders into the secondary, where they hopelessly outnumbered the Seahawk receivers.

The lone touchdown of the first half came in its closing moments at the end of a bizarre series of downs that saw the Steelers stymied with a third-and-28 at the Seahawk 40. Hurrying to his left to escape the clutches of defensive end Grant Winstrom, Roethlisberger was careful to stop just before reaching the line of scrimmage. He turned and threw to his right. Wideout Hines Ward clutched the vital reception for a first-and-goal on the three. Three plays later Roethlisberger lurched in to score on a keeper play.

Holmgren and his men angrily charged that the ball had not crossed the plane of the goal, but the replay films were not conclusive enough for the officials to reverse the call. Pittsburgh led 7-3 at intermission.

Although it was a long afternoon for both quarterbacks, Hasselbeck endured the most frustration as the perfectly tailored and executed Steeler defensive scheme consistently shut down the previously unstoppable Seattle turbocharge on third downs. Still, Pittsburgh's wispy halftime lead meant it was anybody's game.

Although the Seahawk defensive front consistently beat the Steeler offensive line off the ball in the first half, limiting the score, holding the AFC champs without a first down until four minutes into the second quarter and helping offset its own ineffectual offense, the road-happy home team surprised its adversaries with an absurdly simple call on the second play of the third quarter.

Second-year free agent tailback "Fast" Willie Parker took the handoff from Roethlisberger on his own twenty-five and cut behind left guard Alan Faneca's beautiful block on linebacker Leroy Hill and Ward's pulverizing stop of cornerback Andre Dyson. Parker then lived up to his nickname by outdistancing a pack of five more defenders on a Super Bowl-record 75-yard touchdown run.

Holmgren decided it was time to unlimber his full offensive arsenal, and began using Alexander and sending *all* his receivers downfield.

Yet the aroused Pittsburgh defenders managed to shut Alexander out of the end zone, and commenced launching non-bogus blitzes against the now blocker-bereft Hasselbeck. Also, the Seattle offense repeatedly tripped over its own shoelaces.

The Seahawks had a touchdown reception negated by an offensive pass interference call in the end zone, missed two field goals and were plagued by dropped passes. There was also a fatal interception.

Hasselbeck had managed a 16-yard scoring completion to tight end Jerramy Stevens late in the third period to cut the difference to 14-10, and early in the fourth quarter was engineering a promising drive that many observers believed would turn the game in Seattle's favor. Taking the snap at the Pittsburgh twenty-seven on another of the third-and-long situations that were so unkind to him all day he tried to cross up the defense by going for the end zone instead of the first down marker. Cornerback Ike Taylor was not fooled, however, and the ball hit him squarely between his white jersey's numerals on the five-yard line, killing the Seahawk's best chance for victory.

It would take just four more downs for the Super Bowl to witness its most significant Steeler forward pass in twenty-six years. With nine minutes remaining in the game and his team on its opponents' 43-yard line Pitt offensive coordinator Ken Whisenhunt sent in a trick play called Zero Strong Z Short Fake Toss 39 X Reverse Pass.

Parker took a pitch from Roethlisberger and headed to the left. Wide receiver (and one-time University of Indiana quarterback) Antwaan Randle El swung around from his own wide left position and took a handoff from Parker. Randle El rolled out to his right while Ward flew past three befuddled defenders who could not decide whether they should cover him or rush forward to meet Randle El, who did not tip off his intentions by stopping. Never breaking stride he flung what he later called the "prettiest pass" of his life. Ward thought so too as it caught up with him just inside the five-yard line. He flashed into the end zone for the points that gave the game its final score of 21-10. Never before had a wide receiver *thrown* a touchdown pass in a Super Bowl, and for the Steelers it was a great time for this first time.

With an eye toward using up the clock, Cowher now turned to Bettis for the grind-it-out yardage that would deny Seattle a final shot. Carrying the ball seven times, Bettis insured his side maintained possession until the two-minute warning, sealing the victory. It was

Pittsburgh's eighth straight win, with all four postseason victories coming on the road. The Steelers joined the Dallas Cowboys and San Francisco 49ers as the only franchises to win five Super Bowls.

It was a fitting finale for Bettis, who finished this, his thirteenth season, as the NFL's all-time fifth-leading career rusher. He would retire, earning his only Super Bowl ring in his last game. Detroit was a fitting location. A native of the Motor City, he had family and friends in the stands, watching his heroic egress. Also, with Detroit being much closer to Pittsburgh than to Seattle, the crowd was loudly biased in his and his team's favor. The fans made sure his departure was one to cherish.

Roethlisberger's statistics might have best been spoken of in a confessional, but the youngster played a gritty, fearless game, finishing strong and coming through often enough to become the youngest man ever to quarterback a team to a Super Bowl title. En route to the Steelers' victory party he acknowledged that the win coming in spite of his own drab statistics was a hallmark of Cowher's philosophy of team unity.

"For the most part it wasn't the big-name guys offensively and defensively," he said. "That's sort of been the MO of this team, why it's such a special team and why we won."

The bend-but-not-break attitude of the Pittsburgh defense worked to perfection, and the bogus blitzes of the first half were a main ingredient. Seattle's quarterback coach Jim Zorn saw the story in the team statistics. Despite amassing a robust 396 total yards the Seahawks scored only 10 points.

"Relationship of yards to points. The further apart they are, the worse it is for an offense," Zorn said. "I don't think ours was very good tonight."

By stretching just five receptions into 123 yards Ward sufficiently stood out from his teammates to be elected Most Valuable Player. During a pregame team trip to a Detroit nightclub, Ward had classily stayed in the background and allowed Bettis to monopolize the media. With a Most Valuable performance in his pocket he now spoke his mind—with honesty.

"I don't look at myself as a prototypical wide receiver," he said. "I look at myself as a hell of a football player."

He was one of many, and they were a team.

— Like Father... —
2006 Indianapolis Colts versus Chicago Bears

Archie Manning had a sparkling college career at Ole Miss, but his years in the National Football League were spent with the New Orleans Saints and left him with little more than surgical scars as a legacy. He and wife Olivia had three sons, and the middle of this trio, Peyton, loved to hear his father's stories about his collegiate career as a Rebel. Peyton later became a quarterback himself and learned a great deal from his daddy's experience in fending off the assaults of such ferocious middle linebackers as Ray Nitschke, Tommy Nobis, Jack Lambert and Dick Butkus.

Peyton not only was a technical student of the game, but a historian as well. He absorbed the wisdom of his gifted but frustrated sire, who never played for a championship-caliber team. During his first nine years in the league, as quarterback of the Indianapolis Colts, Peyton Manning was surrounded by a splendid cast of teammates who helped him become one of the best signal callers ever to take a snap. He still felt Archie's frustration, though, as season after season his and his brother Colts' best efforts were not enough to spare them a series of painful playoff losses. When they finally managed to get past long-time nemesis New England with a stirring 38-34 victory in the 2006 American Football Conference title game the 30-year-old Manning took the next-to-last step in throwing off the no-championship albatross, but he had a punishing middle linebacker of his own to overcome.

Chicago Bear man in the center Brian Urlacher resembled Manning in how he combined cerebral and athletic ability to the extreme. By being very, very fast and strong and devilishly difficult to outwit, Urlacher and his brother Bruins shut down offense after offense in 2006, but he had a special interest in Manning.

Urlacher still seethed over a 2004 matchup at Chicago's Soldier Field when the Colts rolled over the Bears 41-10 with Manning passing for four touchdowns while the home team's All-Pro middle linebacker, six days after emergency surgery on his left leg, watched the game on television.

"I was mad as hell," he said. "I wanted to be out there playing against him."

His chance had come. Super Bowl XLI in Miami was a singular matchup between the league's best quarterback and best middle linebacker. Both were Hall of Fame shoe-ins who already had 13 Pro Bowl appearances between them. It was obvious which players would be the ones to watch in the big game.

Third-year Chicago head coach Lovie Smith spent the flight to Miami perusing the Indianapolis press guide. After landing he remarked to reporters, "I looked at 18 pages of Peyton Manning."

Although it led the league with 44 takeaways Smith's defense had faded slightly late in the season. Then in the NFC conference championship against New Orleans the Bears stifled the Saints' feared attack in a 39-14 rout. The next offense they would face was ever scarier.

During '06 Manning had thrown 31 touchdowns against just nine interceptions. In fact, he had set a record by never tossing fewer than 25 home run balls in any of his nine pro years, had 275 total, and hung up another record by never amassing less than 3000 passing yards during a season. Yet this was no one-dimensional team.

The Colts' ability to find various ways to win showed up in the first round of the playoffs when the Baltimore Ravens were the first to hold the Ponies without a touchdown in 34 straight games, but still lost 15-6. Despite their success it had been a long year for this team.

After the Super Bowl, amidst riotous celebration, owner Jimmy Irsay spoke tomes when he remarked, "Our bonds have been forged through some real-life tragedies, and those things make you stronger."

In December of 2005 head coach Tony Dungy's 18-year-old son James had committed suicide. The following month came a wrenching home playoff loss to the Patriots. Although Irsay had, year after year, repeatedly written handsome checks to convince his top players to not move on as free agents, after that '05 season All-Pro running back Edgerrin James defected to the Arizona Cardinals. The following September wide receiver Reggie Wayne's brother Rashad was killed in a car crash. Following a 9-0 start in '06 the team hit the skids, losing three of four games, including a 44-17 stomping by the Jacksonville Jaguars in which Indianapolis gave up a humiliating 375 rushing yards. Resolutely rebounding, the Colts knocked off the Kansas City Chiefs and Baltimore in the playoffs before overcoming a 21-3 shortfall to beat New England in the conference title test. Manning was 0-2 versus the Pats in previous postseasons, but by game's end he had passed for a touchdown and 349 yards in this greatest-ever comeback in conference championship history.

Urlacher did not overlook any of his coming opponent's strengths, noting Manning's intelligence, quick release, hawkish eyesight, accuracy, and on-field command presence. He also noted this quarterback's resiliency, having started 156 consecutive games.

"He's a tough guy," said Urlacher. "A lot tougher than people seem to think he is."

Despite the intellect of their lead players, neither Indianapolis' offense or Chicago's defense was real complex. Pre-snap scrimmage line maneuvering was key. Manning would approach center, lean over and shout at the offensive linemen, point to the safeties, pump his right leg or gesticulate with his arms. Defenders often could not tell if he was calling a play or changing one.

"Sometimes," said Urlacher. "He's just screwing around with us."

The Bear middle linebacker, meanwhile, loved to charge into the A-Gap just over center, distractingly get in the quarterback's face and make him wonder if a crushing blitz was coming—which often it was.

Chicago had allowed only 294.1 yards per game in 2006, while Indianapolis' offense had averaged a sterling 379.4 yards per contest. America could hardly wait for the coming showdown between the AFC's best offense and the NFC's best defense. Manning, especially, took the game and its build-up seriously.

The Colts' authoritarian President Bill Polian decreed that although there would be restrictions on who could visit the team in its Fort Lauderdale hotel, players could receive family members and guests in their rooms. His quarterback had something to say about that.

"I don't think we should let anyone up in the rooms," Manning announced to a silent group of teammates and coaches. "This is a business trip, and I don't want any distractions. I don't want any crying kids next to me while I'm trying to study."

Quests

Peyton had his way, but many of the other Ponies were not happy about it. None could argue with the results, though. After the game a delighted cornerback Nick Harper had this to say:

"We were heated. People were saying, 'We're grown men. We've got wives and kids, and we'll make those decisions for ourselves.' But you know, it turned out all right."

It was more than just all right for the Indianapolis quarterback as he shed his can't-win-the-big-one tag and earned a Super Bowl ring to go with his massive collection of individual awards. Working past a so-so start and in spite of a drenching thunderstorm over Dolphin Stadium the seven-time All-Pro was wise enough to not try and do it all himself as he relied heavily on the performances of his fellow champions. Not falling into the many-times-frustrated athlete's trap of being impatient he wisely shared the game with the herd of thoroughbreds around him.

Colt running backs Joseph Addai and Dominic Rhodes made certain the Bruin defenders could not key on their quarterback. Although he never started a game, Addai was the league's leading rookie rusher with 1081 yards during the regular season. On soggy Super Sunday he ran 19 times for 77 steps and caught 10 passes for another 66 yards. Rhodes, meanwhile, rushed 21 times for 113 yards and scored a touchdown. With the Chicago safeties rueful of Manning's right arm and hence playing deep in the second half there were fewer defenders available to contain these young stallions.

"Everybody's got to do his part," Manning crowed in the postgame locker room. "You have to trust them all to do that."

He trusted his defending teammates, too.

The overlooked Colt defense overcame a shaky start to shut down the Windy City offense. After surrendering a 92-yard opening kickoff runback to rookie return man Devin Hester (something that had never before happened on a Super Bowl's first play) and a four-yard touchdown pass from quarterback Rex Grossman to wide receiver Muhsin Muhammad to give the Bears a 14-6 lead with 4:34 still to play in the first quarter, the raucous, overwhelmingly pro-Chicago crowd got quieter and quieter as the game wore on and its team managed only 11 first downs. Other than a third period field goal the NFC would put no more points on the board.

Indianapolis was unsurprised at its pedestrian beginning, and was prepared to respond to it thanks to mental preparation by Dungy. The night before the game he had warned his men they would surely have to overcome a "storm" sometime the next day. Between the downpour and Chicago's strong early showing they rose above two.

It should not have been a surprise. Dungy's "Tampa Two" defensive scheme stations two safeties deep and uses a squad of agile linebackers to help cover receivers throughout the secondary. Versus the Bears his approach was to stymie the running game by frequently stationing an eighth defender near the line of scrimmage, keep an eye open for sneaky running plays on third-and medium yardage downs, and confuse Grossman by varying the alignments in passing situations. When running back Cedric Benson was hurt and left the game in the first period the Bear ground game faded yet further. Bear runner Thomas Jones tried hard, managing 112 yards on 15 carries, but this stingy defense limited Chicago to just 265 total yards, held on seven of 10 third downs, and took away five turnovers. This kept the game from getting out of hand while the offense found its legs.

On the Colts' first play tight end Dallas Clark was supposed to have run a seam pass route in front of the safeties, but mistakenly broke to the inside. When Manning tried to hit him anyway Urlacher slapped the ball off target. Later during this possession Indianapolis was flagged for two false-start infractions, which set them back to their own 41 with a third-and-13. On the next down Manning looked for his favorite target, wideout Marvin Harrison, but overthrew him and strong safety Chris Harris intercepted.

"We looked like a team that had never played in the Super Bowl," said Manning afterward.

Well, they *hadn't*, but they soon started playing like they had.

With 6:58 remaining in the first quarter Indy used a play called 66 D X-Pump that the team had reserved specifically for the Super Bowl. Wayne lined up on the left side and ran an in-and-go route in hopes Bear free safety Danieal Manning would bite on the pump fake, enabling Wayne to get a step on him. It turned out even easier than expected. Danieal Manning paid no heed to Wayne, but followed tight end Ben Utrecht along his inside route. This left Wayne uncovered in the middle of the field, where he picked off Peyton Manning's spiral inside the 20 and cruised into the end zone on a 53-yard score that cut the Bear lead to 7-6. The Colt offense had converted on three third downs during this drive, and despite missing the extra point the team already sensed victory. They kept right on sensing it later in the quarter after the Bears scored their second touchdown.

Late in the period Manning jammed his already-sore right thumb, but did not let it bother him. In fact, he just kept getting better.

"With a wet ball you've got to hold it light to make it go where you want," he later explained. "So the bad thumb kind of helped me because I couldn't grip it real hard."

Sure enough, he finished with 25 completions in 38 attempts for 247 yards and a touchdown. Most of this came after the opening quarter, which he spent figuring out the Chicago defense. By consistently not calling his plays until he lined up over center he kept the Bears back on their heels and unable to react swiftly enough to late-forming offensive alignments. His eagle eye undimmed by the rain, he never failed to notice an open receiver. He hardly ever missed them, either. His offense would roll up 430 total yards, convert on 8 out of 18 third downs versus the league's top-rated defense, eat up more than 38 minutes of the clock despite going no-huddle, and run 81 plays to just 48 by the Bears.

As the Chicago offense bogged down in the morass and under a fearsome assault by the white-shirted Colt defenders, the AFC offense steadily found its rhythm. Although the hard-working Urlacher wound up with 10 tackles, he could not stem the turbocharge facing him as it gained momentum. By halftime the Bears trailed 16-14, but had too much class, skill and determination to collapse.

With 13:38 left in the game they trailed by just 22-17 as they took over on their own 20. Grossman tried to hit Muhammad on a sideline pass, but Chicago native Kelvin Hayden intercepted the soggy skin and ran it back 56 yards for the final points in a 29-17 Indianapolis victory.

Moments later Grossman tried again, but free safety Bob Sanders picked off this pass to squelch the final Chicago flurry. Moments later Dungy swapped his blue-and-white Colts cap for one that read "NFL Champions."

Smith had served as an assistant coach under Dungy in Tampa Bay, and like his former boss he was far too classy to blame an outside agency for a defeat. When facing the press after the game he gave all the credit to the winners.

"The weather was not a factor at all," he said. "They had three and we had five [turnovers.] We are used to playing in this type of weather, and I don't think the weather had any bearing on the outcome of the game."

Hours later, after endless postgame interviews, Most Valuable Player Peyton Manning showered, donned his suit and promptly got soaked again as he strode through the downpour to the team bus. He did not get on immediately, though. He stood in the rain and held the door open for his father.

A Giant Upset
2007 New York Giants versus New England Patriots

No one could have had more right than the New England Patriots to be in the Super Bowl after the 2007 season. Since Labor Day they had averaged more than 40 points per game as they won and won and won. Head Coach Bill Belichick directed his superb cast flawlessly as they amassed a 16-0 regular season record, and now he and Tom Brady stood poised to become only the second head coach-quarterback combo ever to win four Super Bowls (Pittsburgh's Chuck Noll and Terry Bradshaw had done it way back in the 1970s.) After tossing aside their opponents in the American Football Conference divisional and championship games they were *18-0*, and the world was openly assuming a perfect season was around the bend. It had only happened once before. In 1934 and 1942 the Chicago Bears had undefeated regular seasons, but both years they lost the league title game. The impossible came in 1972 when the Miami Dolphins pulled off the mythical perfect season and postseason, but in the decades since nobody else had managed it. Given '07's circumstances fandom may be forgiven for assuming history was finally repeating.

For several years the Patriots had ignored the league's efforts to further equal competition and to prevent dynasties by installing a salary cap and free agency system. Brady was just 30 years old, and already had three championship rings and was a two-time Super Bowl Most Valuable Player. This season he had thrown a league-record 50 touchdown passes, and as a starter this former sixth-round draft choice had a flashy 86-24 won-lost record. Belichick's .833, meanwhile, was second only to the Green Bay Packers' legendary Head Coach Vince Lombardi in postseason winning percentage among head coaches with six or more playoff victories. This Brady-Belichick partnership was the soul of the team.

Not even mass personnel turnovers could derail this powerhouse. Its first title had been six years earlier, in 2001, and it kept right on winning them despite now having only 10 players left over from that first championship roster. Las Vegas installed the Pats as 12-point favorites even though five of their last eight regular season contests had been cliffhangers. In the AFC championship game the injury-riddled San Diego Chargers had intercepted three passes and trailed only 14-12 in the fourth quarter before a long, Brady-orchestrated drive ran out the clock.

Still, few observers construed the Pats' many close calls as signs of vulnerability, but rather as indications that this bunch could (and did) find a way to win in any situation. There is no question that the team's guile and resourcefulness were major assets. In the conference title test New England twice held the Chargers to field goals after San Diego had had first-and-goal. It was emblematic of the 2007 season. Early in the year Brady and his offense captured America's attention with glittering scoring exhibitions, but as the weeks passed and teams began fighting the unbeaten Patriots harder and harder the New Englanders reached into their reserves of selflessness, guts, talent and mutual dependence. Despite the centrality of the Belichick-Brady tandem, no man even thought of himself as standing out from his teammates. They carefully, successfully managed to concentrate on being a winning *team*.

Owner Robert Kraft encapsulated his team's philosophy the week before the big game when he said, "We try to get people who subjugate their egos."

Tight end Kyle Brady had spent 13 years in the NFL, but this was his first with New England. He had seen the ways other teams approached football, but Patriot culture was something that impressed even this grizzled vet.

"There is a professionalism and a businesslike attitude here," he said. "They take film study seriously. They take game-planning seriously. There's an awareness of what's required to be successful that might be pleasantly surprising anywhere else, but here it's just expected."

Still, as they headed for the Super Bowl in the University of Phoenix Stadium in

Glendale, Arizona, the specter of a perfect season was simply too much of a distraction for even the focused Pats to ignore.

Just what did the National Football Conference have to offer up against the SuperBowl-savvy dynasty from America's revolutionary heartland? It had the New York Giants. Although this team had not exactly lived up to its name during most of '07, it did rebound from an 0-2 start to finish with a 10-6 record that earned it the fifth seed in the wild-card playoffs. At this point the New Yorkers found their groove, becoming the first-ever NFC team to make it to the Super Bowl after upsetting three straight playoff opponents *on the road.* After knocking off Tampa Bay and Dallas in hostile arenas, the Giants journeyed to Green Bay and ignored numbing cold to pull out a thrilling 23-20 overtime triumph for the conference title. Counting the playoffs, the Giants were coming into the finale having won ten straight road games. The turnaround changed four-year Head Coach Tom Coughlin from a dour, distant disciplinarian into a fun-loving, palm-slapping cheerleader type who greatly improved his team's morale. Along with his players he had come to feel at home away from home, and Arizona is a long ways from New York. Even so, as Sunday, February 3, 2008 approached, the Giants were once again major underdogs as they prepared to face the undefeated Pats.

New York signal-caller Eli Manning would be the latest star from football's most famous quarterbacking family. His older brother Peyton had been the previous Super Bowl's Most Valuable Player. Versus Green Bay Eli paid no attention to a 23 degrees below zero wind chill as he completed 21-of-40 for 254 yards. Most of his throws went to favored wide receiving target Plaxico Burress, who ignored both the cold and a torn ligament in his right ankle while pulling down 11 receptions for 154 yards.

Burris had been a godsend to his team as he filled the void created when tight end Jeremy Shockey went down with a broken leg late in the season. Also, standout rookie wide receiver Steve Smith missed almost three months with a broken shoulder blade. In spite of this attritition, Manning was the only one of the 12 first-string quarterbacks who started the playoffs to go through them without being intercepted, finishing with a postseason passer rating of 99.2, second only to Brady's 105.7.

Still, no one bragged on himself. Burress and the other Giants gave the credit to Manning, who went through his first 12 postseason quarters completing 62.4% of his throws. Still, aided by the league's fourth-ranked rushing attack, he had only blossomed late in the year. In each of 11 of his first 15 regular season games he had thrown just one scoring pass, or none. Then he took off when it really counted as in the last game of the '07 campaign and the three subsequent playoff games he completed eight touchdown throws with a 105.0 rating for those four afternoons. Manning and his brother New Yorkers had shown through their gritty, gutsy playoff victories and classy reactions to each of them that they were better than their record indicated. Still, Manning's emergence into greatness had started so late in the season that his team finished 21st in passing, while New England ranked first, and as Super Sunday approached nobody seemed to notice much except for New England's gaudy statistics and that 18-0.Maybe this should not have been *too* surprising. After all, New York's last regular season game was played against New England, and even though Brady had dissected the Giant defense for 356 yards passing the Patriots only won by three points. Also, New York had had to come from behind to win eight of their 10 regular season victories, and then sent just one representative to the Pro Bowl—as a reserve. New England boasted seven Pro Bowl starters. All these facts were popular with pre-game prognosticators. It was not until after the Super Bowl that the experts began to remember the winners' less-tangible strengths such as determination, resilience, mental toughness and unwavering courage.

More prosaic was the team's brilliant drafting as all eight of the young men selected by General Manager Jerry Reese the previous spring not only made the team, but also provided major contributions throughout the 2007 campaign, particularly on defense as the Giants led the league with 53 quarterback sacks. The Pats, however, had allowed Brady to be trapped just 21 times.

Seventeen years earlier these two franchises had played in one of the most nail-biting of all pro football championships. Nothing had come easily for either team on that day as the Giants pulled it out on the last play. This match would be more surprising and more of a classic as Super Bowl 42 lived up to its first name. It was the relentless New York defense that gave the first hint that the game might not follow script.

Although the Giants received the opening kickoff, they managed just two possessions in the first quarter. This unwanted Super Bowl record forced the Big Apple's defense to play more than they and Coughlin would have liked, but the defenders of the NFC seemed to relish every moment of it. By combining blitzes from weakside linebacker Kawika Mitchell with constant pressure from the linemen they kept Brady running and his NFL-best-ever offense off-balance all night. After racking up a league record 589 points during the regular season, Brady and his turbocharge would be held to just two scores.

With defensive end Justin Tuck constantly switching positions with his front line mates, Brady had trouble deciding from what direction the rush was likely to come. By game's end Brady had been sacked five times and knocked down another six. Not since September 2003 had any defense gotten to him this much. Playing with the abandon typical of those with nothing to lose and everything to gain the New York defense worked over the New England offensive line in a way it had never experienced. Apart from being unable to protect their quarterback, the linemen could not open holes for very above-average tailback Laurence Maroney, who finished with just 36 yards.

After the Pats went ahead 7-3 on the first play of the second quarter, the defenses choked off *all* scoring for a Super Bowl-record 33 minutes and 52 seconds. What offensive fireworks the game did have it reserved for the fourth period as the by-then-gasping New England defense could not stanch two long, crucial scoring drives.

Panting, rueful Patriot defensive end Richard Seymour would tell postgame reporters, "They would never go away. That's the sign of a champion. It takes heart."

Seymour is a veteran of all three of New England's Super Bowl-winning teams. He knows very well what it takes to be a champion.

The historic fourth quarter started with NY rookie tight end Kevin Boss finding himself all alone when the Patriot defense blew its coverage on him. Manning threw him the ball, and Boss turned the mid-range pass into a 45-yard gainer. Five downs later his quarterback found another open man.

Like many of his teammates, Giants reserve wide receiver David Tyree had endured a season that was painful in more than one way. He missed the year's first two games with a broken left wrist. He was gone for another two weeks when his mother died just before Christmas. He called on a higher power to sustain him and, perhaps, the whole franchise.

"My faith is what kept me going. Ever since my mom went home to be with the Lord this team has been different," he said. "We've been playing with passion. We've been riding the wings of something special."

With 11:05 remaining, Tyree proved to be part of that something special when Manning completed a five-yard touchdown pass to him. The defenses shut down both offenses' next possessions, but at mid-quarter Brady finally got untracked and engineered the prettiest drive of the night as he led his squad 80 yards on 11 plays, finishing with a six-yard scoring throw to wideout Randy Moss. The Patriots now led 14-10, and 2:42 remained on the clock.

Up until this point Manning had directed his offense adequately, but not spectacularly. He had completed 14 of 25 for 178 yards, one touchdown and one interception. Still, he had kept his offense on the field long enough to tire the Pat defense. The 77 yards he would pass for on this last drive would help make him the game's Most Valuable Player.

Starting on his own 17 he drove his offense resolutely, but came up with a 4th-and-1 at his own 37. Offensive coordinator Kevin Gilbride sent in the classic power play when he had Manning hand the ball to 264-pound fullback Brandon Jacobs, who followed 266-pound runner Madison Hedgecock over right guard. Jacobs picked up one yard and one foot.

Three plays later it was 3rd-and-5 at the New York 44 and Manning lined up in shotgun formation. After he caught the snap the worried defenders frantically collapsed the pocket and swarmed him. Manning disappeared in a scrum of dark jerseys, but somehow tore loose. He lobbed the ball towards Tyree in the middle of the field. David had caught just four passes in the regular season, but this play more than made up for his inaction. Frantically fighting veteran strong safety Rodney Harrison for the ball, Tyree managed to trap it against his own helmet. It was not a very attractive reception, but it was legal and gave the Giants a first down on New England's 24.

"Once that ball was in the air, it was mine, mine, mine, like a little kid," said a beaming Tyree later.

Hedgecock added, "Most amazing play I've ever seen on a football field."

Three downs later timeouts-bereft Manning converted on 3rd-and-11 when he completed a 12-yarder to Smith, who also fought his way out of bounds on the Pats' 13, stopping the clock. There were 39 seconds left in the game. It was time for Burris to retake the spotlight, but it was not coming easily.

No one was more aware of the situation and its implications than team doctor Russell Warren. As he watched his patients sacrificing their bodies as they fought both the Patriots and the desert heat he was dismayed by what he saw,

"Guys doubling over, cramping. I didn't think some of them would make it," he said after the game. "Plaxico Burress—my God, what pain he played in. He said, 'Shoot me up for this one if you have to. I'm not going to miss the Super Bowl.'"

Having already played the whole season and post-season on a bad ankle, he had stretched his left knee's medial collateral ligament the Tuesday before the game when he slipped and fell while taking a shower. With Coughlin's blessing he did not practice during the remainder of the week in hopes that rest would heal his aching knee. He did not even run until the pregame warm-ups, and the rehabilitation strategy seemed to work for the eight-year veteran. On the Super Bowl's defining down Manning went to the pass-catcher who had been his bread-and-butter all year.

The play was called simply, "Café," and the New England defense tried to disrupt its timing with a blitz, but Manning refused to be rattled. Also, this strategy forced cornerback Ellis Hobbs into single coverage on Burris. Forced to gamble as to whether Burris would cut to the middle of the field or go for the end zone, Hobbs guessed slant, and was wrong. Burris beat him easily and caught Manning's scoring pass.

There would be no last-second heroics to rescue the New England Patriots from their ultimate humiliation. They would lose 17-14, and for the second straight year a player named Manning would be Super Bowl Most Valuable as he guided his team to the greatest upset in decades.

It was a sweet, direly needed vindication for a young man whose last name and whose status as the number one pick in the entire 2004 draft made others expect greatness from him. The previous year he had been crucified by fans, analysts and writers as the Giants collapsed late in the season. As he savored the postgame victory party he let his feelings of immense relief and delight be known.

"A lot of times I've thought, 'Why have I gotten this treatment? Do I deserve this?' So to come out here and win, not just for me, but for our whole team, is really special," he said. "And for me personally I'd have to say it's kind of sweet."

Moments later he and oldest brother Cooper Manning linked arms and began to sing. The song was *New York, New York*.

Yesterday Once More
2008 Pittsburgh Steelers versus Arizona Cardinals

The Cardinals had long since stopped waiting for next year. The franchise was originally organized in 1890, making it the oldest in the National Football League. At first they played in Chicago, where, in 1947, they won their sole title. A year later they lost to Philadelphia in the lowest-scoring title test the league has ever seen, then sank into an age of invisibility. Forsaking the Windy City they moved to St. Louis in 1960. Aside from a brief spell of respectability in the mid-1970s under the tutelage of offensive wizard head coach Don Coryell their seasons in the Midwest were also forgettable as they made it to just four postseason games—losing each one. After 28 years they took their leave of Missouri and moved to Phoenix, Arizona. Although it took awhile it was here that they finally returned from the past.

It took the Redbirds 20 years in the desert to find their groove, and even when they did it was the end of the 2008 season before the rest of the world realized it. Losing four of their last six games they made the playoffs as a 9-7 Wildcard entry, but the league slowly took note as Phoenix dropped three surprised opponents while scoring a robust 95 points. Although its defense was better than it had been 30-plus years earlier, it was still the offense that found ways to win. One in particular.

Big, strong, fast and sticky-fingered, fifth-year wide receiver Larry Fitzgerald finished the year as an All-Pro and recognized as one of the best pass-catchers ever. During January this University of Pittsburgh alumnus burned the Atlanta Falcons, Carolina Panthers and Philadelphia Eagles for 23 receptions, 419 yards and five touchdowns. Finding an antidote to him was as hard as covering him. When he was single-covered Cardinal quarterback Kurt Warner would loft the ball deep as on a 62-yard scoring bomb that beat the Eagles in the NFC championship game. When double-covered he would use his 6'3 stature and powerful legs to out-jump defenders. He is also more physical than the average wide receiver.

"I've been around some great receivers in 25 years in this league," said Seattle Seahawk head coach Jim Mora. "Jerry Rice ran every route with a purpose. Terrell Owens runs angry. Larry runs with a viciousness. He attacks the defense. He's become a much more physical player this year, but I don't think you can just play him in a physical way exclusively. He's too smart for that."

It would take a receiver of Fitzgerald's stature to make a dent in the pass defense of the Cardinals' opponents in upcoming Super Bowl XLIII. During the 2008 playoffs the Pittsburgh Steelers allowed just one completed pass past their deepest receiver. It took assistance from United Parcel Service to deliver a football beyond the Steelers' secondary. Nobody threw for 300 yards against them, and just three opponents managed 200. Two did not even make it to 100.

Still, Fitzgerald would be a handful for any defense, and there was more than him to this attack. In Anquan Boldin and Steve Breaston the Birds had two additional 1000-yard receivers. Furthermore, their running game had emerged late in the year with the return of their tight ends from injured reserve. After carrying the ball just 36% of the time in the regular season they ran it on 52% of their downs in the playoffs as tailback Edgerrin James suddenly had multiple blockers to escort him downfield. The quarterback was also a voice to be heard—one from the past.

Claimed off the waiver list in 2005, Warner eagerly seized the chance to prove he was not a has-been. He had a champion's ring from his years as a St. Louis Ram and was a two-time league MVP. This year he took full advantage of the brilliant cast around him as he fired 30 touchdown passes and became only the second quarterback to start Super Bowls for different teams. He also won NFL Man of the Year recognition.

"It obviously feels great to be back. You never know if you're going to get these opportunities again," he said. "I think I'm a lot more comfortable this time around, understanding what you're going to deal with."

All this and Fitzgerald, too. In the previous Super Bowl the Giants had pulled off the greatest upset in decades by playing exclusively to their own strengths. Forewarned by this, Pittsburgh's new Steel Curtain defense knew what it had to do, but would it be able to handle an attack with so many weapons?

The main support in the Steeler defensive game plan to choke off the big plays that were Arizona's bread and butter was 30-year-old linebacker James Harrison. In '08 the All-Pro Harrison became the soul of the league's top-ranked defense. With 92 he was the team's second-place tackler, broke the team record for sacks with 16, and became the first-ever undrafted player to be named NFL Defensive Player of the Year.

It was a heady homecoming for an athlete Pittsburgh had cut three times because of his short stature and even shorter fuse. After obscure stints with the Baltimore Ravens and in NFL Europe he came back to the Steelers, buckled down and resolutely earned a starting spot in a defense that positively terrified the rest of the league. He had one more game to play to finally prove his status.

Twenty-nine years earlier Pittsburgh had played a 9-7 team in a Super Bowl. That squad had tried hard, but could not overcome the dynasty of the seventies. Now that the franchise had rebounded and earned a fifth championship ring it had its heart set on an unprecedented sixth, and the players and coaches would not take the unheralded Cardinals lightly. This was very wise.

Steeler quarterback Ben Roethlisberger had no intention of overlooking the Arizona *defense*. He knows what it is like to be unfairly taken lightly. Three years later many said his team had won the Super Bowl *in spite* of him. He had been a wide-eyed 23-year-old then, but much had since happened that matured him and honed his considerable football talents. Apart from the positive development brought by three more years as starting quarterback, something totally removed from football had changed his outlook.

He was not wearing a helmet while riding his motorcycle through downtown Pittsburgh one day in June of 2006. When he had a one-sided collision with a Chrysler New Yorker he came away with serious facial injuries that required two-inch titanium plates and screws to fix. Now he takes nothing lightly.

"It's a trophy to be alive every day," he says.

He and second-year head coach Mike Tomlin were closer than most brothers, and the faith Tomlin had in him helped banish his problem with self-confidence. Roethlisberger's blue-collar, hard-working style of play landed him in few highlights films, but his way of toiling relentlessly on both the practice and playing fields could not help but win games. His unselfish nature came through in how he constantly defended an offensive line that allowed him to be sacked a whopping 46 times in 2008. He just kept climbing back to his feet. When he trotted onto Tampa, Florida's Raymond James Stadium on the evening February 1, 2009 he felt the confidence of a champion.

Yet through a push-and-shove first half it was the 37-year-old Warner who radiated poise and professionalism despite hardly having a chance to play in a Steeler-dominated first quarter that ended with Arizona trailing 10-0, and Pitt was known as a team that never blew a lead.

Card head coach Ken Whisenhunt was a former Steeler assistant. He had anticipated the opposition game plan. When the Steelers predictably stacked their secondary against Fitzgerald, Warner coolly connected with Boldin and Breaston while occasionally slipping the ball to James on sneaky running plays rather than trying to force passes to covered receivers. As the second quarter wound down, Warner moved his offense to Pittsburgh's one-yard line, where he connected with tight end Ben Patrick for the touchdown, cutting the Steeler lead to 10-7. Moments later Roethlisberger had a pass deflected and intercepted. The underdog Cardinals had a priceless opportunity to score and take a promising lead into halftime. What happened instead was the most incredible *defensive* play this game has ever seen.

Warner smoothly moved his offense back to Pittsburgh's one-yard line as the heavily pro-Steelers crowd fell silent. Eighteen seconds remained in the half as Kurt bent over center. He expected pass-rushing specialist Harrison to come charging at him, but the linebacker refused to be predictable. He dropped back in pass coverage, jumped in front of Boldin, intercepted Warner's pass at the goal line and took off downfield.

Shaking off Warner, Fitzgerald, Breston, left tackle Mike Gandy, tight end Leonard Pope and guard Reggie Wells he also collided repeatedly with his own teammates as he churned along the right sideline. When Fitzgerald caught up with him again far downfield Harrison somersaulted over the astounded wide receiver, landing on his head in the Arizona end zone. Exhausted by his 100-yard interception return for a touchdown, he lay on his back until Tomlin helped him to his feet and walked him back to the bench and iced Gatorade after the longest play in Super Bowl history. Most thought this unexpected bolt from the blue would break Arizona's will to continue, but the Birds were not quite ready to fly south.

Too few of the AFC champs had noticed that Fitzgerald had so far caught just one pass. The third quarter was no kinder to him as penalties repeatedly aborted Arizona drives, but in the fourth quarter this magnificent competitor began to shake off the confident Steeler defensive backs. In the game's final 11 minutes he caught six passes for 115 yards and two touchdowns. The first was a one-yard score over cornerback Ike Taylor on a fade route. This capped an 87-yard drive on which Warner completed all eight of the passes he threw for all the yards. This stunning combo had plenty more to show.

With 2:37 remaining in the game Fitzgerald took a short slant pass and outran the entire Pittsburgh secondary for a 64-yard touchdown. During this stretch of time Arizona was also awarded a safety when the Steelers offense was flagged for holding in its own end zone. At the two-minute warning the Cardinals suddenly owned a 23-20 lead, and never had his team so needed Roethlisberger's confidence.

Some of his teammates may have been rattled by the sudden turnaround, but Big Ben was not—even though he had to start his final drive at his own 12-yard line. Lining up in the ancient Shotgun formation he repeatedly threw the coverage off his receivers by pump-faking and moving around in the pocket while his offensive line put on its best performance of the year. Overcoming what could have been a killing holding infraction, he passed his unit to the Arizona 46, from where he connected with wide receiver Santonio Holmes about 10 yards downfield. The third-year vet cradled the ball, turned and raced down the left sideline to the Cardinal six. It was first-and-goal, and there were 48 tics on the clock.

Although they were scared and tired, the Arizona defenders were fighting desperately. On the next play, forced to throw over the red-jerseyed rush line, Roethlisberger overthrew Holmes in the back of the end zone. On second down his first and second reads, running back Willie Parker and wide receiver Nate Washington, were surrounded by defenders, so he again looked to Holmes. Three defenders were converging on him as he sprinted for the right rear corner of the end zone, but his quarterback was confident in his teammates as well as in himself. Roethlisberger wafted a soft pop fly high and outside. Holmes caught it with his fingertips and scraped his toes along the very last of the green grass before they hit white chalk. It was his fourth reception of this drive, his ninth for the game, scored the game-winning touchdown and made him Super Bowl Most Valuable Player as his side won 27-23. Although just barely, the Steelers had accomplished their standard goal of imposing their will on their foes.

The 36-year-old Tomlin became the youngest head coach ever to win this game, and those around him knew how he had done it. A year earlier Pittsburgh had lost in the playoffs at home to the Jacksonville Jaguars. There were those who thought Tomlin worked his players too hard in practices, and that by the end of the season they were fatigued. In '08 he eased up, even allowing some older players to skip midweek workouts. One of these was 12-year linebacker James Farrior, who, in a madcap postgame locker room, described his coach's successful new outlook.

"This year [he's known] when to push our buttons and when to lay off. When he gives us breaks we all feel like we have to uphold the responsibility and not be the guy who goes out and gets in trouble."

It was a sure recipe for success as the Steelers played their hearts out until the final gun of every game, earned a record sixth Vince Lombardi Trophy and joined the Dallas Cowboys as the only franchises to win it all under three different head coaches. These were the only head coaches the team had employed during the past 40 years, and all three had won Super Bowls. The Cards had no reason to feel ashamed. They had crashed into an institution.

Meanwhile, back in Pittsburgh, team owner Dan Rooney bought a bigger trophy case.

Bibliography

Alzado, Lyle. Zimmerman, Paul. *Mile High: The Story of Lyle Alzado and the Amazing Denver Broncos*, Berkley Publishing Corporation, 1978.

Anderson, Dave. *Great Quarterbacks of the NFL*, Random House, 1965.

Anderson, Dave. *Great Pass Receivers of the NFL*, Random House, 1966.

Archer, Todd. *The Dallas Morning News*, 2-2-04, 2-6-06, 2-5-07, 2-3-08, 2-4-08.

Associated Press. 1-26-87, 2-1-88, 1-28-92, 2-1-93, 1-31-94, 1-21-96, 1-13-97, 1-26-97, 1-27-97, 1-26-98, 2-4-02, 1-27-03, 2-2-04, 2-6-06.

Attner, Paul. *The Sporting News*, 2-3-99.

Barra, Allen. *The Wall Street Journal*, 1-12-01.

Baum, Bob. Associated Press/*Tyler Morning Telegraph*, 1-21-09.

Baxley, Andrew. *USA Today*, 2-1-88.

Bayless, Skip. *The Dallas Times Herald*, 1-30-90.

Bayless, Skip. *The Chicago Tribune*, 1-31-00.

Bell, Jarrett. *USA Today*, 2-1-93, 1-31-94, 1-29-96, 1-26-98, 2-1-99, 2-4-02, 1-27-03, 2-1-08.

Berger, Phil. *Championship Teams of the NFL*, Random House, 1965.

Bleier, Rocky. O'Neill, Terry. *Fighting Back*, Warner Books, 1975.

Blount, Terry. *The Houston Chronicle*, 2-1-99.

Bock, Hal. *The Houston Chronicle*, 1-27-92, 2-1-99.

Bock, Hal. *The Houston Post*, 2-1-93, 1-30-95.

Bortstein, Larry. *Len Dawson: Super Bowl Quarterback*, Tempo Books, 1970.

Bortstein, Larry. *Football Stars of 1971*, Pyramid Books, 1971.

Brondfield, Jerry. *All-Pro Football Stars '79*, Scholastic Books Services, 1979.

Brown, Chip. *The Dallas Morning News*, 1-27-03.

Buchanan, Olin. *Tyler Courier Times/Tyler Morning Telegraph*, 1-29-93.

Buck, Ray. *The Houston Post*, 1-21-85, 1-31-94.

Burwell, Bryan. *USA Today*, 2-1-93, 1-31-94, 1-27-97.

Campbell, Dave. *Dallas Cowboys Annual*, Sports Communications, Inc., 1971, 1972, 1976, 1978, 1979 issues.

Chandler, Charles. *The Dallas Morning News*, 2-2-04.

Clary, Jack. *Pro Football's Greatest Moments*, Bonanza Books, 1981.

Coffey, Wayne. *All-Pro's Greatest Football Players*, Scholastic Inc., 1983.

Cohen, Richard. Deutsch, Jordan. Neft, David. *The Scrapbook History of Pro Football*, Bobbs Merrill, 1979.

Cowlishaw, Tim. *The Dallas Morning News*, 1-29-90, 1-28-91, 1-27-92, 2-1-93, 1-31-94, 2-1-99, 1-31-00, 1-29-01, 2-4-02, 1-27-03, 2-7-05, 2-6-06, 2-5-07, 2-4-08, 2-2-09.

Czarnecki, John. *The National Sports Daily*, 1-26-91, 1-29-91.

Davis, Nate. *USA Today*, 2-1-08.

Davis, Mac. *Football's Unforgettables*, Bantam Pathfinder Edition, 1971.

Dent, Jim. *The Dallas Times Herald*, 1-27-86, 1-26-87, 2-1-88.

DiMeglio, Steve. *USA Today*, 2-6-06.

Dodd, Mike. *USA Today*, 2-1-93, 2-1-08.

Easterbrook, Greg. *The Wall Street Journal*, 1-26-01.

Eskenazi, Gerald. *The Dallas Morning News*, 2-1-99.

Fagan, Greg. *TV Guide*, 1-30-93.

Forbes, Gordon. *USA Today*, 1-23-89, 1-28-91, 1-26-98, 2-1-99, 2-4-02, 1-27-03, 2-5-07.

Fowler, Ed. *The Houston Chronicle*, 1-27-86, 1-29-90, 1-28-91.

Fraley, Gerry. *The Dallas Morning News*, 2-1-93, 2-2-04.

Freeman, Denne. *The Houston Post*, 2-1-93, 1-30-95.

Friend, Tom. *The New York Times,* 1-30-95.

Galloway, Randy. *The Dallas Morning News,* 1-26-87, 1-23-89, 2-1-93, 1-31-94, 1-29-96, 1-28-98.

Gano, Rick. *Associated Press/Tyler Morning Telegraph,* 1-29-07.

Gano, Rick. *Associated Press/Dallas Morning News,* 2-5-07.

Gifford, Frank. *NFL-AFL Football Guide 1968,* New American Library, Inc., 1968.

Glauber, Bob. *Newsday,* 1-30-95.

Goldberg, Dave. *Longview News-Journal,* 2-2-04.

Goldberg, Dave. *Tyler Morning Telegraph,* 1-15-06, 1-17-06, 2-1-06.

Goldstein, Jody. *The Houston Chronicle,* 2-1-99.

Gosselin, Rick. *The Dallas Morning News,* 1-28-91, 1-31-94, 1-30-95, 1-29-96, 1-27-97, 1-26-98, 2-1-99, 1-31-00, 1-29-01, 2-4-02, 1-20-03, 1-27-03, 2-2-04, 2-6-06, 2-5-07, 2-3-08

Grant, Evan. *The Dallas Morning News,* 1-27-97, 1-27-03.

Gutman, Bill. *The Signal Callers: Sipe, Jaworski, Ferguson, Bartkowski,* Ace Tempo Books, Grosset & Dunlap, 1981.

Hack, Damon. *Are Super!/Sports Illustrated,* 2-9-09.

Hauser, Melanie. *The Houston Post,* 1-31-94, 1-30-95.

Herndon, Booton. *Football's Greatest Quarterbacks,* Sport Magazine Library, 1961.

Hershey, Steve. *USA Today,* 2-1-93.

Herskowitz, Mickey. *Pro!,* January 1984.

Hicks, Phil. *The Tyler Morning Telegraph,* 2-1-93, 1-31-94, 2-2-04, 2-5-07.

Hollander, Zander (compiled by.) *Great Moments in Pro Football,* Scholastic Book Services, 1969.

Hollander, Zander and Phyllis (edited by.) *Touchdown! Football's Most Dramatic Scoring Feats,* Random House Sports Library, 1982.

Izenberg, Jerry. *Championship: The NFL Title Games Plus Super Bowl,* Scholastic Book Services, 1973.

Jenkins, Chris. *The Sporting News,* 2-3-99.

Jenkins, Lee. *Woe, Be Gone/Sports Illustrated,* 2/2/09.

Johnson, Chuck. *USA Today,* 1-29-96.

Justice, Richard. *The Houston Chronicle,* 2-4-02, 1-27-03.

King, Peter. *Sports Illustrated: That Super Season (The Dallas Cowboys' Return to Glory,)* February 1993.

King, Peter. *Sports Illustrated/Perfect Timing,* 2-3-03.

King, Peter. *Sports Illustrated/A Father's Wish,* 2-12-07.

King, Peter. *Sports Illustrated/Destiny's Chill,* 1-28-08.

King, Peter. *Sports Illustrated/XLIII: Cardinals versus Steelers,* 2-2-09.

King, Peter. *Sports Illustrated/Work in Progress,* 2-9-09.

Klein, Frederick C. *The Wall Street Journal,* 1-16-01.

Kramer, Jerry. *Instant Replay: The Green Bay Packers Diary of Jerry Kramer,* Signet Books, 1968.

Lawrence, Andrew. *Sports Illustrated/No Surrender,* 2-2-09.

Layden, Tim. *Sports Illustrated/XLI,* 2-5-07.

Layden, Tim. *Sports Illustrated/And One For All,* 1-28-08.

Layden, Tim. *Sports Illustrated/They're History,* 2-11-08.

Layden, Tim. *Sports Illustrated/We Are Family,* 2-2-09.

Linicome, Bernie. *The Chicago Tribune,* 1-31-00.

Liss, Howard. *Playoff!,* Dell Publishing Company, Inc., 1966.

Litke, Jim. *The Dallas Morning News,* 2-4-02.

Loftis, Randy Lee. *The Dallas Morning News,* 1-31-94.

Lopez, John P. *The Houston Chronicle,* 1-31-94.

Lopresti, Mike. *USA Today,* 2-2-09.

Luksa, Frank. *The Dallas Morning News,* 1-27-97, 2-1-99.

Lunsford, J. Lynn. *The Dallas Morning News,* 1-31-94.

Lupica, Mike. *The National Sports Daily,* 1-16-91, 1-29-91.

Maadd, Rob. *Longview News-Journal,* 2-7-05.

Marot, Michael. *Associated Press/Longview News-Journal,* 2-5-07

Marot, Michael. *Associated Press/Tyler Morning Telegraph*, 2-5-07.

McClain, John. *The Houston Chronicle*, 1-29-90, 1-27-92, 2-1-93, 1-31-94, 1-30-95, 1-29-96, 1-27-97, 2-1-99, 1-29-01, 2-4-02, 1-27-03.

McDonald's. *History of the Super Bowl*, Volumes I, II and III, National Football League Properties, Inc., 1977.

Mihoces, Gary. *USA Today*, 2-1-88, 2-1-93, 1-31-94, 1-30-95, 2-4-02, 1-27-03, 2-1-08.

Miklasc, Bernie. *The Dallas Morning News*, 1-23-89.

Montgomery, Chris. *The National Sports Daily*, 1-26-91.

Moore, David. *The Dallas Morning News*, 2-1-93, 2-1-99.

Moore, David Leon. *USA Today*, 1-31-94.

Mortensen, Chris. *The National Sports Daily*, 1-29-91.

Myers, Gary. *The Dallas Morning News*, 1-21-85, 2-1-88, 1-23-89.

Nadel, John. *The Houston Post*, 2-1-93.

Newberry, Paul. *USA Today*, 1-27-97.

NFL Films. *Super Sundays: A History of the Super Bowl*, 1988.

Pedulla, Tom. *USA Today*, 1-29-94, 2-1-99, 2-1-08.

Pells, Eddie. *Associated Press/Tyler Morning Telegraph*, 1-23-06, 1-22-07.

Pierson, Don. *The Chicago Tribune*, 1-31-00.

Plimpton, George. *Paper Lion*, Signet Books, 1964.

Rapoport, Ken. *Super Sundays*, Tempo Books, 1980.

Reilly, Rick. *Sports Illustrated: That Super Season (The Dallas Cowboys' Return to Glory,)* February 1993.

Roberts, Selena. *Sports Illustrated/The Weight of the World*, 2-11-08.

Robertson, Dale. *The Houston Chronicle*, 1-27-92, 2-1-93, 1-30-95, 1-29-96, 1-27-97, 2-1-99, 1-27-03.

Robinson, Alan. *Longview News-Journal*, 2-6-06.

Robinson, Alan. Associated Press/*Tyler Morning Telegraph*, 1-24-09.

Rogers, Phil. *The Dallas Morning News*, 2-1-93.

Rubin, Bob. *Little Men of the NFL*, Random House, 1974.

Sabino, David. *Sports Illustrated/Super Stats*, 2-5-07.

Sahadi, Lou. *The Long Pass*, Bantam Books, 1969.

Sahadi, Lou. *Super Sundays I-XIII*, Contemporary Books, Inc., 1979.

Saraceno, Jon. *USA Today*, 1-27-97, 1-26-98, 1-29-01, 2-4-02, 1-27-03, 2-5-07.

Schefter, Adam. Scripps Howard News Service, 1-28-96.

Shattuck, Harry. *The Houston Chronicle*, 1-27-92.

Sherrington, Kevin. *The Dallas Morning News*, 2-1-93.

Sherrod, Blackie. *The Dallas Morning News*, 1-29-90, 1-31-94.

Silver, Michael. *Sports Illustrated/Return to Glory*, 2-3-97.

Silver, Michael. *Sports Illustrated/Seven Up*, 2-2-98.

Silver, Michael. *Sports Illustrated*, 1-25-99.

Silver, Michael. *Sports Illustrated/The Magnificent 7*, 2-8-99.

Silver, Michael. *Sports Illustrated/The Greatest*, 2-7-00.

Silver, Michael. *Sports Illustrated/Talk of the Town*, 2-5-01.

Silver, Michael. *Sports Illustrated/Pat Answer*, 2-11-02.

Silver, Michael. *Sports Illustrated/What a Steal!*, 2-3-03.

Silver, Michael. *Sports Illustrated/Fight to the Finish*, 2-9-04.

Silver, Michael. *Sports Illustrated/Three-Ring Circus*, 2-14-05.

Silver, Michael. *Sports Illustrated/Hearts of Steel*, 2-13-06.

Silver, Michael. *Sports Illustrated/Bringing It Home*, 2-12-07.

Sins, Ken. *The Dallas Morning News*, 2-1-93.

Smith, Robert. *Illustrated History of Pro Football*, Grosset & Dunlap, 1977.

Somers, Kent. *USA Today*, 2-2-09.

Spagnola, Mickey. *The Dallas Times Herald*, 1-28-91.

Sullivan, Bill. *The Houston Chronicle,* 1-29-90, 2-1-93, 1-29-96.

Tarkenton, Fran. *Better Scramble Than Lose,* Scholastic Book Services, 1969.

Taylor, Jean-Jacques. *The Dallas Morning News,* 1-27-97, 2-4-02, 1-20-03, 2-2-04, 2-7-05, 2-6-06, 2-3-08, 2-4-08, 2-2-09.

Thompson, Carlton. *The Houston Chronicle,* 1-29-01.

Trotter, Jim. *Sports Illustrated/The Incredibles,* 2-11-08.

Trotter, Jim. *Sports Illustrated/Above and Beyond,* 2-2-09.

Ward, Bob. *Longview News Journal,* 2-2-04.

Weiner, Richard. *The Houston Post,* 1-31-94.

Weiner, Richard. *USA Today,* 1-29-01, 2-4-02, 1-27-03.

Weir, Richard. *USA Today,* 1-27-92, 1-31-94.

Weir, Tom. *USA Today,* 2-1-08.

Weisman, Larry. *USA Today,* 2-1-88, 1-29-90, 1-27-92, 1-30-95, 1-29-96, 1-27-97, 1-26-98, 2-4-02, 1-27-03, 2-7-05, 2-6-06, 2-5-07, 2-1-08, 2-2-09.

Wilner, Barry. *Associated Press/Longview News-Journal,* 2-2-04, 2-5-07.

Wilner, Barry. *Associated Press/Tyler Morning Telegraph,* 2-7-05, 1-23-06, 1-24-06, 2-6-06, 1-22-07, 2-5-07, 2-2-09.

Wine, Steven. *Associated Press/Longview News-Journal,* 2-5-07.

Wine, Stephen. *Associated Press/Tyler Morning Telegraph*, 2-5-07.

Wood, Skip. *USA Today*, 2-4-02, 1-27-03, 2-1-08.

Zanger, Jack. *Pro Football*, Pocket Books, 1970.

Zillgitt, Jeff. *USA Today*, 2-2-09.

Zimmerman, Paul. *Sports Illustrated/That Super Season (The Dallas Cowboys' Return to Glory,)* February 1993.

Zimmerman, Paul. *Sports Illustrated/Defying Logic*, 2-7-00.

Zimmerman, Paul. *Sports Illustrated/They Came Prepared*, 2-3-03.

Zimmerman, Paul. *Sports Illustrated/Possession Obsession*, 2-12-07.

Zimmerman, Paul. *Sports Illustrated/Two-Minute Thrill*, 2-11-08.